Norbert Pfaffinger

Processing Recursively Structured Data

Norbert Pfaffinger

Processing Recursively Structured Data

A Generic Approach to Parsing and Transforming Data with a Recursive Structure, Illustrated by a Practical Implementation

VDM Verlag Dr. Müller

Imprint

Bibliographic information by the German National Library: The German National Library lists this publication at the German National Bibliography; detailed bibliographic information is available on the Internet at http://dnb.d-nb.de.

Any brand names and product names mentioned in this book are subject to trademark, brand or patent protection and are trademarks or registered trademarks of their respective holders. The use of brand names, product names, common names, trade names, product descriptions etc. even without a particular marking in this works is in no way to be construed to mean that such names may be regarded as unrestricted in respect of trademark and brand protection legislation and could thus be used by anyone.

Cover image: www.purestockx.com

Publisher:
VDM Verlag Dr. Müller Aktiengesellschaft & Co. KG, Dudweiler Landstr. 125 a, 66123 Saarbrücken, Germany,
Phone +49 681 9100-698, Fax +49 681 9100-988,
Email: info@vdm-verlag.de

Produced in USA and UK by:
Lightning Source Inc., La Vergne, Tennessee, USA
Lightning Source UK Ltd., Milton Keynes, UK
BookSurge LLC, 5341 Dorchester Road, Suite 16, North Charleston, SC 29418, USA

ISBN: 978-3-8364-9150-1

Contents

1	**Introduction**	**3**
2	**Conception and Realisation of Smute**	**6**
	2.1 Overview	6
	2.2 The Smute Language	8
	2.2.1 Smute Functions, Smute Modules and Smute Packages	10
	2.3 Data I/O Conception	11
	2.3.1 Textual Input Data Specifications in Context-Free Languages	11
	2.3.2 Data I/O in CARGOTREE Exchange Format	16
	2.3.3 Visualisation Output in the Graph Description Language	18
	2.4 The Smute Interpreter	18
	2.4.1 Technical Notes	19
	2.5 The Smute Assembler	19
	2.5.1 Technical Notes	21
	2.6 Discussion of Alternatives	21
	2.7 Related Solutions	23
3	**Invoking Smute Functions**	**26**
	3.1 Step-by-Step Smute Function Usage	26
	3.2 Smute Launch File Documentation	30
	3.2.1 Smute Launch File Syntax	31
4	**Writing Smute Functions**	**33**
	4.1 The Smute Language	33
	4.1.1 Virtual Machine Characteristics	33
	4.1.2 Resources	34
	4.1.3 Instructions	37
	4.2 CARGOTREE-Schemes	64
	4.3 Data I/O	65
	4.3.1 CARGOTREE Exchange Format	65
	4.3.2 Data Input through an LALR-language	66
	4.4 Core Functions and Wrapper Functions	68
	4.5 Smute Assembler Usage	68
5	**Support for the Interaction of External Applications with Smute**	**71**
	5.1 File Layout for the CARGOTREE Exchange Format	71
6	**Reductions-to-QBFs Background**	**74**
	6.1 Propositional Logic	74
	6.2 Quantified Boolean Formulas	75
	6.3 Nonmonotonic Reasoning Formalisms	77
	6.3.1 Default Logic	77

	6.3.2	Classical Abduction	78
	6.3.3	Equilibrium Logic	78
	6.3.4	Paraconsistent Reasoning via Signed Systems	80
	6.3.5	Paraconsistent Reasoning via Three-Valued Logic	81
6.4	An Example Reduction-to-QBF	82

7 Smute Interpreter Logic Edition   **86**
   7.1 Logic Edition Launch File Syntax 86
   7.2 Logic Edition Preprocessing Functions and CARGOTREE-Schemes 87

8 Reduction-to-QBF Smute Package Documentation   **94**
   8.1 Overview 94
   8.2 Smute Function Invocation Example 95
   8.3 The Smute Function Interfaces 96

9 Details on the Implementation of Reductions-to-QBFs   **145**
   9.1 Documented Source Code of a Reduction-to-QBF 145
   9.2 Technical Notes 153

10 Conclusion and Discussion   **154**

Chapter 1

Introduction

SAT, the satisfiability problem of classical propositional logic, is known to be NP-complete. This means that any problem which is in NP, i.e., any problem that can be solved by a nondeterministic Turing machine working in polynomial time, is expressible as SAT-instance with polynomial effort. Several knowledge representation tasks (KR-tasks in short) are in NP. This allows for a uniform principle of KR-task-solver realisation: To re-express the task as SAT-instance and invoke an existing SAT-solver. Constrained-based planning problems [18] are an example where this principle has been successfully deployed.

An analogous method can be applied to problems beyond NP—in particular, many KR-tasks have been shown to be in Σ_2^p or Π_2^p (cf. [11, 12, 13, 16]). For tasks with this computational complexity it is possible to express them in polynomial time as Quantified Boolean Formulas (QBFs). Efficient solvers for QBFs do exist (boole [2], Decide [28], QSolve [14], etc.) and get further developed. A KR-task-solver could thus perform a reduction-to-QBF, i.e., a re-expression as QBF, and then execute one of the existing QBF-solvers.

Several polynomial reductions-to-QBFs have been presented in recent years ([6, 7, 9, 10, 22]). The implementation of such reductions, i.e., the development of programs performing the reductions, raises several difficulties, among them the following:

- The KR-task data instances are recursively structured and many reduction-to-QBF functions are recursively defined. This poses several problems: For example, in most programming languages the implementation of recursively defined reductions-to-QBFs via recursive function calls should be deprecated, as static stacks limit the recursive depth and for high-level programming languages there is an uncontrollable waste of stack-space (for local variables of functions). Another difficulty is the implementation of recursive data structures such that both memory-efficiency and the support of typical operations, like the concatenation of formulas, are provided.

- For many KR-tasks there are task-specific types of data. Thus, for the implementation a specification format must be devised, and functions for reading and writing files in the respective format must be written. This often turns out to be laborious.

QUIP [10], a program developed at the Vienna University of Technology, implements several reductions-to-QBFs. In QUIP, the reductions-to-QBFs are realised individually and heterogeneously, without a general solution of the aforementioned difficulties.

The goal for this thesis was to simplify and automate reduction-to-QBF implementation via a uniform approach, namely by designing a language with the following essential properties:

- The language should be expressive enough to support the specification of any reduction-to-QBF, existing ones as well as ones that might yet be devised.

- Specifications in the language should be as simple and concise as possible, relieving the author of caring about implementation details.

3

- For functions specified in that language it should be possible to automatically generate their implementation.

- The function implementations should not be restricted to trivial data instances, i.e., with regard to the data instances' size and recursive depth there should be as few limitations as possible.

The language introduced in this thesis is called *Smute Language* and meets all the criteria. It is a language for the specification of functions working with recursively structured data. This means a great generalisation: Functions written in the Smute Language, so-called *Smute Functions*, do not need to be related to reductions-to-QBFs at all. The following are examples for the diversity of tasks that can be performed with Smute Functions:

- Manipulation/evaluation of arithmetic expressions;

- Compilation of programming-language source-codes;

- Extraction/Conversion of data from files in structured formats such as XML.

This generalisation has of course not been an arbitrary decision. In fact, there are no common properties of reductions-to-QBFs which would allow for a more specialised custom-tailored solution.

The Smute Language is a new abstract layer—specifications in this language are platform-independent and there is no interrelationship with existing programming languages. The language is optimised for direct interpretability. There is an interpreter for Smute Language code, the so-called *Smute Interpreter*. A compiler does not exist.

Among the key ideas in the development of the Smute Language were the following:

- A resource called `CARGOTREE`, on the one hand primitive, on the other hand versatile, is used for the representation of any recursively structured data. With this uniform representation a few primitive `CARGOTREE` instructions allow to perform arbitrary operations on recursively structured data instances, plus it enables memory-efficient implementation, together with a second resource called `CARGOTREEMEM`. Furthermore, due to the uniform representation, functions working with arbitrary recursively structured data can be written. A trivial example is a function creating a copy of a data instance, independently of its actual recursive structure. This function is readily provided as instruction of the Smute Language.

- All stack-operations at the Smute Language level, including calling-stack operations (function calls and returning from functions) are implemented through dynamic stacks and all stack-usage is explicit. The dynamic stacks permit to support data instances of arbitrary recursive depth, only limited by the host-machine's (the computer running the Smute Function) available memory—which thanks to virtual memory architectures usually is huge. Furthermore, the explicit stack usage allows for recursive function calls in the Smute Language due to stack memory efficiency.

- Most failure conditions, like insufficient memory, are hidden from the Smute Language level. They are correctly treated at the implementation level by aborting the whole top-level Smute Function. This can be regarded as default exception handling. It should be observed that without this automated treatment code specifications would either have to be much more intricate, or incorrect (for example, crashing if data instances become too large).

Smute also handles the difficulty of input data processing and output data generation. For the author of Smute Functions, so-called *Smute Function Developers*, this comprises two tasks: The specification of formats (or the reuse of existing formats), and the processing/generation of data in the respective format. Both tasks are automated, most notably even in the case of textual input processing.

4

Apart from Smute, this thesis also presents the implementation of numerous reductions-to-QBFs, grouped together in the *Reduction-to-QBF Smute Package*. These reductions-to-QBFs can be regarded as test cases, proving the serviceability of Smute. The Smute Functions of the Reduction-to-QBF Smute Package are largely based on reduction-to-QBF specifications presented in [6, 7, 10, 22].

The thesis is laid out as follows: In Chapter 2 the basic conceptions of Smute and important aspects of its realisation are outlined. It includes a discussion of alternatives and a comparison with related solutions. As the user-interface of Smute Functions is to a large extent provided by Smute, the invocation of Smute Functions follows a uniform pattern, which is described in Chapter 3. Chapter 4 documents how to write Smute Functions. It contains the detailed descriptions of the Smute Language, explaining each of its instructions. Smute supports the interaction of Smute Functions with external applications. The respective solutions are documented in Chapter 5. Chapter 6 presents the background to reductions-to-QBFs, including propositional logic, Quantified Boolean Formulas, and an example-reduction. Smute Interpreter Logic Edition has special support for the specification of logic-related data-instances and is documented in Chapter 7. Chapter 8 documents the Reduction-to-QBF Smute Package, and includes the description of all the Smute Functions of this Smute Package. Details on how reductions-to-QBFs have been implemented in the Reduction-to-QBF Smute Package are given in Chapter 9. It contains documented Smute Language source-code for a complete reduction-to-QBF Smute Function, serving as illustration for function-implementation. Finally, Chapter 10 concludes the thesis. It includes a summary of Smute's features and a discussion of potential extensions.

Chapter 2

Conception and Realisation of Smute

An overview of the Smute conception is given in Section 2.1. Essential constituent parts are the Smute Language, the Data I/O Conception, the Smute Interpreter, and the Smute Assembler, which are introduced in Sections 2.2, 2.3, 2.4, and 2.5 respectively. Finally, Section 2.7 contains a comparison of Smute with related solutions.

2.1 Overview

The *Smute Language* is a programming language for the specification of functions processing structured data, with special support for the case of recursively structured data. A programming language is of course not self-contained: For example, a compiler or interpreter is required. The Smute Language and these related components are subsumed as *Smute*.

Example 2.1 (Function working with recursively structured data) A prototypical example for recursively structured data are arithmetic expressions, like the following:

- $17 + 26 * (15/(8 - 3))$;

- $x^2 + 3xy + 3y^2$.

A function for the simplification of arithmetic expressions, performing the replacements listed below, is thus a trivial example for a function working with recursively structured data ('E' stands for an arbitrary sub-expression):

$$
\begin{array}{rcl}
E * 1 \text{ and } 1 * E & \rightarrow & E; \\
E + 0 \text{ and } 0 + E & \rightarrow & E; \\
E * 0 \text{ and } 0 * E & \rightarrow & 0; \\
E^0 & \rightarrow & 1; \\
E^1 & \rightarrow & E; \\
\text{etc.} & & \hfill \square
\end{array}
$$

The main purpose of the Smute Language is the simplified implementation of functions working with recursively structured data (compared to an implementation via an existing programming language). Short and concise specifications are possible through a high level of abstraction. For example, the Smute Language is completely platform independent. The abstraction is however only provided to an extent that does not conflict with implementation efficiency. Thus, the Smute Language does not impose any restrictions on the size or recursive depth of data instances.

A function written in the Smute Language is called *Smute Function*. Authors of Smute Functions are called *Smute Function Developers*. Users of Smute Functions, i.e., those who invoke Smute Functions, are called *Smute Function Users*. The basic principle of a Smute Function is depicted in Figure 2.1. Smute provides support to expose a Smute Function's functionality to

Figure 2.1: Smute Function principle

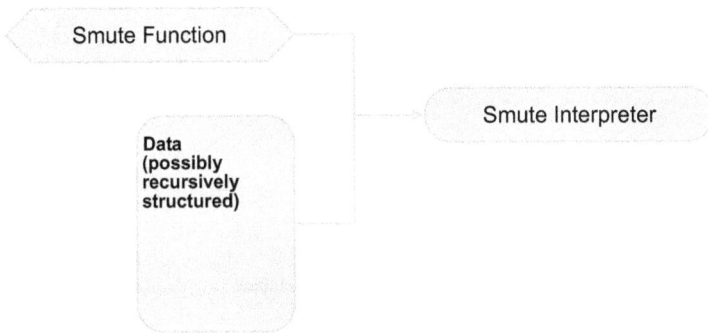

Figure 2.2: Smute Function invocation

a Smute Function User. This is why—as opposed to most other programming languages—the term "program" is not used here: There is no need to develop a user interface for the intended functionality—the user interface to Smute Functions is to a large extent provided by Smute. Of course, in analogy to programs, a Smute Function can call "internal" Smute Functions, i.e., Smute Functions that are invisible to Smute Function Users.

Smute Functions can be executed by interpretation via the *Smute Interpreter*. A Smute Function User invokes a Smute Function with specific input data by passing both the function and the data to the Smute Interpreter, as illustrated in Figure 2.2. The Smute Language is optimised for interpretability. It can thus be seen as low-level language, i.e., as machine language for the virtual machine which is implemented by the Smute Interpreter.

A *Smute Module* is a file containing Smute Language code. Smute Functions of a Smute Module can be *exported*, which means that they are made accessible. A Smute Function Developer can do so for two reasons: To expose the function to Smute Function Users, or to make the function available for calling it from other Smute Functions. An illustration of Smute Modules is given in Figure 2.3

The Smute Interpreter expects Smute Modules in binary format. A Smute Function Developer creates binary Smute Modules by passing textual mnemonics to the *Smute Assembler*, as depicted in Figure 2.4.

A Smute Function User specifies input to Smute Functions (if there is any) in files, and receives the output (if there is any) in files. For Smute Function Developers there is various support for reading input and for writing output. This is subsumed as *Smute Data I/O Conception* and explained in Section 2.3.

7

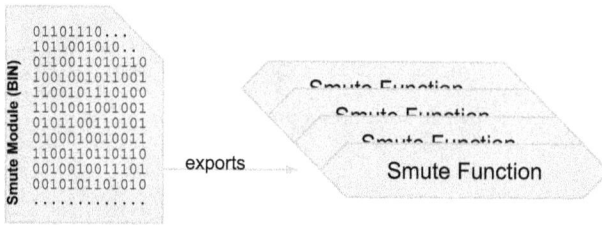

Figure 2.3: Smute Module

Figure 2.4: Smute Assembler

2.2 The Smute Language

The Smute Language provides a set of *instructions*, Smute Language code is a sequence of Smute Language instructions. The majority of Smute Language instructions is of one of the following two types: Either general-purpose instructions (like arithmetic instructions) or instructions for recursively structured data. Some additional instructions are provided for data input and data output. A list of all instructions can be found in the Smute Function Developer Manual.

"Implementation" refers to computer code carrying out Smute Language code. It is, on the one hand, an important principle of the Smute Language to be detached from the implementation layer, i.e., specifications in the Smute Language are made without regard of implementation details. An example are conditions of insufficient memory, which are treated within the implementation layer (by aborting the whole top-level Smute Function) and are therefore invisible to Smute Function Developers. On the other hand, the language is designed to allow for efficient implementations. Some implementation aspects are therefore more or less anticipated, as deviations would result in reduced efficiency. An example is memory requirement of stack operations. The Smute Language allows to very efficiently implement these operations. Of course this efficiency is anticipated, even if all the details remain undetermined by the Smute Language itself.

Most Smute Language instructions operate with *registers*, the main data storage locations. Currently there are 64 registers, each with a width of 32 bits.

There are various types of *resources* in the Smute Language. CARGOTREE is one of them. It is used to represent recursively structured data. Instructions working with CARGOTREE-*nodes* allow to specify operations on those data instances. A CARGOTREE is one of the following:

- an integer-leaf where one 32-bit integer value can be stored;

- a string-leaf where one string, i.e., byte-array, can be stored;

- an inner node with a non-empty array of (sub-)CARGOTREEs.

8

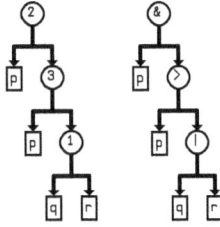

Figure 2.5: CARGOTREE visualisations

All these nodes provide so-called *ids*. These are integer values allowing to encode structural information. The simplicity of this format allows to provide instructions that work with arbitrary CARGOTREEs, and hence are independent of the data instance's actual recursive structure. For example, instructions for creating copies of a CARGOTREE are provided. There are CARGOTREE-node instructions for reading/setting a node's children, for reading/setting a leaf's value, for creating a new node, etc.

Example 2.2 (CARGOTREE) In Figure 4.1 visualisations of a CARGOTREE representing propositional formula $p \wedge (p \rightarrow (q \vee r))$ are shown. The two visualisations are of the same CARGOTREE. In the right one CARGOTREE-node-ids are replaced with symbols for better readability. □

A Smute Function Developer must define a convention (or use existing conventions) laying down how data with a specific structure (for example, arithmetic expressions) is represented with CARGOTREEs. Such a convention is called *CARGOTREE-Scheme*. Currently this is an informal specification.

Resources, such as CARGOTREE-nodes, require machine resources of the computer a Smute Function is executed on. For example, a CARGOTREE-node obviously requires memory for storing its associated data. Smute Function Developers must discard resources that are not required any longer. For implementation efficiency reasons, several resources cannot be created and discarded separately, but only as parts of other resources. An important example for this principle are CARGOTREE-nodes, which are always part of a so-called *CARGOTREEMEM*-instance. When creating a new CARGOTREE-node, a CARGOTREEMEM-instance must be specified wherein the node is allocated. Individual discarding of CARGOTREE-nodes is not possible. Instead, by discarding a CARGOTREEMEM-instance all associated CARGOTREE-nodes are automatically discarded. This conception is essential for memory-efficient implementations: For any block of memory which can be deallocated separately there is a memory overhead. This is of course crucial when there are thousands of mini-allocations, as is the case with CARGOTREE-nodes. To quantify the benefit of the CARGOTREEMEM-architecture: On typical computer systems the overhead-per-node decreases from 8 bytes to less than 0.02 bytes. Thus, for a CARGOTREE with 100000 nodes the overhead shrinks from 800000 bytes (781KB) to less than 2000 bytes. Furthermore, a large number of allocations via the operating system's memory management can cause drastic slow-downs. This is prevented with the CARGOTREEMEM-resource. Apart from its implementation efficiency benefits, CARGOTREEMEM also aids in writing short and concise code. For example, a whole CARGOTREE, whatever its size, can be discarded with a single instruction if all the nodes are allocated from the same CARGOTREEMEM-instance.

There are two *Stack*-resources provided: A *calling-stack* and a *data-stack*. For the Smute Language there is no resource-usage which is not explicitly specified by the Smute Function Developer. This also holds for the Stack-resources: For the calling-stack only a branch-to-subroutine consumes stack-space and only a return-from-subroutine returns stack-space. For the data-stack it is data explicitly pushed onto or popped off the stack. Implementation comes in the form of dynamic stacks. Dynamic means there is no fixed size—these stacks can grow as long as there is memory available. The dynamic implementation is essential, as stack-requirements are usually proportional to the recursive depth of the data processed with Smute Functions. Any limitation of stack-size would hence impose a limitation of the data instances' recursive depth. The explicit stack-usage and the dynamic implementation ensures that there are no disadvantages or restrictions for recursive function-calls in the Smute Language. This is an essential feature, which sets the Smute Language apart from most existing languages, including all machine languages and all the common high-level-languages, such as C. Recursive function-calls in those languages can for the following reasons not be regarded as proper solution: For machine languages (processor code) there is the problem of static calling-stacks. For higher-level languages there is an additional grave disadvantage, namely implicit uncontrollable stack usage. For example, a C-compiler reserves stack-space for a function's local variables. This is troublesome insofar, as wasted stack-space cumulates with each (recursive) level of function-calls.

The functionality of the so-called *Hash*-resources is as follows: A Hash-resource is an initially empty collection of *hash-entries*. A hash-entry is composed of an integer or string, the so-called *hash-key*, plus optional additional data. Any integer or string can occur at most once as a hash-entry's key in a Hash-resource. For any integer or string it is possible to tell if it occurs as key in a Hash-resource, and if so, to access the according hash-entry's associated data-fields. Any number of hash-entries can be added to a Hash-resource. These are essential operations for all Smute Functions operating on recursively structured data with identifiers, like propositional variable-identifiers in formulas of propositional logic. Most types of hash-entries cannot be discarded individually. This is the same as with CARGOTREE-nodes, and has got the same reasons. The name—Hash-resource—comes from the typical way of implementation, namely with hash-tables.

Support for array-operations comes with the ARRAY resource. It is especially useful for Smute Functions working with arrays of recursively structured data, where such arrays are not part of the recursive data structure itself.

2.2.1 Smute Functions, Smute Modules and Smute Packages

A *Smute Module* is a file containing Smute Language code. A *label* is a string identifying a position in a Smute Module. Labels are used with the flow control instructions in order to specify positions, e.g., to specify where to branch to.

Now the term *Smute Function* can be clarified: It is a position in a Smute Module where it is possible to BSR (branch-to-subroutine) to. The shortest possible Smute Function is thus a single Return instruction.

Labels can be *exported* from a Smute Module. This means they are made "visible" to the outside, i.e., they can be referenced from outside the Smute Module. The functionality provided by a Smute Module is thus given by its exports. Smute Module code can contain branches (usually BSRs) to *external* labels, i.e., to exports of other modules. A full reference to another modules' export—called *import*—consists of a (module-name, label-name)-tuple.

References to Smute Module-internal positions via labels are used for convenient specification of Smute Language code with its textual mnemonics. They get resolved by the Smute Assembler, i.e., when creating the binary Smute Module. In the binary Smute Module hence only exported labels are stored.

If code of Smute Module b references an export of Smute Module a, then b is said to *directly depend* on a. b is said to *depend* on a, if either

- b directly depends on a or

- there is a Smute Module c directly depending on a, and b depends on c.

A dependency graph for Smute Modules is generated as follows: Each Smute Module is a node. Each direct dependency is a (directed) edge. For proper Smute Modules the dependency graph is a tree—although circular dependencies are of course possible, they must be considered poor Smute Module design. This is why in the rest of this document the term *dependency tree* will be used.

Obviously the import/export-architecture is destined for modularity. Different functions, even if completely independent of each other, often require common subroutines. Instead of redundantly including common subroutines in each of the independent Smute Modules, these functions can be imported.

Publishing and distribution of Smute Functions is usually done via *Smute Packages*. A Smute Package consists of one or more Smute Modules and related files, e.g., documentation.

2.3 Data I/O Conception

According to the design of the Smute Language, with CARGOTREEs as one of the fundamental concepts, a function with recursively structured input and output could be implemented as follows:

1. Input data instances are read in order to create a CARGOTREE-representation. The following cases need to be distinguished:

   (a) Input data instances are provided in binary format.

   (b) Input data instances are provided through textual specifications.

2. The function processing the data gets executed. This function is independent of input/output-formats and works with recursively structured data only in its CARGOTREE-representation.

3. Resulting CARGOTREEs are saved in the desired output format. Again there is a distinction between:

   (a) Output is provided in binary format.

   (b) Output is provided in a textual format.

Proper support is as yet "only" provided for point 1b, i.e., textual input specification. Compared to the difficulty of points 1a, 3a, and 3b, this was of course the real tough nut to crack. The missing points are of course subject to further Smute development.

Smute introduces a new standardised binary file format for recursively structured data, the *CARGOTREE Exchange Format*. Any CARGOTREE can be saved to CARGOTREE Exchange Format with a single instruction of the Smute Language. Furthermore Smute can automatically create a CARGOTREE from a file in CARGOTREE Exchange Format. This new file format serves multiple purposes. For example, it makes it possible to write applications that seamlessly work together with Smute Functions.

2.3.1 Textual Input Data Specifications in Context-Free Languages

This section is divided into two parts. The first is a compact introduction to languages, grammars, and parsers. For a more comprehensive discussion of these important topics of computer science refer to [4]. The second part explains the Smute Data I/O concept for textual input specification and processing. It is of course based on the theoretical background of the first part.

Background

Let A be a set. A *string* over A is a (possibly empty) finite sequence of elements from A. The *empty string*, denoted ϵ, is defined as empty sequence of elements. For $a \in A$, the string solely consisting of a is denoted a. The *length* of a string u, denoted $|u|$, is defined as follows:

- If $u = \epsilon$ then $|u|:=0$;

- If $u = av$, where $a \in A$ and v is a string, then $|u|:=|v| + 1$.

The *concatenation* of strings u and v, denoted uv, is obtained by appending the sequence of string v to the sequence of string u. A string x is called *substring* of string y, if there are strings u and v such that $y = uxv$. A string x is called *prefix* of string y, if there is a string v such that $y = xv$. A string x is called *suffix* of string y, if there is a string u such that $y = ux$. For a set A, the *Kleene closure* of A, denoted A^*, is the set of all strings over A, including ϵ.

Let A be a set. A *formal language* L over A is a (possibly empty) set of strings over A, i.e., $L \subseteq A^*$. A is called the *alphabet* of L.

A *formal grammar* G is a quadruple (N, T, P, S) of

- a finite set N of *nonterminals*;

- a finite set T of *terminals* that is disjoint from N;

- a finite set P of *productions*, where a production is of the form $s_l \rightarrow s_r$ with

  - $s_l, s_r \in (T \cup N)^*$ and
  - s_l contains at least one nonterminal.

  s_l is referred to as the production's *left side*, s_r as the production's *right side*;

- a symbol $S \in N$ designated as *start symbol*.

Let $s_1, s_2, s_l, s_r \in (T \cup N)^*$ be strings and $s_l \rightarrow s_r$ be a production. Then *applying* a production $s_l \rightarrow s_r$ to a string $s_1 s_l s_2$ means to replace it with the string $s_1 s_r s_2$. In this case $s_1 s_r s_2$ is said to be *derived* from $s_1 s_l s_2$ in one step, denoted $s_1 s_l s_2 \Rightarrow s_1 s_r s_2$. A string $r \in (T \cup N)^*$ *derives* a string $s \in (T \cup N)^*$, denoted $r \overset{*}{\Rightarrow} s$, if s can be generated from r by repeatedly (zero or more times) applying productions from P. A sequence of such replacements is called *derivation*. The *language* of a formal grammar, denoted $L(G)$, is defined as the set of terminal-strings, i.e., strings from T^*, that can be derived from the start symbol. A formal grammar is called *unambiguous* if for each string of its language there is exactly one derivation.

A *context-free grammar* G is a formal grammar (N, T, P, S), where each production's left side consists of a single nonterminal only. A formal language is called *context-free language*, if it is the language of a context-free grammar (i.e., if it can be generated with the productions of a context-free grammar). A derivation with productions of a context-free grammar is called *leftmost*, if in each replacement step the leftmost nonterminal gets replaced with a production's right side. It is called *rightmost*, if in each replacement step the rightmost nonterminal gets replaced.

Example 2.3 (Context-free grammar) For the following context-free grammar the set of nonterminals is $\{S, T, F\}$, the start symbol is S, and the set of terminals is $\{+, -, *, (,), x, y, z\}$. Usually these are not explicitly specified, but implicitly given through the set of productions, which are listed below.

$S \rightarrow S + T$;
$S \rightarrow S - T$;
$S \rightarrow T$;
$T \rightarrow T * F$;
$T \rightarrow F$;
$F \rightarrow (S)$;
$F \rightarrow x$;
$F \rightarrow y$;
$F \rightarrow z$.

"$x * y * (y + z)$" is a string of the context-free grammar's language, as the following rightmost derivation from the start symbol shows:

$$S \Rightarrow T$$
$$\Rightarrow T * F$$
$$\Rightarrow T * (S)$$
$$\Rightarrow T * (S + T)$$
$$\Rightarrow T * (S + F)$$
$$\Rightarrow T * (S + z)$$
$$\Rightarrow T * (T + z)$$
$$\Rightarrow T * (F + z)$$
$$\Rightarrow T * (y + z)$$
$$\Rightarrow T * F * (y + z)$$
$$\Rightarrow T * y * (y + z)$$
$$\Rightarrow F * y * (y + z)$$
$$\Rightarrow x * y * (y + z).$$
□

A *Backus-Naur form* is a convention for the specification of context-free grammars in text-files. Character-strings within angular brackets, such as `<formula>`, are used to specify and identify nonterminals. Strings delimited with quotation marks, such as `'if'`, are used to specify terminals. For productions the left side and the right side are separated with the string "`::=`", as illustrated below:

```
<stmt> ::= 'if' <expr> 'then' <stmt>
```

Multiple productions with an equal left side nonterminal can be grouped together with the "`|`" character as illustrated below:

```
<expr> ::= <expr> '*' <expr> | '-' <expr> | <expr> '+' <expr>
```

The analysis of the grammatical structure of an input with respect to a given formal grammar is called *parsing*. A *top-down* parser creates a derivation by starting with the start symbol and trying to recreate the input with repeated application of productions. A *bottom-up* parser creates a derivation by repeated inverse application of productions to the input until only the start symbol is left. Common types of top-down parsers are so-called *LL*-parsers and *recursive descent* parsers. See [4] for a description. A common type of bottom-up parsers is the *LR*-parser-type. LR-parsers are introduced in the following paragraphs.

A *shift-reduce* parser is a bottom-up parser for context-free grammars which works as follows: It implements a stack where terminals and nonterminals can be stored. It reads the input from the left to the right. The parsing is done via 2 actions called *shift* and *reduce*.

- In a *shift*-action the parser shifts the next input terminal onto the top of the stack.

- In a *reduce*-action a certain number of symbols (terminals and nonterminals) on top of the stack correspond to the right side of a production which can be applied in the derivation of the input. The symbols are thus popped from the stack and replaced with the nonterminal from the production's left side.

A shift-reduce parser uses k input-terminals not yet used for shifting/reducing, the so-called *lookahead-symbols*, to decide on whether to shift or reduce, and in the latter case according to which production to reduce. The following errors can occur in shift-reduce parsers: A *shift/reduce-conflict* (knowing the stack content and the lookahead-symbols it is not possible to decide whether to shift or reduce), and *reduce/reduce*-conflicts (knowing the stack content and the lookahead-symbols it is not possible to elect one of several reductions).

An *LR(k) parser* (the 'L' stands for reading input from the left to the right, the 'R' stands for creating rightmost derivations) is a shift-reduce parser with k symbols of lookahead. *LR* is an abbreviation for LR(1). Here only the LR(1)-parser algorithm is introduced in full detail. The relevance of LR(1)-parsers and their superiority to other well-known parsing algorithms are discussed in [4].

An LR-parser determines the next action (shift or reduce) from a so-called *LR-parsing-table*, the next input-symbol, and its current *state*. The algorithm is best explained with a simple example:

Example 2.4 (LR-parser)

```
(1) <expr> ::= <expr> '+' <bool>
(2) <expr> ::= <bool>
(3) <bool> ::= '0'
(4) <bool> ::= '1'
```

The LR-parsing-table for this grammar is as follows:

state	action				goto	
	0	1	+	$	\<expr>	\<bool>
0	s3	s4			1	2
1			s5	acc		
2			r2	r2		
3			r3	r3		
4			r4	r4		
5	s3	s4				6
6			r1	r1		

The $-terminal serves as end-of-input identification. The entries in the action-table have the following meaning:

- $s\langle i \rangle$: Shift and continue with state i.

- $r\langle i \rangle$: Reduce according to rule i.

- acc: Accept the input.

The numbers in the goto-table refer to the state in which to continue after a reduction with the specified left-hand side nonterminal has been performed.

The parsing-algorithm uses a stack in which it remembers its states. The top-of-the-stack is its current state. Its initial state is 0. For each shift-action the new state is shifted onto the stack. For a reduction the number of right-hand side symbols (nonterminals and terminals) determines the number of states to walk back, i.e., to pop from the stack. The new state is then determined by this state's goto-table entries.

The following is an illustration of the algorithm for input string "0+1":

	stack	input	action
(step1)	[0]	0 (↪0+1)	s3
(step2)	[0 3]	+ (0↪+1)	r3
(step3)	[0 2]	+ (0↪+1)	r2
(step4)	[0 1]	+ (0↪+1)	s5
(step5)	[0 1 5]	1 (0+↪1)	s4
(step6)	[0 1 5 4]	$ (0+1↪)	r4
(step7)	[0 1 5 6]	$ (0+1↪)	r1
(step8)	[0 1]	$ (0+1↪)	acc

Thus, the following derivation is returned (reductions in reverse order):

14

$$\text{<expr>} \overset{r1}{\Rightarrow} \text{<expr> '+' <bool>}$$
$$\overset{r4}{\Rightarrow} \text{<expr> '+' '1'}$$
$$\overset{r2}{\Rightarrow} \text{<bool> '+' '1'}$$
$$\overset{r3}{\Rightarrow} \text{'0' '+' '1'}$$

In (step1) the current state is 0, and the current input symbol is '0'. The according action-table entry is "s3". Thus, state 3 is shifted onto the stack (and hence made the current state), and input processing continues with symbol '+'. This is displayed in (step2). Here the action-table entry is "r3", i.e., reduction according to rule `<bool> ::= '0'`. This rule has got one right-hand-side symbol. Hence one state is popped from the stack (state 3), which means that state 0 is the top of the stack. For the continuation after applying the reduction it is hence necessary to go to the state stored in the goto-table for state 0 and nonterminal `<bool>` (the rule's left-hand-side), i.e., state 2. This is displayed in (step3). The other steps follow the same pattern.

All empty action-table entries correspond to parsing-errors. For example, when parsing string "0++1", the next input-symbol when the parser reaches state 5 is '+'. The action-table entry for this configuration is empty, the parser would thus correctly report an unexpected '+'-terminal. □

There are context-free grammars that cannot be parsed with an LR-parser—even unambiguous ones. This is because the decision whether to shift or reduce (or which reduction to apply respectively) could depend on other input symbols than the first one, but only the first one is taken into account. Those context-free grammars which can be parsed with an LR-parser are called *LR-grammars*. In practice, e.g., for most programming languages, LR-grammars are sufficient.

The algorithm which for a given LR-grammar calculates the LR-parsing-table is beyond the scope of this document. Refer to [4] for a comprehensive description.

An *LALR-parser* (*lookahead-LR parser*) works like an LR-parser, but instead of an LR-parsing-table uses an *LALR-parsing-table*. As LR-parsing-tables are becoming quite large for non-trivial grammars, such as programming-language grammars, there have been various attempts for size-reduction. The most widespread solution are LALR-parsing-tables. Their structure is exactly the same as the LR-parsing-table structure. Though certain states of an LR-parsing table are "merged" into just one state in an LALR-parsing-table. Of course this cannot be done in a lossless way (otherwise the LR-parsing-tables would be constructed redundantly)—the "loss" is as follows:

- Some parsing-errors are not detected when they occur, but at a later point of time (in this case LALR-parsers cannot tell the original cause of a parsing error).

- For some LR-grammars it is not possible to generate an LALR-parsing-table, because it would contain reduce/reduce-conflicts.

LALR-grammars, i.e., grammars that can be parsed with LALR-parsers, are thus a proper subset of LR-grammars. Nevertheless LALR-grammars are usually sufficient. For example, most compilers for programming languages parse with LALR-parsers. For the details of LALR-parsing-table construction refer to [4].

The Smute Solution

In principle the processing of recursively structured data specified in a text-file (in a specific language) is the task of a Smute Function Developer. For example, it would be sufficient if the Smute Language permits to write parsers. This is however not the case. Instead, Smute offers full automation—a Smute Function Developer never needs to write a parser.

The Smute solution works as follows:

1. The Smute Function Developer specifies an LALR-grammar by writing a Backus-Naur form.

2. The Smute Function Developer passes the Backus-Naur form to a utility program which creates the LALR-parsing-table. This parsing-table is distributed together with the Smute Modules.

3. A Smute Function User specifies input in the respective language and references the appropriate LALR-parsing-table. The parsing of the source is performed by Smute. If successful, a CARGOTREE representing the input in an LALR-grammar-dependent CARGOTREE-Scheme is created.

4. The Smute Function Developer provides Smute Functions working with CARGOTREEs in the LALR-grammar dependent CARGOTREE-Scheme. The recommended way is to develop a *Preprocessing Function* in the Smute Language. A Preprocessing Function creates from a CARGOTREE in an LALR-grammar-dependent CARGOTREE-Scheme a CARGOTREE representation in a grammar-independent CARGOTREE-Scheme. Typically a core Smute Function works with CARGOTREEs in the independent scheme. A "wrapper" Smute Function performs preprocessing (by invoking the Preprocessing Function), and then calls the core Smute Function.

With only two simple tasks, namely writing a Backus-Naur form and writing a Preprocessing Function (a typical Preprocessing Function is approximately hundred lines long), a Smute Function Developer can support textual specifications in any desired LALR-language. Also note the implementation independence: Support for textual specifications is automatically available with all implementations, e.g., for different computer systems.

The principle of textual input processing with Smute is depicted in Figure 2.6. Here the utilisation of a Preprocessing Function is assumed.

Fortunately, a freely available program called GOLD Parser [3] proved to be perfectly suitable for the LALR-parsing-table creation. This definitely saved some months of work. Although several parser source codes are offered freely as well, due to the special requirements (like memory efficiency) and for neat integration into the other code the Smute LALR-parser is an own development.

2.3.2 Data I/O in CARGOTREE Exchange Format

Smute Function code can save a CARGOTREE to a file in a new standardised binary format, the CARGOTREE Exchange Format. Such files can of course be used as input to Smute Functions again.

The purposes are the following:

- For Smute Function Users: Consecutive Translations. A Smute Function User might want to pass the output of one Smute Function to another Smute Function. Smute Function Developers can support such consecutive translation calls by CARGOTREE Exchange File output and input, with only a few lines of Smute Language code - independently of syntactic input/output conventions.

- CARGOTREE Exchange Format permits to write applications that seamlessly work together with Smute. The following are examples:

  - As mentioned on page 11, support of input from and output to arbitrary binary or textual formats is not yet possible with Smute. Smute Function Developers can circumvent this current limitation by providing small tools converting to/from CARGOTREE Exchange Format.

  - Where Smute Functions are used as part of a tool-chain, data can be passed via files in CARGOTREE Exchange Format.

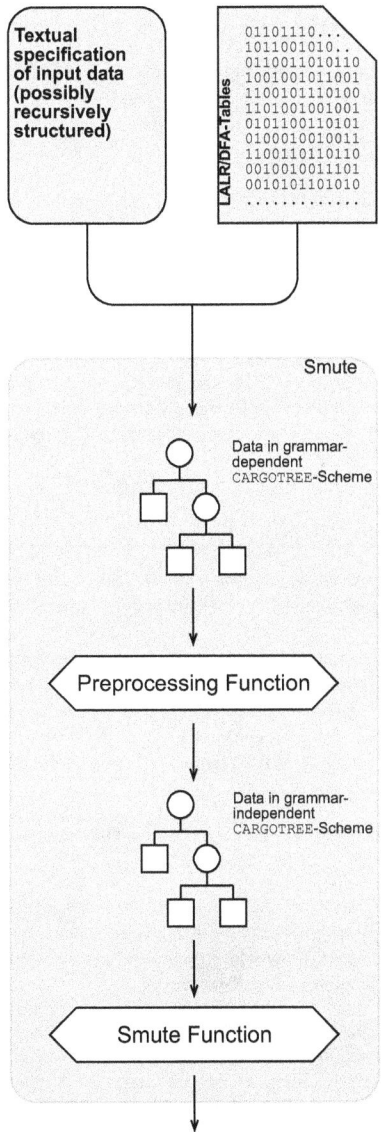

Figure 2.6: Textual input processing

2.3.3 Visualisation Output in the Graph Description Language

The recursive structure of data is best displayed in the form of a tree. From string-representations it is however difficult to decipher the recursive structure. For example, imagine a random arithmetic expression with hundreds of variables. In the form of a string it is a hardly comprehensible sequence of brackets, operator symbols, variable symbols, and numbers. During the development of function code, regardless of the programming language, it is a common task to display internal data instances in order to verify their correctness. The same is necessary for recursively structured data instances of Smute Functions. Thus it was self-evident that Smute had to support tree visualisations.

Smute supports the visualisation of recursively structured data with instructions for saving CARGOTREE descriptions in the so-called *Graph Description Language*. The Graph Description Language is used by graph visualisation software aiSee [1]. See Figure 4.1 on page 65 for an example visualisation (all CARGOTREE visualisations in this document are created with aiSee).

For internal CARGOTREE-nodes the integer id is displayed in the visualisation. Depending on the CARGOTREE-Scheme a visualisation could however be "decrypted" by displaying certain symbols instead. For example, a plus-symbol ('+') could be displayed for a CARGOTREE-node representing an arithmetic formula '$l + r$'. Though this requires visualisation-related CARGOTREE-Scheme meta-information, and is not implemented yet. Only for CARGOTREEs in 'QBF'-Scheme (a CARGOTREE-Scheme for the representation of Quantified Boolean Formulas) is there currently a "decrypted" visualisation output available.

2.4 The Smute Interpreter

Smute Functions can be executed via the *Smute Interpreter*. As the name Smute Interpreter suggests, Smute Functions are executed by interpretation of their code (as opposed to the compilation-approach).

The many parameters passed to the Smute Interpreter—namely which Smute Functions from which Smute Modules to invoke with which parameters—have to be specified in a file, the so-called *Smute Launch File*. The Smute Launch File syntax is presented in Chapter 3.

Input to Smute Functions can be specified via references to files, i.e., via the specification of file-names, in Smute Launch Files. It is an important feature of the Smute Interpreter that it can process the input for certain types of data:

- From files in CARGOTREE Exchange Format the Smute Interpreter can automatically create CARGOTREEs.

- From files in LALR-languages the Smute Interpreter can—if provided with the respective LALR-parsing-table—automatically create a grammar-dependent CARGOTREE representation. LALR-parsing-tables are provided by Smute Function Developers in order to support the specification of input in an LALR-language.

For the sake of convenient input specification are there special *Smute Interpreter Editions*. They permit textual specifications of certain recursively structured data directly within the Smute Launch File. Smute Interpreter Editions come with one or more Smute Modules containing Pre-processing Functions for the recursively structured data in question. An example is *Smute Interpreter Logic Edition*: It allows formulas of propositional logic and other logic-related data instances to be specified directly within the Smute Launch File. As it requires changes in the Smute Interpreter, a new Smute Interpreter Edition (or changes in an existing one) can only be manufactured by the author of the Smute Interpreter, but not by Smute Function Developers.

Smute Launch File grammars are subject to changes (for example, extension with additional specification syntax). Therefore data specified in Smute Launch Files must be preprocessed with the Preprocessing Functions that come with the respective Smute Interpreter Edition. Otherwise Smute Functions are rendered useless with changes in the Smute Launch File grammar.

Figure 2.7 on page 20 illustrates the Smute Interpreter.

2.4.1 Technical Notes

The Smute Interpreter is written in C. A few constructs of C++, like function-templates, have been used, but essentially it is plain C. The code has been developed from scratch, the only libraries used are the ANSI Standard C libraries. Thus the Smute Interpreter can be compiled for various platforms.

A 32-bit addressing architecture is required on the target platform (wider addresses are not supported). 16-bit datatypes are only addressed at 16-bit boundaries, 32-bit values at 32-bit boundaries. Depending on the target platform processor such alignments can be required or advantageous.

The Smute Interpreter is currently available for Intel Pentium/Windows and Intel Pentium/Linux platforms.

The ANSI Standard C library calls are completely encapsulated. Thus the Smute Interpreter can be easily detached from ANSI Standard C in order to create a different version, for example, a Windows-version with graphical user-interface. Currently no such versions are planned though.

As pointed out in Section 2.2, the Smute Language is designed to allow for efficient implementations. All the implementation characteristics that have been demanded there (for example, dynamic stacks, efficient memory handling, etc.) are realised with the Smute Interpreter.

For user-friendliness the Smute Interpreter applies a cumulative error notification technique, i.e., multiple errors (for example, typing errors in the Smute Launch File) can be notified at once.

2.5 The Smute Assembler

For textual specifications of Smute Language code the *Smute Assembler* is required in order to create the binary Smute Modules. Like with existing assemblers, the textual mnemonics only serve the ease of specification.

A Smute Assembler application is not yet available. Instead, the so-called *Smute Assembler Library* can be used. The Smute Assembler Library is a static library which can be used with C-programs, i.e., there is a C-header-file available. Smute Language instructions can be specified in a C source-code file via respective Smute Assembler Library function-calls. Compilation of the C source-code yields an executable, which, when executed, generates the binary Smute Module.

Example 2.5 (Smute Language code specification via Smute Assembler Library function-calls) The following listing displays a small Smute Function in "native" Smute Language:

```
Label(Not);
Move(R01,R02);
NewConClsImm(1,R00,R01,0);
PlugImm(R01,R02,0);
Return;
```

For usage with the Smute Assembler Library it must be specified as follows:

```
TMMWrite_WLabel(ptmmw,(PuCHAR)"Not",3);
TMMWrite_WMove(ptmmw,R01,R02);
TMMWrite_WNewConClsImm(ptmmw,1,R00,R01,0);
TMMWrite_WPlugImm(ptmmw,R01,R02,0);
TMMWrite_WReturn(ptmmw);
```

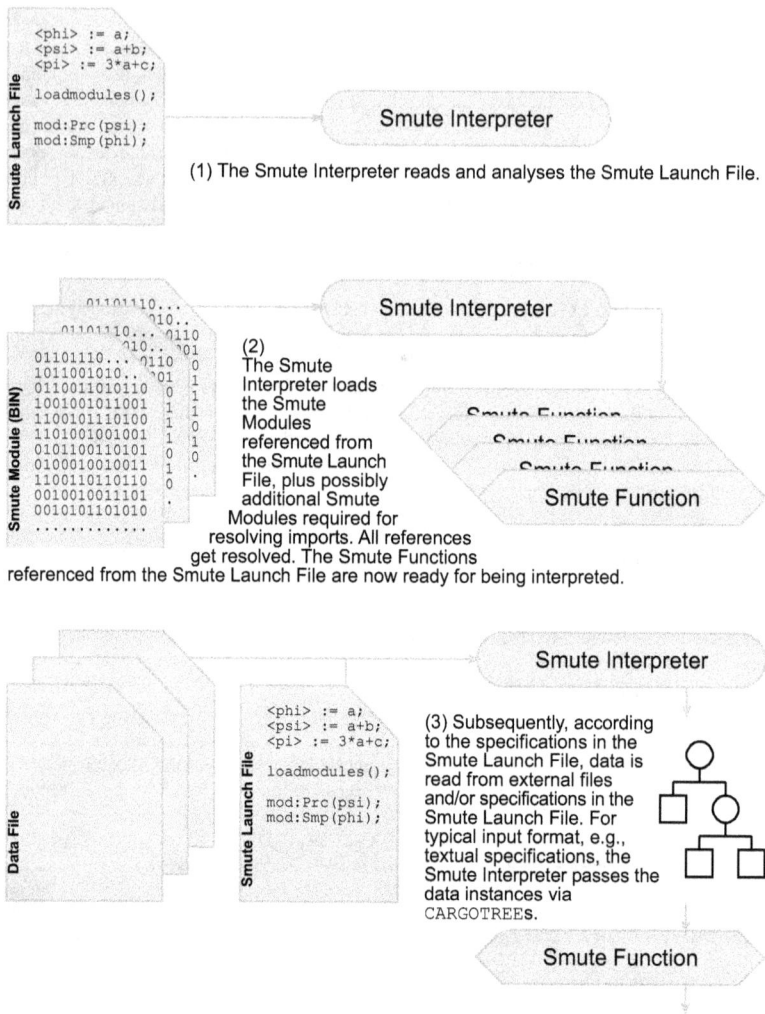

Figure 2.7: Smute Interpreter

For the compilation with a C-compiler a few additional framing instructions are required. □

The Smute Assembler Library is documented in the Smute Function Developer Manual. The Smute Assembler Library is only a tentative solution for the not yet developed Smute Assembler application. Throughout this document Smute Language code is hence presented in its native form, not in the form of Smute Assembler Library function-calls.

2.5.1 Technical Notes

Like the Smute Interpreter, the Smute Assembler Library is basically written in plain C, with the rare exception of using C++ extensions. Again, the only libraries used are the ANSI Standard C libraries. An encapsulation of ANSI Standard C library calls identical to the one of the Smute Interpreter is implemented. The code has been written with the future development of a Smute Assembler in mind, i.e., in large parts the code can be reused for the development of such a program.

2.6 Discussion of Alternatives

This section discusses the most important alternatives that occurred in the conception of Smute.

Compiler vs. Interpreter

For a language supporting the specification of functions processing recursively structured data there are two implementation options: compilation and interpretation. For compilation there are two different sub-options, namely a standard compiler, i.e., a compiler creating code for a certain microprocessor, and a *compiler-compiler*, i.e., a compiler generating code of a certain programming language. The following is a list of disadvantages for the compiler-approach (some specific for either standard compilers or compiler-compilers) in comparison to the interpretation approach:

- Recursive function calls in the specification language cannot be implemented via recursive function calls in the host programming language, due to the stack problem (as discussed on page 10). This has a tremendous effect on the whole implementation:

  - For compiler-compilers this means that just one big function (or a few ones) with numerous internal flow-control destinations (for the functions of the specification language) must be created. With C, function-internal flow-control destination handling is rather limited and intricate, because labels can only be used directly with a few instructions (most notably "goto"), but not be accessed as data.

  - For standard compilers it has the effect that recursively structured functions cannot be implemented as functions (with a return-instruction). Alternative solutions are however more feasible than with compiler-compilers.

- Common functionality provided at the specification language layer must either be redundantly linked to each application, or these applications use an external common core-file. In any case is there a certain static frame. For function users this has the unpleasant effect that applications compiled with different versions of the compiler can differ in their user interfaces.

- For compiler-compilers there is a general problem: There is very limited influence on the second compilation step. Compilers for the second step differ from each other. It cannot be guaranteed that the second compilation step works flawlessly and that the resulting code is correct. Furthermore, usually certain settings for the second compilation step are required. There are however no standardised ways for the specification of compiler settings. In the case of a faulty implementation it is difficult to detect whether the error is caused by the second compilation step, or if the original specification is faulty.

- For compiler-compilers recompilations are required for different computer platforms.

- For standard compilers there is the disadvantage that they generate applications for one platform only.

- For standard compilers the development effort is enormous, even more so if code optimisation is performed.

The disadvantages of interpretation:

- Runtime overhead caused by interpreting. In a properly designed specification language this is only a small disadvantage, as all the efficiency-critical tasks are encapsulated in the implementation layer and not performed via code of the specification layer.

Smute applies interpretation. The realisation of a compiler (alongside the interpreter) is not ruled out by the Smute conception, though it is not planned. See Chapter 10 for a discussion.

Static linking vs. Dynamic linking

The disadvantages of static linking are as follows:

- Smute Modules commonly used get redundantly linked. All the typical disadvantages of redundancy apply: Waste of space, different versions of the code, updates only through re-linking, etc.

- Static linking cannot work function-wise, as this would require program flow analysis. Thus always a complete Smute Module gets linked, which is a waste of space.

- For testing Smute Functions during the development of Smute Modules it is not only necessary to assemble the Smute Module, but also to link it.

The disadvantages of dynamic linking:

- In order to invoke Smute Functions, a Smute Function User needs all the Smute Modules from the dependency-tree.

Smute applies dynamic linking. Of course a static linker could be implemented alongside the existing dynamic linking solution. Currently this is not planned.

Higher-level language vs. Lower-level language

As Smute uses an interpretation approach, it was obvious that there had to be a language which could be efficiently interpreted. This is realised with the Smute Language, which can thus be regarded as lower-level language. This is however not a decision against a higher-level language: For the implementation of a higher-level language a compiler creating Smute Language code would be required. Currently there is no higher-level language in the Smute framework, but it can be considered as potential extension. This is discussed in Chapter 10.

Parsing-Table Creation Alternatives

Dozens of applications to aid in parser development have been reviewed, but only GOLD Parser [3] has a strict separation between parsing-tables and parsers as it is required for Smute. Most other applications are compiler-compilers creating parser-code in one of various programming languages. GOLD Parser has grammar-testing capabilities, an excellent user-interface, it is well documented, and publicly available. As GOLD Parser proved to be sufficient for the current purposes, its usage was preferable to the only other alternative, namely writing an own parsing-table-creation utility. If however in the further development of Smute more advanced features are required, for example, the specification of parsing-error-recovery, then GOLD Parser must be abolished.

Recursively Structured Data Visualisation Alternatives

Several programs have been reviewed with regard to their tree visualisation capabilities: aiSee, CharGer, GraphViz, GVF and VGJ. aiSee [1] proved to be the by far most suitable one. Some of its advantages:

- fully configurable visualisations (colors, shapes, layout, etc.);

- excellent on-screen display, with zoom- and scrolling-features;

- various export options (for example, in Postscript- and in GIF-format);

- availability for multiple computer platforms; and

- student license conditions.

Most of aiSee's sophisticated features, like graph layout algorithms for arbitrary graphs, are not even used with CARGOTREE visualisations.

2.7 Related Solutions

Prior to the development of Smute has there been an extensive research with regard to existing software suitable for the specification and implementation of functions processing recursively structured data. The existing software solutions which have been found and reviewed in this research are at best partially suited for this task. This section gives an overview and discusses common insufficiencies.

Smute-related solutions have typically one of the following two backgrounds:

- The solution is intended for parser-generation and is extended to provide support for the transformation of parse-trees.

- The solution provides programming language specification and compilation support.

The solution which is closest to meeting the requirements is called TXL (Transformation by Example, www.txl.ca) [8] and belongs to the latter category. It is one of the few Smute-related solutions where transformations are entirely expressed in a language designed for this purpose. The more common case is a mixture of using a new language and an existing programming language. One of the better-suited examples with parser-generation background is ANTLR (www.antlr.org) [20]. The following is a list of other software packages that have been reviewed:

- AnaGram
  (www.parsifalsoft.com)

- ASF+SDF Meta Environment
  (www.cwi.nl/projects/MetaEnv)

- ClearParse
  (www.clearjump.com)

- EAG (Extended Affix Grammars Project)
  (www.cs.kun.nl/~kees/eag)

- Elkhound
  (www.cs.berkeley.edu/~smcpeak/elkhound)

- Gentle
  (www.first.gmd.de/gentle)

- Haskell Language
  (www.haskell.org)

- iburg
  (www.cs.princeton.edu/software/iburg)

- IParse
  (home.planet.nl/~faase009/MM.html)

- Precc
  (vl.fmnet.info/precc)

- ProGrammar
  (www.programmar.com)

- SLK Parser Generator
  (www.parsers.org)

- SPIRIT
  (spirit.sourceforge.net)

- Stratego Language (Strategies for Program Transformation)
  (www.stratego-language.org)

- STYX
  (www.speculate.de/styx)

- SYNTAX System
  (www-rocq.inria.fr/oscar/www/syntax/syntax-eng.htm)

- Visual Parse++
  (www.sand-stone.com)

While these software packages are related to Smute, none is suitable for the specification of functions processing recursively structured data as required for reductions-to-QBFs. The following is a list of typical insufficiencies:

- The package does not introduce a new language, but only aids in writing code of an existing programming language. This has several severe disadvantages, including the problem of recursive function calls (as discussed on page 10).

24

- There is no support for identifier-related operations, such as the introduction of new unused variables or the substitution of variables. This is true for all the reviewed languages. It is either not possible to implement such operations, or they can be implemented only via extremely inefficient workarounds (linear search, etc.).

- The language-design makes (runtime- or memory-)efficient implementations impossible. For example, there are languages following a functional approach instead of a procedural (imperative) one. For the functions typically implemented with Smute this is unnecessary and reduces efficiency.

- The package does not distinguish between textual specification of data and its recursive structure. This usually has the effect of ill-suited representation of data during transformations.

- The language is missing modularity, e.g, all specifications have to be provided within one file.

- The language is not powerful enough—it only supports a certain kind of operations on recursively structured data, e.g., syntactic pattern-match replacements. There are too many presumptions with regard to, for example, the tree-traversal.

Although in many cases aimed at different goals, Smute can be used as replacement for some of the software packages listed above. Most of Smute's features, like support for identifier operations and for visualisation of recursively structured data, set it apart from existing solutions.

Chapter 3

Invoking Smute Functions

The user-interface to Smute Functions is to a large extent provided by Smute. This saves work for Smute Function Developers, but also allows for a uniform usage of Smute Functions. This chapter documents the uniform usage. Section 3.1 lists the necessary steps for Smute Function invocation, from obtaining the necessary files to the execution of Smute Functions via the Smute Interpreter. These steps are illustrated with a running example. A comprehensive description of Smute Launch Files follows in Section 3.2. It includes their Backus-Naur form.

3.1 Step-by-Step Smute Function Usage

The steps of Smute Function invocation are illustrated with the following trivial running example: For arithmetic expressions a Smute Function User wants to visualise the grammar-dependent CARGOTREEs. Although the respective Smute Function is rather useless, it is well-suited for the illustration of general Smute Function invocation principles.

Step 1: Gather the necessary files and read the documentation

Smute Functions are usually distributed in the form of Smute Packages. The most important files in a Smute Package are the Smute Modules ('.tmm'-files) containing the desired Smute Functions. Apart from these Smute Modules a Smute Package typically contains additional files like the following:

- additional Smute Modules containing Smute Functions that are called from within the main Smute Functions (in other words: Smute Modules from the dependency tree);

- Compiled Grammar Tables ('.cgt'-files) in order to support the specification of data in the respective languages;

- example Smute Launch Files invoking Smute Functions of the Smute Package;

- example data instance files in binary format or text format; and

- documentation files.

For each Smute Module all the additional Smute Modules it depends on (if any) are required. Usually these additional Smute Modules are part of the Smute Package. In some cases however, due to copyright reasons, it might be up to the Smute Function User to obtain additional Smute Modules. Missing Smute Modules are reported to the Smute Function User on Smute Function invocation.

Most Smute Packages already contain the Smute Interpreter. For others it must be obtained separately. In the latter case care has to be taken to choose the correct Smute Interpreter Edition. For Smute Packages not requiring a special Smute Interpreter Edition, any edition suffices.

Here is a summary of the standard procedure for gathering the necessary files:

1. Obtain the Smute Package (Smute Modules plus other files).

2. Find out about the following:

    (a) Is the Smute Package self-contained, or are there additional Smute Modules or Smute Packages required? In the latter case, where can those additional files be obtained from?

    (b) Is the Smute Interpreter contained in the Smute Package? If not, is a special Smute Interpreter Edition required, and if so, which one?

According to the answers to these questions it might be necessary to obtain additional files. Note that it might be necessary to repeat this step for additional Smute Packages or Smute Modules.

Example 3.1 In the running example the Smute Package consists of the following files:

```
m_devutil.tmm
expr.cgt
smute.exe
10000.txt
expr00.txt
readme.txt
```

- "m_devutil.tmm" is a Smute Module. Smute Module-filenames always have prefix 'm_' and suffix '.tmm'. As it is the only Smute Module of this Smute Package, it is this Smute Module which exports the desired Smute Function creating visualisations of grammar-dependent CARGOTREEs.

- "expr.cgt" is a "Compiled Grammar Table". Compiled Grammar Tables are LALR-parsing tables created by GOLD Parser Builder [3]. "expr.cgt" is an LALR-parsing table for arithmetic expressions.

- "smute.exe" is the Smute Interpreter (Windows version).

- "10000.txt" is an example Smute Launch File.

- "expr00.txt" is an example input specification, i.e., a specification of an arithmetic expression.

- "readme.txt" is a documentation file. In this trivial example it just states that the function for CARGOTREE-visualisation is called **DumpCargoTree** and that the Smute Package is self-contained, i.e., that no additional files are required. It also documents the syntax for input specifications. □

Step 2: Prepare a working directory

The Smute Interpreter is a command-line program which expects all its input files in the 'current directory', and writes all output files to that directory. The following files are read by the Smute Interpreter: Smute Launch Files, Smute Modules ('.tmm'-files), Compiled Grammar Tables ('.cgt'-files), and external data specification files. It is recommended to retain all these files in one directory, which should be the 'current directory' at the time of running the Smute Interpreter. Documentation files are of course unaffected by the Smute Interpreter and can be stored in different locations.

Example 3.2 For the running example all the files as listed in Example 3.1 are assumed to be copied to one directory. □

Step 3: Write data specifications and a Smute Launch File

Which parameters a Smute Function takes and how they are specified is explained in the Smute Package documentation. The typical way of learning about input data specification syntax is to take a look at example specifications. For the details the Smute Package documentation should be read: It contains the Backus-Naur forms of the according specification languages.

For input data specified in a Smute Launch File, the syntax is documented with the respective Smute Interpreter Edition.

In many cases the easiest way of writing new Smute Launch Files is to copy existing example-Smute Launch Files and alter them.

Example 3.3 Example Smute Launch File "10000.txt" is listed below[1]:

```
(1)    // example translation launch file
(2)    <expr0>      := #load("expr00.txt","expr.cgt")
(3)
(4)    loadmodules(devutil);
(5)
(6)    devutil:DumpCargoTree(expr0,40);
```

Obvserve the following structure of a Smute Launch File:

1. Data declaration and/or specification;

2. Smute Module load declaration;

3. Smute Function calls.

Line comments start with "//". Line (2) states that data identifier "expr0" is assigned the content of file "expr00.txt", which is parsed with the LALR-parsing-table "expr.cgt". Thus "expr0" identifies a CARGOTREE in a grammar-dependent CARGOTREE-Scheme. In line (6) this CARGOTREE is then passed as first parameter to Smute Function **DumpCargoTree** of Smute Module "m_devutil.tmm". Note that in a Smute Module reference the prefix "m_" and the suffix ".tmm" are omitted. The second parameter determines the filename of the output-file—for example, for value 40 a file named "tree0040.gdl" is created. Line (4) declares which Smute Modules are used. This declaration mainly serves the awareness of which Smute Modules are required, including potential Smute Modules from the dependency tree. The "loadmodules"-declaration is not handled very strictly by the Smute Interpreter: For Smute Modules missing in the declaration only a warning-message is issued. The syntax of Smute Launch Files is documented in full detail in Section 3.2.1 on pages 31ff.

Data specification file "expr00.txt" consists of the following line:

```
2*x^2+3*y
```

It is the specification of arithmetic expression $2x^2 + 3y$. Now it should be obvious how to specify new input data, e.g., arithmetic expression $a^{4b+5c} + 7bc$:

---

[1]The line-numbers are not part of the Smute Launch File, but only added here for referencation purposes.

```
a^(4*b+5*c)+7*b*c
```

If this is saved as "`expr01.txt`", then it can be passed to the Smute Function **DumpCargoTree** by altering the Smute Launch File as follows:

```
// example translation launch file
<expr0>     := #load("expr00.txt","expr.cgt")
<expr1>     := #load("expr01.txt","expr.cgt")

loadmodules(devutil);

devutil:DumpCargoTree(expr0,40);
devutil:DumpCargoTree(expr1,41);
```

□

Generally it is not necessary to be careful with specifications in a Smute Launch File or in text files used as input data: For example, in the case of mistyped Smute Module-names or Smute Function-names a notification about their non-existence is issued. Only with the specification of Smute Function parameters care needs to be taken, as there is no type-checking[2]:

! WARNING !

There is no type-checking whatsoever for parameters passed to Smute Functions. In all of the following cases the Smute Interpreter crashes:

- An `INTEGER`-parameter is passed where a `CARGOTREE` is expected.

- A `CARGOTREE`-parameter does not comply with the expected `CARGOTREE`-Scheme (for example, an arithmetic expression is provided in the place of a propositional formula).

- Fewer parameters than expected are specified.

Step 5: Launch the Smute Functions and view the results

A Smute Function can be invoked by passing a Smute Launch File to the Smute Interpreter, i.e., the name of a Smute Launch File is the only (command-line-)parameter of the Smute Interpreter. The sequence of Smute Function calls specified in the Smute Launch File is then executed one after another. For each Smute Function messages indicate as to whether it has been successfully executed or why execution failed. Usually each invoked Smute Function creates one or more output-files. In most cases the names of such output-files are determined by Smute Function parameters. Alongside files in other formats many Smute Functions create output in Graph Description Language (GDL). GDL-files permit to visualise the output with the graph visualisation software `aiSee` [1].

Example 3.4 Open a command-line interface. Example for many Windows-versions: Click "Start", then "Run...", type "`cmd.exe`", then click "OK". Change the current directory to the Smute working directory. Call the Smute Interpreter and pass the Smute Launch File.

```
>cd smutedir
>smute 10000.txt
```

Now successful executions, errors, and warnings are reported. The output should be as follows:

---

[2]The implementation of parameter type-checking would require lots of additional effort and is currently not planned.

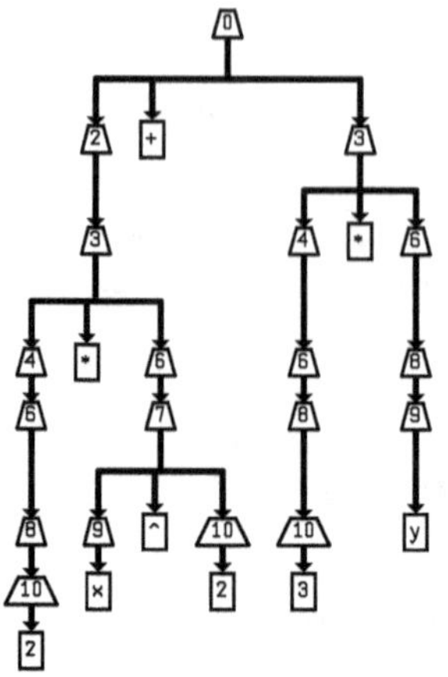

Figure 3.1: CARGOTREE in grammar-dependent CARGOTREE-Scheme

```
Executing function "devutil:DumpCargoTree(expr0,40)"...
Done.
```

As explained in Example 3.3, for Smute Function **DumpCargoTree** the second parameter determines the output-filename, here—for a value of 40—it is "tree0040.gdl". In this example the output is the visualisation of the grammar-dependent CARGOTREE representing the expression stored in file "expr00.txt", namely $2x^2 + 3y$. Loading file "tree0040.gdl" with aiSee yields the visualisation of Figure 4.2. □

3.2 Smute Launch File Documentation

Smute Functions are launched by writing the appropriate specifications, namely which function to invoke with which input, in a Smute Launch File, and then passing the Smute Launch File to the Smute Interpreter.

Examples for Smute Launch Files have been given in Section 3.1. This section provides a short summary of Smute Launch Files. Smute Launch Files consist of three parts: The *data declaration* part, the *loadmodules declaration*, and the *function calls*. In the data declaration part data instances are assigned to variables. Currently there are the following options for assignment:

- A #load-instruction with one parameter, namely the filename of a file in CARGOTREE Exchange Format. This file is automatically loaded into a CARGOTREE by Smute.

- A #load-instruction with two parameters, the first the filename of a text-file in an LALR-language, and the second the filename of a Compiled Grammar Table, i.e., an LALR-parsing-table for that language. The text-file is automatically loaded into a CARGOTREE in grammar-dependent CARGOTREE-Scheme by Smute.

- Various Smute Interpreter Editions allow the specification of text in certain LALR-languages directly within the Smute Launch File. Such a specification is automatically loaded into a CARGOTREE in grammar-dependent CARGOTREE-Scheme by Smute.

In the `loadmodules` declaration the required Smute Modules are listed. All the Smute Modules referenced in the function call part should be listed, plus additional Smute Modules from the dependency trees. The `loadmodules` declaration serves the awareness of required Smute Modules.

The function calls part contains a sequence of Smute Function calls. Instances of recursively structured data are passed via the variables of the data declaration part.

3.2.1 Smute Launch File Syntax

Printed below is the Backus-Naur form for Smute Launch Files: Start symbol is `comb`. The grammar is specified in the GOLD Parser [3] Backus-Naur form syntax. `Letter` and `Digit` are predefined character sets for GOLD Parser containing ASCII letters a-z, A-Z and ASCII digits 0-9 respectively. A line-comment is started with '`//`' (two slashes). Block-comments are currently not supported, neither in Smute Launch Files, nor in data specification files parsed by the Smute Interpreter.

```
{hexdigit}              = {Digit} + [abcdefABCDEF]
{id_head}               = {Letter} + [_]
{id_tail}               = {id_head} + {Digit}
{stringchar}            = {any}-["]

decliteral              = {Digit}+
hexliteral              = 0x{hexdigit}+
id                      = {id_head}{id_tail}*
string                  = '"' {stringchar}* '"'


!----------------------------------------------------------------
! combined specification
!----------------------------------------------------------------

<comb>                  ::= <declarray> <modloade> <fnccallarray>


!----------------------------------------------------------------
! declarations
!----------------------------------------------------------------

<cmdparam>              ::= decliteral
                          | hexliteral
                          | string

<cmdparamarray>         ::= <cmdparam> ',' <cmdparamarray>
                          | <cmdparam>

<cmdparamarraye>        ::= <cmdparamarray>
                          |

<command>               ::= '#' id '(' <cmdparamarraye> ')'

<declarray>             ::= <decl> <declarray>
                          |

<decl>                  ::= '<' id '>' ':=' <declrhs>
```

```
<declrhs>                    ::= <command>


!-----------------------------------------------------------------
! module load instruction
!-----------------------------------------------------------------

<modidarray>                 ::= id ',' <modidarray>
                             | id

<modload>                    ::= 'loadmodules' '(' <modidarray> ')' ';'

<modloade>                   ::= <modload>
                             |


!-----------------------------------------------------------------
! generic rules
!-----------------------------------------------------------------

<numberval>                  ::= decliteral
                             | hexliteral


!-----------------------------------------------------------------
! (translation) function calls
!-----------------------------------------------------------------

<fncref>                     ::= id ':' id

<varspec>                    ::= id
                             | <fncref>
                             | <numberval>

<varspecarray>               ::= <varspec> ',' <varspecarray>
                             | <varspec>

<varspecarraye>              ::= <varspecarray>
                             |

<fnccall>                    ::= id ':' id '(' <varspecarraye> ')' ';'

<fnccallarray>               ::= <fnccall> <fnccallarray>
                             |
```

For other editions than the Standard Edition the rule for declrhs is:

```
<declrhs>                    ::= <command>
                             | <data>
```

The rules for data depend on the edition.

Chapter 4

Writing Smute Functions

Using a text-editor, Smute Function Developers write Smute Functions as sequences of Smute Language instructions in their textual mnemonics. From these textual specifications Smute Modules can be created with the Smute Assembler.

The Smute Language with all its instructions is documented in Section 4.1. Section 4.2 describes CARGOTREE-Schemes, i.e., conventions for the representation of data with a specific recursive structure using CARGOTREEs. Data I/O for Smute Functions is covered in Section 4.3. Section 4.4 presents guidelines for writing modular Smute Functions. Finally, Section 4.5 documents the usage of the Smute Assembler.

4.1   The Smute Language

As has been mentioned in the Smute Function User Manual, the Smute Language is a machine language for a virtual machine. This virtual machine provides functionality that is typically required when working with recursively structured data. It introduces an abstract layer, where it is possible to specify *what* should be done with the recursively structured data, without having to care *how* this is done.

4.1.1   Virtual Machine Characteristics

Almost every instruction of the Smute Language operates on some of the virtual machine's *registers*. In its current version the machine has got 64 registers, each with a size of 32 bits. In the Smute Language these registers are referenced with identifiers 'R00' to 'R63'. Of course the machine supports all the usual 32-bit integer (arithmetic) operations, like 'addition', 'multiplication', 'bitwise and', etc. Not yet available are floating-point operations. Like with common microprocessors there is also a status register, its flags indicating the results of, for example, comparisons. The virtual machine provides several so-called *resources*. As indicated by the name 'resource', these are of limited availability. Most of these resources require memory on the host machine the translation is executed on, which means limitations come from the host machine's available memory. A (register's) *datatype* refers to the way a value is interpreted: For example, INTEGER for the interpretation as integer value, or HASHINT for the interpretation as resource identifier for a HASHINT resource. Many implementation details are hidden from the virtual machine layer. For example, adding a new node to a CARGOTREE could fail on the host machine due to unavailable memory. Though the virtual machine instruction "pretends" it could not fail. Instead, such errors are automatically treated at the implementation layer—the whole top-level Smute Function is aborted if one occurs.

4.1.2 Resources

Stack

The *Stack*-resource is one of the key-concepts of the Smute Language. In the Smute virtual machine there are currently 2 stacks, the *calling-stack* and the *data-stack*. Whenever a subroutine is called, the *return address* is pushed on the calling stack. The return-address is the address of the instruction following the subroutine-call. Whenever a 'return from subroutine' instruction is encountered, a return address is popped from the calling stack and execution continues there. For the data-stack there are push-/pop-instructions in the Smute Language.

The important point about the stacks is their implementation side: First of all, there is no implicit stack-usage (subroutine-calling and -returning is considered explicit). Thus, a Smute Function Developer has full control over the byte-size of stack-requirements in the implementation. Second, the stacks are implemented as dynamic stacks, meaning their size is limited only by the available memory on the host machine. This is essential, as the amount of stack-space actually required for the execution of a Smute Function is usually proportional to the recursive depth of the data it processes. Especially for Smute Functions that get recursively called, unnecessary (or unnecessarily large) stack-allocations must be avoided, as they cumulate with each recursive level.

CARGOTREE

The Smute Language introduces so-called *CARGOTREE-node*-resources. Every CARGOTREE-node has a *type*. Additional data associated with a CARGOTREE-node depends on its type. There are the following types (*I8*, *I32*, and *STR* identify datatypes, namely 8-bit-integer, 32-bit integer, and byte-array respectively):

type	full name	associated data
ConCls	Classic Connector	*id* (I8), child-array
ConArr	Array Connector	*id* (I8), child-array
Int	Integer Leaf	*id* (I8), *value* (I32)
Str	String Leaf	*id* (I8), *value* (STR)
LocalCon	Local Connector	*id* (I8), child-array
LocalInt	Local Integer Leaf	*id* (I8), *value* (I32)
LocalStr	Local String Leaf	*id* (I8), *value* (STR)
GrammarRule	Grammar Rule	*rule-id* (I32), child-array
GrammarToken	Grammar Token	*token-id* (I32), *value* (STR), *line* (I32), *column* (I32)
PseudoRoot	Pseudo Root	child-array (of size 1)

Smute is designed to support the introduction of new node-types in future versions. ConCls, ConArr, LocalCon, GrammarRule, and PseudoRoot nodes, which are classified as *inner* CARGOTREE-nodes, have an associated array (array-size$\geq$1) of references to other CARGOTREE-nodes. A CARGOTREE-node referenced from an inner node is called *child* of the inner node. The individual children are referenced with the array-index, for n children valid indices are $0, 1, \ldots, n-1$. A CARGOTREE-node a is called *parent* of CARGOTREE-node b if b is a child of a. CARGOTREE-nodes that are not inner nodes, i.e., CARGOTREE-nodes without children, are called *leaves*. A CARGOTREE-node b is called *descendant* of CARGOTREE-node a if

- b is a child of a or

- there is a child c of a of which b is a descendant.

A CARGOTREE-node a is called *ascendant* of CARGOTREE-node b if b is a descendant of a.

If a CARGOTREE-node a is fully initialised, i.e., if all the data associated with a is initialised, including—in the case of an inner node—all children, and if all descendants of a are fully initialised as well, then a together with all its descendants is called a *CARGOTREE*, and a is called the *root* of that CARGOTREE. In the Smute Language the identifier of a CARGOTREE is the identifier of its root-node. As opposed to CARGOTREE-node instructions, for CARGOTREE-instructions it is essential that the node and all its descendants are properly initialised in order to represent a CARGOTREE.

A CARGOTREE generated by the Smute parser consists of GrammarRule and GrammarToken nodes only, and reflects with this data structure the syntax-tree of the parsed sentence. GrammarRule and GrammarToken nodes cannot be created with instructions of the Smute Language.

The 'local' nodes LocalCon, LocalInt and LocalStr are intended for local (or temporary) usage in Smute Functions. With the local nodes a Smute Function can assign node-ids independent of already existing ids for non-local nodes. This can be useful especially for Smute Functions working with different CARGOTREE-Schemes.

Currently there is no difference between ConCls and ConArr nodes. However, ConCls should be used where for a given id the number of children is fixed, ConArr where for a given id there are multiple possibilities for the number of children. The distinction is made because Smute (theoretically) does not need to store the number of children for ConCls with each node, but only once for a given id. Thus storage space could be saved.

Obviously, node-types, ids, and the tree-structure (children) are intended for the representation of the structure of recursively structured data instances. The restriction for ids to be 8-bit only has to do with memory-efficiency of the implementation. For many common recursive data structures, like propositional formulas and arithmetic expressions, this available id range is absolutely sufficient. For Smute Function Developers working with recursive data structures where 8-bit ids are insufficient there are the following options:

- Structure information is stored in newly added Integer Leaves. This option is not recommended, because of more intricate access to the data and an unnecessary increase of memory usage on the implementation side.

- The Smute Language author is contacted, demanding the implementation of new node-types with 32-bit ids (a relatively simple task).

PseudoRoot nodes are provided for Smute Functions performing node replacement. If prior to node replacement a CARGOTREE is re-rooted with a PseudoRoot, then the CARGOTREE's original root can be replaced just like any other node (by assigning a new child to the parent node). This permits a considerable simplification of node replacement.

Smute Functions with CARGOTREE input and CARGOTREE output might use CARGOTREE-nodes of an input-CARGOTREE in an output-CARGOTREE. If this is the case then the Smute Function is said to *utilise* the input-CARGOTREE. For each input-CARGOTREE a Smute Function description must clearly state whether it is utilised or not.

CARGOTREEMEM

The CARGOTREEMEM is an important conception mainly for the implementation layer, but also aids in writing clear and simple specifications in the Smute Language.

Obviously nodes of CARGOTREEs require storage locations. Each time a new CARGOTREE-node is created, it is allocated from a CARGOTREEMEM. That is, nodes are not allocated from a "global memory", but grouped to allocations from CARGOTREEMEMs. The important point is that nodes can *not* be deallocated from CARGOTREEMEMs, instead, it is always a complete CARGOTREEMEM which is discarded.

For Smute Function Developers this has the advantage that whole CARGOTREEs, consisting possibly of hundreds of thousands of nodes, can be discarded with one single built-in instruction of the Smute Language (if all the nodes are allocated from the same CARGOTREEMEM).

As a PseudoRoot node is always of temporary nature (attached before applying replacement functions, removed afterwards), PseudoRoot nodes are *not* allocated from CARGOTREEMEMs. Instead, PseudoRoot nodes are resources of their own and have to be discarded separately.

ARRAY

The Smute Language provides an *ARRAY* resource with the very basic array functionality: indexed element access. An ARRAY is always an array of 32-bit-values. For the ARRAY resource the array-size is determined at the time of array-creation. There is no built-in support for growing/shrinking array-sizes. If required by Smute Function Developers, future versions of the Smute Language could implement such functionality with either the ARRAY datatype, or a new array datatype. The ARRAY-resource can, for example, be useful in Smute Functions working with arrays of recursively structured data where such arrays are not part of the recursive data structure.

Hash resources

The Hash-resources are provided for functions working with recursively structured data that involves identifiers, like variable names in arithmetic expressions. Typical identifier-operations are illustrated with the following example expression:

```
x^2+3*x+5*y
```

Essential tasks (required, for example, in substitutions) are:

- *re-identification*: tell that in subexpression `3*x` the same variable is referenced like in subexpression `x^2`, while in subexpression `5*y` it is a different one.

- *collection*: tell that there are 2 variables occurring in the expression, and that their names are x and y.

The Hash-resources and its associated instructions of the Smute Language provide these features. The name, Hash-resources, comes from an efficient implementation technique, namely hash-tables. Hash-table knowledge is not required for an understanding of the Smute Language. For those interested anyway, almost any computer science related book features hash-tables. The following resources are subsumed as *Hash*-resources:

- HASHSTRCOL,

- HASHINT,

- HASHINTCOL,

- HASHINTSTACK.

The different Hash-resources are very similar, with only slight variations of their features. In fact, some Hash-resources only extend other Hash-resource's features. As simpler Hash-types allow for a more efficient implementation, Smute Function Developers should always use the Hash-resource with minimal sufficient functionality.

For a Hash-resource there is a collection of so-called *Hash-entries*. Upon creation, Hash-instances are empty. An arbitrary number of Hash-entries can be sequentially added. For every Hash-entry there is an identifier, called the *key*. The crucial property of the Hash-resources is that any key can occur only once in a Hash, i.e., at most in one Hash-entry. In addition to the key arbitrary data can be stored in a Hash-Entry.

Those Hash-resources with 'STR' in their name work with string-keys, while those with 'INT' in their name work with integer-keys. Each Hash-resource has its own Hash-entry-resources, namely HASHSTRCOLENTRY, HASHINTENTRY, etc.

For a Hash-instance and any string or any integer respectively, there are two possibilities: Either the string/integer is a key occurring in the Hash (once), or it does not occur. One can find out by passing the string or integer to a 'Find'-instruction, which returns the Hash-entry if there is one with that key, and otherwise informs about the key's non-occurrence. In the Smute Language the instructions for adding entries to Hashes never add a key more than once. Instead, for a key already occurring in the Hash the according existing Hash-entry is returned. It should be obvious how these features can be used for re-identification.

Those Hash-resources with 'COL' (abbreviating 'collection') in their name permit to browse through all the Hash-entries. This can, for example, be used to copy the keys occurring in the Hash to an array[1]. When browsing through 'COL'-Hashes, entries appear in the order they have been added. They can be browsed forward (starting with the first Hash-entry that has been added) and backward (starting with the last Hash-entry that has been added). Obviously, a 'COL'-Hash only extends the original Hash's features. For example, there is nothing one can do with HASHINT that could not be done with a HASHINTCOL. As mentioned above, a Smute Function Developer should always use the Hash-resource with minimal sufficient functionality, as simpler Hash-resources are implemented more efficiently. For HASHINT and HASHINTCOL this means that if browsing through Hash-entries is not required, then HASHINT should be used.

In order to describe the HASHINTSTACK-resource a detail of the previously introduced Hashes needs to be focussed. So far only adding Hash-entries and retrieving them has been mentioned. Though there might be situations where one wants to add an entry temporarily, which means it must be removable again. In this context it should be known that in the implementation Hash-entries are not allocated and deallocated individually, for the same reasons this is not done with CARGOTREE-nodes, namely allocation overhead. Instead, all Hash-entries are deallocated 'at once' when the Hash gets discarded. So while a Hash-entry could be removed (it is technically possible), it would still waste memory. Thus adding and removing of Hash-entries should not occur at a frequent basis with these Hash-types. Currently there are no instructions for removing Hash-entries from these Hash-resources anyway.

HASHINTSTACK provides the same features as HASHINT plus a special Hash-entry-removal. With HASHINTSTACK it is possible to always remove the last Hash-entry (the one last added to the Hash). The removed Hash-entry does *not* waste any memory and for the implementation allocation efficiency is practically the same as with HASHINT. HASHINTSTACK is typically used when processing identifiers of a CARGOTREE with the following method: the CARGOTREE is traversed with depth-first traversal, integer-identifiers are added on entering a subtree and removed on leaving a subtree. Then it is always the last Hash-entry that needs to be removed, which means that HASHINTSTACK is sufficient.

HASHSTR- and HASHSTRSTACK-resources are postponed to future versions.

4.1.3 Instructions

This section lists all the Smute Language instructions. It starts with an overview and is followed by detailed descriptions on page 42. The instructions are sorted by their type of functionality.

- Flow control instructions:

  - Label (p.42): Declare a Smute Module position identifier (label).
  - BSR (p.42): Branch To Subroutine.
  - BRA (p.42): Unconditional Branch.
  - BEQ (p.42): Conditional Branch (Equal).
  - BNE (p.42): Conditional Branch (Not Equal).

---

[1]With the other Hash-resources this is not possible, because there the entries can only be retrieved with their keys. As these keys are unknown, every potential key would have to be tested for occurrence in the Hash. There are however 2^{32} integer keys, and a theoretically infinite number of string keys.

- `BLT` (p.42): Conditional Branch (Less Than).
- `BGT` (p.43): Conditional Branch (Greater Than).
- `BLE` (p.43): Conditional Branch (Less or Equal).
- `BGE` (p.43): Conditional Branch (Greater or Equal).
- `JumpTab` (p.43): Conditional branches determined by a register's value.
- `FarBSR` (p.44): Far Branch To Subroutine.
- `FarBRA` (p.44): Far Unconditional Branch.
- `Return` (p.44): Return From Subroutine.

- Basic data transfer instructions:

  - `Clear` (p.44): Set a register to 0x00000000.
  - `Set` (p.44): Set a register to 0xFFFFFFFF.
  - `Swap` (p.44): Exchange two registers' contents.
  - `Move` (p.44): Copy the content of one register to another register.
  - `MoveImm` (p.45): Set a register to a specified integer value.

- Arithmetic instructions:

  - `CMP` (p.45): Compare the integer values of two registers.
  - `TST` (p.45): Test if a register contains value 0x00000000.
  - `Add` (p.45): Add the integer value of one register to that of another register.
  - `Sub` (p.45): Subtract the integer value of one register from that of another register.
  - `Mul` (p.45): Multiply the integer value of one register by that of another register.
  - `Div` (p.45): Divide the integer value of one register by that of another register.
  - `Mod` (p.46): Perform the integer modulo operation on two registers' values.
  - `And` (p.46): Perform the operation "bitwise and" on two registers' values.
  - `Or` (p.46): Perform the operation "bitwise or" on two registers' values.
  - `XOr` (p.46): Perform the operation "bitwise exclusive or" on two registers' values.
  - `Not` (p.46): Perform the operation "bitwise not" on a register's value.
  - `AddImm` (p.47): Add an integer value to the integer value of a register.
  - `SubImm` (p.47): Subtract an integer value from the integer value of a register.
  - `Add1` (p.47): Add 1 to the integer value of a register.
  - `Sub1` (p.47): Subtract 1 from the integer value of a register.
  - `AndTST` (p.47): Commands `And` and `TST` in one.
  - `LSL1` (p.47): Logical Shift Left (1 bit).
  - `LSR1` (p.48): Logical Shift Right (1 bit).

- Stack instructions:

  - `Push` (p.48): Allocate Stack-space.
  - `Pop` (p.48): Deallocate Stack-space.
  - `MoveToStack` (p.48): Store a register to the Stack.
  - `MoveFromStack` (p.48): Store a stack-value to a register.
  - `LSP` (p.49): Load the Stack Pointer into a register.

- Array instructions:

  - `NewArray` (p.49): Create a new ARRAY.
  - `DiscardArray` (p.49): Discard an ARRAY.

- ArraySize (p.49): Return the size of an ARRAY.
- ArraySet (p.49): Set an ARRAY element.
- ArrayGet (p.49): Get an ARRAY element.

- CARGOTREEMEM instructions:

  - NewCargoTreeMem (p.49): Create a new CARGOTREEMEM.
  - DiscardCargoTreeMem (p.50): Discard a CARGOTREEMEM.

- CARGOTREE-node instructions:

  - NewConClsImm (p.50): Create a new ConCls-node (Classic Connector).
  - NewConArrImm (p.50): Create a new ConArr-node (Array Connector).
  - NewIntImm (p.50): Create a new Int-node (Integer Leaf).
  - NewStrImm (p.50): Create a new Str-node (String Leaf).
  - NewIntImmSetVal (p.50): Create a new Int-node (Integer Leaf) and initialise its value.
  - NewPseudoRoot (p.51): Create a new PseudoRoot node.
  - DiscardPseudoRoot (p.51): Discard a PseudoRoot node.
  - GetNodeType (p.51): Return the type of a CARGOTREE-node.
  - GetNodeId (p.51): Return the id of a CARGOTREE-node.
  - SetNodeIdImm (p.51): Set the id of a CARGOTREE-node.
  - SetNodeId (p.51): Set the id of a CARGOTREE-node.
  - GetRuleId (p.51): Return the rule-id of a GrammarRule-node.
  - GetNumChildren (p.52): Return the number of children of a CARGOTREE-node.
  - GetChildImm (p.52): Return a child-node of a CARGOTREE-node.
  - GetChild (p.52): Return a child-node of a CARGOTREE-node.
  - GetRuleChildImm (p.52): Return a child-node of a GrammarRule-node.
  - GetRuleChild (p.52): Return a child-node of a GrammarRule-node.
  - PlugImm (p.52): Set a CARGOTREE-node's child node.
  - Plug (p.52): Set a CARGOTREE-node's child node.
  - RefToken (p.53): Re-reference the value of a GrammarToken-node in a Str-node.
  - RefStr (p.53): Re-reference the value of a Str-node in another Str-node.
  - GetVal (p.53): Return the value of an Int-node.
  - SetVal (p.53): Set the value of an Int-node.
  - SetValImm (p.53): Set the value of an Int-node.

- HASHSTRCOL instructions:

  - NewHashStrCol (p.53): Create a new HASHSTRCOL.
  - DiscardHashStrCol (p.53): Discard a HASHSTRCOL.
  - HashStrColAdd (p.54): Add a new HASHSTRCOLENTRY or return the existing one.
  - HashStrColFind (p.54): For a given key find the appropriate HASHSTRCOLENTRY.
  - MoveToHashStrColEntry (p.54): Store a register to a HASHSTRCOLENTRY data-field.
  - MoveFromHashStrColEntry (p.54): Store a HASHSTRCOLENTRY data-field to a register.
  - HashStrColNumEntries (p.54): Return a HASHSTRCOL's number of entries.
  - HashStrColBrowseInit (p.54): Get a handle for browsing through a HASHSTRCOL's entries.
  - HashStrColBrowseNext (p.54): Browse to the next entry of a HASHSTRCOL.

- `HashStrColBrowsePrev` (p.55): Browse to the previous entry of a `HASHSTRCOL`.

- `HASHINT` instructions:

  - `NewHashInt` (p.55): Create a new `HASHINT`.
  - `DiscardHashInt` (p.55): Discard a `HASHINT`.
  - `HashIntAddImm` (p.55): Add a new `HASHINTENTRY` or return the existing one.
  - `HashIntAdd` (p.55): Add a new `HASHINTENTRY` or return the existing one.
  - `HashIntFind` (p.55): For a given key find the appropriate `HASHINTENTRY`.
  - `HashIntEntryGetKey` (p.56): Return the key of a `HASHINTENTRY`.
  - `MoveToHashIntEntry` (p.56): Store a register to a `HASHINTENTRY` data-field.
  - `MoveFromHashIntEntry` (p.56): Store a `HASHINTENTRY` data-field to a register.
  - `HashIntNumEntries` (p.56): Return a `HASHINT`'s number of entries.

- `HASHINTCOL` instructions:

  - `NewHashIntCol` (p.56): Create a new `HASHINTCOL`.
  - `DiscardHashIntCol` (p.56): Discard a `HASHINTCOL`.
  - `HashIntColAddImm` (p.56): Add a new `HASHINTCOLENTRY` or return the existing one.
  - `HashIntColAdd` (p.57): Add a new `HASHINTCOLENTRY` or return the existing one.
  - `HashIntColFind` (p.57): For a given key find the appropriate `HASHINTCOLENTRY`.
  - `HashIntColEntryGetKey` (p.57): Return the key of a `HASHINTCOLENTRY`.
  - `MoveToHashIntColEntry` (p.57): Store a register to a `HASHINTCOLENTRY` data-field.
  - `MoveFromHashIntColEntry` (p.57): Store a `HASHINTCOLENTRY` data-field to a register.
  - `HashIntColNumEntries` (p.57): Return a `HASHINTCOL`'s number of entries.
  - `HashIntColBrowseInit` (p.57): Get a handle for browsing through a `HASHINTCOL`'s entries.
  - `HashIntColBrowseNext` (p.58): Browse to the next entry of a `HASHINTCOL`.
  - `HashIntColBrowsePrev` (p.58): Browse to the previous entry of a `HASHINTCOL`.

- `HASHINTSTACK` instructions:

  - `NewHashIntStack` (p.58): Create a new `HASHINTSTACK`.
  - `DiscardHashIntStack` (p.58): Discard a `HASHINTSTACK`.
  - `HashIntStackAdd` (p.58): Add a new `HASHINTSTACKENTRY` or return the existing one.
  - `HashIntStackRemove` (p.58): Remove the top-of-the-stack `HASHINTSTACKENTRY`.
  - `HashIntStackFind` (p.59): For a given key find the appropriate `HASHINTSTACKENTRY`.
  - `MoveToHashIntStackEntry` (p.59): Store a register to a `HASHINTSTACKENTRY` data-field.
  - `MoveFromHashIntStackEntry` (p.59): Store a `HASHINTSTACKENTRY` data-field to a register.

- `CARGOTREE` instructions:

  - `CopyCargoTree` (p.59): Create a copy of a `CARGOTREE`.
  - `CollectIntVal` (p.59): Create a new `HASHINTCOL` containing selected Int-values of a `CARGOTREE`.
  - `HashIntVal` (p.60): Create a new `HASHINT` containing selected Int-values of a `CARGOTREE`.
  - `HashIntValCont` (p.60): Add selected Int-values of a `CARGOTREE` to a `HASHINT`.

- SubstIntAscA (p.60): Perform substitution of selected Int-values of a CARGOTREE according to a HASHINTCOL.
- CopySubstIntAscA (p.60): Create a copy of a CARGOTREE in which selected Int-values are replaced according to a HASHINTCOL.
- CopySubstIntAscB (p.60): Create a copy of a CARGOTREE in which selected Int-values are replaced according to a HASHINT.
- CopyColSubstIntAscB (p.61): Create a copy of a CARGOTREE in which selected Int-values are replaced according to a HASHINT. The hash is extended if necessary.
- CopyColSubstIntAscBM (p.61): Create a copy of a CARGOTREE in which selected Int-values are replaced according to a HASHINT. The hash is extended if necessary.

- CARGOTREE export instructions:

  - WriteCargoTreeCGE (p.61): Store a CARGOTREE into a file in CARGOTREE Exchange Format.

- CARGOTREE visualisation export instructions:

  - WriteCargoTreeGDL (p.61): Store a CARGOTREE into a file in Graph Description Language.
  - WriteCargoTreeGDLImm (p.61): Store a CARGOTREE into a file in Graph Description Language.

- Developer instructions:

  - DevDumpReg (p.62): Dump a register.
  - DevDumpRegNote (p.62): Dump a register and mark it with a note-character.
  - DevDumpRegs (p.62): Dump subsequent registers.
  - DevDumpHashIntColImm (p.62): Dump a HASHINTCOL.
  - DevDumpStack (p.62): Dump entries of the main data stack.
  - DevDumpResourceSummary (p.62): Dump a summary of the number of resources in use.

- Smute Interpreter Logic Edition special instructions:

  - WriteCargoTreeBooleRaw (p.63): Store a QBF-CARGOTREE into a file in raw 'boole' QBF-format.
  - WriteCargoTreeBooleRawImm (p.63): Store a QBF-CARGOTREE into a file in raw 'boole' QBF-format.
  - WriteCargoTreeBoole (p.63): Store a QBF-CARGOTREE into a file in 'boole' QBF-format.
  - WriteCargoTreeBooleImm (p.63): Store a QBF-CARGOTREE into a file in 'boole' QBF-format.
  - WriteCargoTreeGDL_QBFS (p.63): Store a QBFS-CARGOTREE into a file in Graph Description Language.
  - WriteCargoTreeGDL_QBFSImm (p.63): Store a QBFS-CARGOTREE into a file in Graph Description Language.
  - WriteCargoTreeGDL_QBF (p.63): Store a QBF-CARGOTREE into a file in Graph Description Language.
  - WriteCargoTreeGDL_QBFImm (p.64): Store a QBF-CARGOTREE into a file in Graph Description Language.

This concludes the overview. Following next are the instruction descriptions.

Label

Declare a Smute Module position identifier (label).

Synopsis: Label(*label*);

Declares a label. Labels are used with flow control instructions like (conditional or unconditional) branches (BRA, BGE, ...). Labels must be module-wide unique. Functions are nothing else than (entry-point-)labels one can BSR (branch-to-subroutine) to. Smute Module exports are declared with the function's entry-point-label. *label* is a non-empty string of arbitrary length which must comply with the following naming conventions:

- The first character is one of a-z, A-Z (lowercase or uppercase letter), or '_' (underscore).

- The other characters (if any) are one of a-z, A-Z, '_' (underscore), or 0-9 (digit).

Note that Label is a textual mnemonic for Smute Module position specification and referencing, but not a real command.

BSR

Branch To Subroutine.

Synopsis: BSR(*label*);

Pushes the position following the BSR-command onto the calling-stack and continues execution at the position referenced with *label*. Also see Label and Return.

BRA

Unconditional Branch.

Synopsis: BRA(*label*);

Continues execution at the position referenced with *label*. Also see Label.

BEQ

Conditional Branch (Equal).

Synopsis: BEQ(*label*);

Continues execution at the position referenced with *label* if the Z (Zero) condition flag is set. Otherwise continues with the instruction following BEQ. Also see Label and CMP.

BNE

Conditional Branch (Not Equal).

Synopsis: BNE(*label*);

Continues execution at the position referenced with *label* if the Z (Zero) condition flag is cleared. Otherwise continues with the instruction following BNE. Also see Label and CMP.

BLT

Conditional Branch (Less Than).

Synopsis: BLT(*label*);

Continues execution at the position referenced with *label* if the V (Overflow) condition flag is set and the Z (Zero) condition flag is cleared. Otherwise continues with the instruction following BLT. Also see Label and CMP.

BGT

Conditional Branch (Greater Than).
Synopsis: BGT(*label*);
Continues execution at the position referenced with *label* if both the V (Overflow) condition flag and the Z (Zero) condition flag are cleared. Otherwise continues with the instruction following BGT. Also see Label and CMP.

BLE

Conditional Branch (Less Or Equal).
Synopsis: BLE(*label*);
Continues execution at the position referenced with *label* if at least one of the V (Overflow) condition flag and the Z (Zero) condition flag is set. Otherwise continues with the instruction following BLE. Also see Label and CMP.

BGE

Conditional Branch (Greater or Equal).
Synopsis: BGE(*label*);
Continues execution at the position referenced with *label* if the V (Overflow) condition flag is cleared or the Z (Zero) condition flag is set. Otherwise continues with the instruction following BGE. Also see Label and CMP.

JumpTab

Conditional branches determined by a register's value.
Synopsis: JumpTab(*regsrc*,
                         val0,label0,
                         val1,label1,
                         ...,...);
A JumpTab has the same effect like the sequence of commands

```
MoveImm(val0,regcmp);
CMP(regsrc,regcmp);
BEQ(label0);
MoveImm(val1,regcmp);
CMP(regsrc,regcmp);
BEQ(label1);
...
```

where *val0*, *val1* are integers. Not only is using the JumpTab command more convenient, the Smute Interpreter also interprets it more efficiently than a code segment like the one above: Whatever the actual value of *regsrc*, the execution effort is the same. However, there are prerequisites for using this command. Let *vall* be the lowest (unsigned integer order) and *valh* be the highest of the integers *val0*, *val1*, etc. Then the prerequisites can be expressed as follows:

- It is known that *regsrc* takes no value lower than *vall* and no value higher than *valh*. If this condition is not met, the Smute Function crashes during the execution of the JumpTab command.

- *valh-vall* is a small value, i.e., all the different values are from within a relatively small range. This constraint is caused by storage requirement, which is proportional to (*valh-vall*). If the range is too large the Smute Module cannot be successfully assembled.

43

Integer identifiers that could be used to determine flow control should consequently always be taken from a small range. This is especially true for CARGOTREE-Scheme node-ids, which otherwise cannot be used as JumpTab-parameters.

FarBSR

Far Branch To Subroutine.
Synopsis: FarBSR(*module*,*label*);
Pushes the position following the FarBSR-command onto the calling-stack and continues execution at the position referenced with *label* in the Smute Module referenced with *module*. The *module*-reference is written without the prefix 'm_' and the suffix '.tmm' of module-filenames. Also see Label and Return.

FarBRA

Far Unconditional Branch.
Synopsis: FarBRA(*module*,*label*);
Continues execution at the position referenced with *label* in the Smute Module referenced with *module*. The *module*-reference is written without the prefix 'm_' and the suffix '.tmm' of module-filenames. Also see Label.

Return

Return From Subroutine.
Synopsis: Return;
Pops a return-position from the calling-stack and continues execution there. Also see BSR and FarBSR.

Clear

Set a register to 0x00000000.
Synopsis: Clear(*regdst*);
Sets *regdst* to value 0x00000000.

Set

Set a register to 0xFFFFFFFF.
Synopsis: Set(*regdst*);
Sets *regdst* to value 0xFFFFFFFF.

Swap

Exchange two registers' contents.
Synopsis: Swap(*reg0*,*reg1*);
Exchanges the contents of registers *reg0* and *reg1*.

Move

Copy the content of one register to another register.
Synopsis: Move(*regsrc*,*regdst*);
Sets *regdst* to the content of *regsrc*. *regsrc* is left unchanged.

MoveImm

Set a register to a specified integer value.
Synopsis: MoveImm(*val*,*regdst*);
Sets *regdst* to *val*.

CMP

Compare the integer values of two registers.
Synopsis: CMP(*reg0*,*reg1*);
Compares the integer in *reg1* to the integer in *reg0* (unsigned integer order) and sets the condition flags Z (Zero) and V (Overflow) accordingly.
Examples (lowercase letters z and v for cleared, uppercase for set):

reg0	*reg1*	condition flags	
1	2	zv	(for example, BGT would branch, BLE would not)
2	2	Zv	(for example, BEQ would branch, BLT would not)
3	2	zV	(for example, BLE would branch, BGT would not)

TST

Test if a register contains value $0x00000000$.
Synopsis: TST(*reg*);
Sets the Z (Zero) condition flag if *reg* contains value $0x00000000$, otherwise clears it. In most cases the instruction following TST is either BEQ or BNE.

Add

Add the integer value of one register to that of another register.
Synopsis: Add(*regsrc*,*regdst*);
Adds the integer of *regsrc* to the integer of *regdst* (the result is stored there). The addition is performed within $\mathbb{Z}_{0x100000000}$. This command does *not* affect condition flags.

Sub

Subtract the integer value of one register from that of another register.
Synopsis: Sub(*regsrc*,*regdst*);
Subtracts the integer of *regsrc* from the integer of *regdst* (the result is stored there). The subtraction is performed within $\mathbb{Z}_{0x100000000}$. This command does *not* affect condition flags.

Mul

Multiply the integer value of one register by that of another register.
Synopsis: Mul(*regsrc*,*regdst*);
Multiplies the integer of *regsrc* by the integer of *regdst* (the result is stored there). The multiplication is performed within $\mathbb{Z}_{0x100000000}$. This command does *not* affect condition flags.

Div

Divide the integer value of one register by that of another register.
Synopsis: Div(*regsrc*,*regdst*);
Divides the integer of *regdst* by the integer of *regsrc*, the result is stored in *regdst*. The usual integer division is applied, which means that, if the integer value of *regsrc* is called i and the integer value of *regdst* is called j, the result is $\frac{j-(j \bmod i)}{i}$. The behaviour for a *regsrc* value of 0 is undefined, calling Div with that value must be avoided. This command does *not* affect condition flags.

Mod

Perform the integer modulo operation on two registers' values.

Synopsis: Mod(*regsrc,regdst*);

If the integer value of *regsrc* is called i and the integer value of *regdst* is called j, then $j \bmod i$ is calculated and stored in register *regdst*. The behaviour for a *regsrc* value of 0 is undefined, calling Mod with that value must be avoided. This command does *not* affect condition flags.

And

Perform the operation "bitwise and" on two registers' values.

Synopsis: And(*regsrc,regdst*);

"bitwise and" is defined as follows:

bit0	bit1	bitwiseand(bit0,bit1)
0	0	0
0	1	0
1	0	0
1	1	1

It is applied to the 32 bits of registers *regsrc* and *regdst* and stored in register *regdst*. This command does *not* affect condition flags.

Or

Perform the operation "bitwise or" on two registers' values.

Synopsis: Or(*regsrc,regdst*);

"bitwise or" is defined as follows:

bit0	bit1	bitwiseor(bit0,bit1)
0	0	0
0	1	1
1	0	1
1	1	1

It is applied to the 32 bits of registers *regsrc* and *regdst* and stored in register *regdst*. This command does *not* affect condition flags.

XOr

Perform the operation "bitwise exclusive or" on two registers' values.

Synopsis: XOr(*regsrc,regdst*);

"bitwise exclusive or" is defined as follows:

bit0	bit1	bitwisexor(bit0,bit1)
0	0	0
0	1	1
1	0	1
1	1	0

It is applied to the 32 bits of registers *regsrc* and *regdst* and stored in register *regdst*. This command does *not* affect condition flags.

Not

Perform the operation "bitwise not" on a register's value.

Synopsis: Not(*regdst*);

"bitwise not" is defined as follows:

bit	bitwisenot(bit)
0	1
1	0

It is applied to the 32 bits of register *regdst* (and stored there). This command does *not* affect condition flags.

AddImm

Add an integer value to the integer value of a register.
Synopsis: `AddImm`(*val,regdst*);
Adds the integer *val* to the integer of *regdst* (the result is stored there). The addition is performed within $\mathbb{Z}_{0x100000000}$. This command does *not* affect condition flags.

SubImm

Subtract an integer value from the integer value of a register.
Synopsis: `SubImm`(*val,regdst*);
Subtracts the integer *val* from the integer of *regdst* (the result is stored there). The subtraction is performed within $\mathbb{Z}_{0x100000000}$. This command does *not* affect condition flags.

Add1

Add 1 the integer value of a register.
Synopsis: `Add1`(*regdst*);
Adds 1 to the integer of *regdst* (the result is stored there). The addition is performed within $\mathbb{Z}_{0x100000000}$. This command does *not* affect condition flags.

Sub1

Subtract 1 from the integer value of a register.
Synopsis: `Sub1`(*regdst*);
Subtracts 1 from the integer of *regdst* (the result is stored there). The subtraction is performed within $\mathbb{Z}_{0x100000000}$. This command does *not* affect condition flags.

AndTST

Commands `And` and `TST` in one.
Synopsis: `AndTST`(*regsrc,regdst*);
Has exactly the same effects as

```
And(regsrc,regdst);
TST(regdst);
```

See `And` and `TST` for further description.

LSL1

Logical Shift Left (1 bit).
Synopsis: `LSL1`(*regdst*);
Shifts the bits of *regdst* to the left by 1 bit. The rightmost bit (bit 0) is cleared. This command does *not* affect condition flags.

LSR1

Logical Shift Right (1 bit).
Synopsis: LSR1(*regdst*);
Shifts the bits of *regdst* to the right by 1 bit. The leftmost bit (bit 31) is cleared. This command does *not* affect condition flags.

Push

Allocate Stack-space.
Synopsis: Push(*numdata*);
numdata is an integer specification determining the number of 32-bit storage locations allocated on the stack. Also see Pop, MoveToStack and MoveFromStack.

Pop

Deallocate Stack-space.
Synopsis: Pop(*numdata*);
numdata is an integer specification determining the number of 32-bit storage locations deallocated from the stack. It must exactly match a previous Push. Also see Push, MoveToStack and MoveFromStack.

MoveToStack

Store a register to the Stack.
Synopsis: MoveToStack(*regsrc,stackidx*);
Stores the register *regsrc* to one of the storage locations that have been allocated with Push. The storage location is selected with an index *stackidx*. If n storage locations have been allocated with Push(n), then available storage location indices are $0,1,\ldots,n-1$. Using an invalid storage index causes a runtime crash (i.e., it is not detected by the Smute Assembler). The data stored to the stack can be re-retrieved with MoveFromStack. Also see Push, Pop and MoveFromStack.

MoveFromStack

Store a stack-value to a register.
Synopsis: MoveFromStack(*stackidx,regdst*);
Stores the value from the stack-location referenced with *stackidx* to the register *regdst*. This only makes sense if a value has been stored there before. See MoveToStack for an explanation of stack storage location selection with parameter *stackidx*. Here is example code that implements a swap, that is exchanging two registers' (R00 and R01) values, without affecting any other registers:

```
Push(1);
MoveToStack(R00,0);
Move(R01,R00);
MoveFromStack(0,R01);
Pop(1);
```

This example is intended for illustration. The code is not required, as, for example, the Swap instruction could be used instead. Also see Push, Pop and MoveToStack.

LSP

Load the Stack Pointer into a register.
Synopsis: LSP(*regdst*);
Nothing can be done with the Stack Pointer except comparing it (see CMP). This can be used for detecting a "top (bottom) of the stack reached"-situation. This instruction will rarely be required.

NewArray

Create a new ARRAY.
Synopsis: NewArray(*regsize,regdst*);
Creates a new uninitialised array. The array-size is determined by the integer value in register *regsize*, an array identifier (ARRAY datatype) gets stored in register *regdst*. Like all resources, ARRAYs should be discarded as soon as they are not required any more. Also see DiscardArray.

DiscardArray

Discard an ARRAY.
Synopsis: DiscardArray(*regarray*);
Discards the ARRAY referenced via register *regarray*. Also see NewArray.

ArraySize

Return the size of an ARRAY.
Synopsis: ArraySize(*regarray,regdst*);
Stores the size of the ARRAY referenced via register *regarray* in register *regdst*.

ArraySet

Set an ARRAY element.
Synopsis: ArraySet(*regarray,regsrc,regidx*);
regarray is the register identifying the ARRAY, *regsrc* is the register containing the value written to the array, *regidx* is the register containing the ARRAY destination index. For an array of size n valid array indices are $0, 1, \ldots, n - 1$.

ArrayGet

Get an ARRAY element.
Synopsis: ArrayGet(*regarray,regidx,regdst*);
regarray is the register identifying the ARRAY, *regidx* is the register containing the ARRAY source index, *regdst* is the register the ARRAY-value gets written to. For an array of size n valid array indices are $0, 1, \ldots, n - 1$.

NewCargoTreeMem

Create a new CARGOTREEMEM.
Synopsis: NewCargoTreeMem(*regdst*);
Creates a new CARGOTREEMEM and stores its identifier in register *regdst*. Like all resources, CARGOTREEMEMs should be discarded as soon as they are not required any more. Also see DiscardCargoTreeMem.

DiscardCargoTreeMem

Discard a CARGOTREEMEM.

Synopsis: DiscardCargoTreeMem(*regmem*);

Discards the CARGOTREEMEM referenced via register *regmem*. All CARGOTREE-nodes allocated in that CARGOTREEMEM are auto-discarded, all references to such nodes become invalid. Attempts of accessing such nodes after their CARGOTREEMEM has been discarded is a severe programming error, resulting in untreated runtime failure (crash). Also see NewCargoTreeMem.

NewConClsImm

Create a new ConCls-node (Classic Connector).

Synopsis: NewConClsImm(*numchild,regmem,regdst,id*);

Creates a new Classic Connector within the CARGOTREEMEM referenced with register *regmem*. The number of at first uninitialised children is determined by *numchild*, the id is set to *id*. *numchild* must contain an integer in the range 1 to 65535, *id* has to be an integer in the range 0 to 255. The resulting node identifier is stored in register *regdst*. Also see Plug and PlugImm.

NewConArrImm

Create a new ConArr-node (Array Connector).

Synopsis: NewConArrImm(*regnumchild,regmem,regdst,id*);

Creates a new Array Connector within the CARGOTREEMEM referenced with register *regmem*. The number of at first uninitialised children is determined by the integer in register *regnumchild*, the id is set to *id*. *regnumchild* must contain an integer in the range 1 to 65535, *id* has to be an integer in the range 0 to 255. The resulting node identifier is stored in register *regdst*. Also see Plug and PlugImm.

NewIntImm

Create a new Int-node (Integer Leaf).

Synopsis: NewIntImm(*regmem,regdst,id*);

Creates a new Integer Leaf within the CARGOTREEMEM referenced with register *regmem*, and sets its id to *id*. *id* has to be an integer in the range 0 to 255. The resulting node identifier is stored in register *regdst*. The Integer Leaf's value remains uninitialised. Also see SetVal and GetVal.

NewStrImm

Create a new Str-node (String Leaf).

Synopsis: NewStrImm(*regmem,regdst,id*);

Creates a new String Leaf within the CARGOTREEMEM referenced with register *regmem*, and sets its id to *id*. *id* has to be an integer in the range 0 to 255. The resulting node identifier is stored in register *regdst*. The String Leaf's value remains uninitialised.

NewIntImmSetVal

Create a new Int-node (Integer Leaf) and initialise its value.

Synopsis: NewIntImmSetVal(*regmem,regdst,id,regval*);

Creates a new Integer Leaf within the CARGOTREEMEM referenced with register *regmem*, and sets its id to *id*. *id* has to be an integer in the range 0 to 255. The resulting node identifier is stored in register *regdst*. The Integer Leaf's value is initialised with the integer of register *regval*. NewIntImmSetVal is a shortcut for using the two instructions NewIntImm and SetVal. Also see GetVal and SetVal.

NewPseudoRoot

Create a new PseudoRoot node.
Synopsis: NewPseudoRoot(*regnodechild,regdst*);
Creates a new PseudoRoot, sets its only child to the node referenced via register *regnodechild*, and stores the PseudoRoot identifier in register *regdst*. Note that a PseudoRoot-node is a resource of its own and needs to be discarded when not used anymore. Also see DiscardPseudoRoot.

DiscardPseudoRoot

Discard a PseudoRoot node.
Synopsis: DiscardPseudoRoot(*regnode*);
Discards the PseudoRoot-node referenced via register *regnode*. Also see NewPseudoRoot.

GetNodeType

Return the type of a CARGOTREE-node.
Synopsis: GetNodeType(*regnode,regdst*);
Returns in register *regdst* the type identifier of the node referenced via register *regnode*. This instruction can be used with CARGOTREE-nodes of any type.

GetNodeId

Return the id of a CARGOTREE-node.
Synopsis: GetNodeId(*regnode,regdst*);
Returns in register *regdst* the id of the node referenced via register *regnode*. Supported node types are ConCls, ConArr, Int, Str, LocalCon, LocalInt, and LocalStr. Other types do not provide an id.

SetNodeIdImm

Set the id of a CARGOTREE-node.
Synopsis: SetNodeIdImm(*regnode,id*);
For the node referenced via register *regnode* the id is set to *id*. Supported node types are ConCls, ConArr, Int, Str, LocalCon, LocalInt, and LocalStr. Other types do not provide an id. *id* has to be an integer in the range 0 to 255.

SetNodeId

Set the id of a CARGOTREE-node.
Synopsis: SetNodeId(*regnode,regid*);
For the node referenced via register *regnode* the id is set to the value of register *regid*. Supported node types are ConCls, ConArr, Int, Str, LocalCon, LocalInt, and LocalStr. Other types do not provide an id. *regid* must contain an integer in the range 0 to 255.

GetRuleId

Return the rule-id of a GrammarRule-node.
Synopsis: GetRuleId(*regnode,regdst*);
Returns in register *regdst* the rule-id of the GrammarRule-node referenced via register *regnode*.

GetNumChildren

Return the number of children of a CARGOTREE-node.
Synopsis: GetNumChildren(*regnode,regdst*);
Returns in register *regdst* the number of children of the node referenced via register *regnode*. Supported node types are ConCls, ConArr, LocalCon, PseudoRoot and GrammarRule. Also see GetChild and GetChildImm.

GetChildImm

Return a child-node of a CARGOTREE-node.
Synopsis: GetChildImm(*regnode,idx,regdst*);
Returns in register *regdst* the child with index *idx* of the node referenced via register *regnode*. Supported node types are ConCls, ConArr, LocalCon and PseudoRoot. For a node with n children, valid child indices are $0, 1, \ldots, n - 1$. Also see Plug and PlugImm.

GetChild

Return a child-node of a CARGOTREE-node.
Synopsis: GetChild(*regnode,regidx,regdst*);
Register *regidx* contains value *idx*. GetChild returns in register *regdst* the child with index *idx* of the node referenced via register *regnode*. Supported node types are ConCls, ConArr, LocalCon and PseudoRoot. For a node with n children, valid child indices are $0, 1, \ldots, n - 1$. Also see Plug and PlugImm.

GetRuleChildImm

Return a child-node of a GrammarRule-node.
Synopsis: GetRuleChildImm(*regnode,idx,regdst*);
Returns in register *regdst* the child with index *idx* of the GrammarRule-node referenced via register *regnode*. For a GrammarRule-node with n children, valid child indices are $0, 1, \ldots, n - 1$.

GetRuleChild

Return a child-node of a GrammarRule-node.
Synopsis: GetRuleChild(*regnode,regidx,regdst*);
Register *regidx* contains value *idx*. GetRuleChild returns in register *regdst* the child with index *idx* of the GrammarRule-node referenced via register *regnode*. For a GrammarRule-node with n children, valid child indices are $0, 1, \ldots, n - 1$.

PlugImm

Set a CARGOTREE-node's child node.
Synopsis: PlugImm(*regnodeparent,regnodechild,idx*);
The node referenced via register *regnodechild* is set the idx^{th} child of the node referenced via register *regnodeparent* ("plugged into the parent node"). The parent node must be one of ConCls, ConArr, LocalCon or PseudoRoot. For a parent node with n children, valid indices are $0, 1, \ldots, n - 1$. Also see GetChild and GetChildImm.

Plug

Set a CARGOTREE-node's child node.
Synopsis: Plug(*regnodeparent,regnodechild,regidx*);

Register *regidx* contains value *idx*. The node referenced via register *regnodechild* is set the idx^{th} child of the node referenced via register *regnodeparent* ("plugged into the parent node"). The parent node must be one of ConCls, ConArr, LocalCon or PseudoRoot. For a parent node with n children, valid indices are $0, 1, \ldots, n-1$. Also see `GetChild` and `GetChildImm`.

RefToken

Re-reference the value of a GrammarToken-node in a Str-node.
Synopsis: `RefToken`(*regnodesrctoken,regnodedststr*);
Sets the value of the Str-node referenced via register *regnodedststr* to the value of the Grammar-Token referenced via register *regnodesrctoken*. The string is not copied, but only re-referenced. Care has to be taken to avoid premature discarding of the string while still being referenced.

RefStr

Re-reference the value of a Str-node in another Str-node.
Synopsis: `RefStr`(*regnodesrcstr,regnodedststr*);
Sets the value of the Str-node referenced via register *regnodedststr* to the value of the Str-node referenced via register *regnodesrcstr*. The string is not copied, but only re-referenced. Care has to be taken to avoid premature discarding of the string while still being referenced.

GetVal

Return the value of an Int-node.
Synopsis: `GetVal`(*regnode,regdst*);
Returns in register *regdst* the value of the Int-node referenced via register *regnode*. Also see `SetVal` and `SetValImm`.

SetVal

Set the value of an Int-node.
Synopsis: `SetVal`(*regval,regnode*);
Sets the value of the Int-node referenced via register *regnode* to the integer in register *regval*. Also see `GetVal` and `SetValImm`.

SetValImm

Set the value of an Int-node.
Synopsis: `SetValImm`(*val,regnode*);
Sets the value of the Int-node referenced via register *regnode* to *val*. Also see `GetVal` and `SetVal`.

NewHashStrCol

Create a new `HASHSTRCOL`.
Synopsis: `NewHashStrCol`(*regdst*);
Creates a new empty `HASHSTRCOL` and stores its identifier in register *regdst*. Also see `Discard-HashStrCol`.

DiscardHashStrCol

Discard a `HASHSTRCOL`.
Synopsis: `DiscardHashStrCol`(*reghash*);
Discards the `HASHSTRCOL` referenced via register *reghash*. Also see `NewHashStrCol`.

HashStrColAdd

Add a new HASHSTRCOLENTRY or return the existing one.
Synopsis: HashStrColAdd(*reghash*,*regnodestr*,*numdata*,*regdst*);
This instruction uses the value of the Str-node referenced via *regnodestr* as string identifier. If a hash-entry with this string key is found in the hash referenced via *reghash* it is returned in register *regdst* and the Z (Zero) condition flag is set. Otherwise a new hash-entry with *numdata* additional data-fields is created, its identifier returned in register *regdst*, and the Z condition flag is cleared.

HashStrColFind

For a given key find the appropriate HASHSTRCOLENTRY.
Synopsis: HashStrColFind(*reghash*,*regnodestr*,*regdst*);
Register *regnodestr* references a Str-node, its string-value is *val*. HashStrColFind tries to find a hash-entry with key *val* in the HASHSTRCOL referenced via register *reghash*. If such an entry is found, its identifier is stored in register *regdst* and the Z condition flags is cleared. Otherwise the Z condition flag is set and register *regdst* remains unaffected.

MoveToHashStrColEntry

Store a register to a HASHSTRCOLENTRY data-field.
Synopsis: MoveToHashStrColEntry(*regentry*,*regsrc*,*idxdst*);
Stores the value of register *regsrc* in the *idxdst*[th] data-field of the hash-entry referenced via register *regentry*. For a HASHSTRCOLENTRY with n data-fields valid indices are $0, 1, \ldots, n - 1$. Also see MoveFromHashStrColEntry.

MoveFromHashStrColEntry

Store a HASHSTRCOLENTRY data-field to a register.
Synopsis: MoveFromHashStrColEntry(*regentry*,*idxsrc*,*regdst*);
Stores the *idxsrc*[th] data-field of the hash-entry referenced via register *regentry* in register *regdst*. For a HASHSTRCOLENTRY with n data-fields valid indices are $0, 1, \ldots, n - 1$. Also see Move-ToHashStrColEntry.

HashStrColNumEntries

Return a HASHSTRCOL's number of entries.
Synopsis: HashStrColNumEntries(*reghash*,*regdst*);
Returns the number of entries (keys) of the hash referenced via register *reghash* in register *regdst*. For example, upon HASHSTRCOL-creation the number of entries is zero.

HashStrColBrowseInit

Get a handle for browsing through a HASHSTRCOL's entries.
Synopsis: HashStrColBrowseInit(*reghash*,*regdst*);
Stores a handle for browsing through the entries of the hash identified with register *reghash* in register *regdst*. This handle can then be used with HashStrColBrowseNext and HashStr-ColBrowsePrev.

HashStrColBrowseNext

Browse to the next entry of a HASHSTRCOL.
Synopsis: HashStrColBrowseNext(*reghash*,*regentry*);

regentry may either contain a HASHSTRCOLENTRY identifier or a browse-handle as returned by HashStrColBrowseInit. In the latter case it is attempted to return the hash's first entry, otherwise it is attempted to return the entry following the specified entry. If such a hash-entry (first or following) exists, the Z flag is cleared and the entry-identifier is returned in register *regentry*. Otherwise the Z flag is set and register *regentry* remains unaffected.

HashStrColBrowsePrev

Browse to the previous entry of a HASHSTRCOL.
Synopsis: HashStrColBrowsePrev(*reghash*,*regentry*);
regentry may either contain a HASHSTRCOLENTRY identifier or a browse-handle as returned by HashStrColBrowseInit. In the latter case it is attempted to return the hash's last entry, otherwise it is attempted to return the entry preceding the specified entry. If such a hash-entry (last or preceding) exists, the Z flag is cleared and the entry-identifier is returned in register *regentry*. Otherwise the Z flag is set and register *regentry* remains unaffected.

NewHashInt

Create a new HASHINT.
Synopsis: NewHashInt(*regdst*);
Creates a new empty HASHINT and stores its identifier in register *regdst*. Also see Discard-HashInt.

DiscardHashInt

Discard a HASHINT.
Synopsis: DiscardHashInt(*reghash*);
Discards the HASHINT referenced via register *reghash*. Also see NewHashInt.

HashIntAddImm

Add a new HASHINTENTRY or return the existing one.
Synopsis: HashIntAddImm(*reghash*,*regval*,*numdata*,*regdst*);
Register *regval* contains integer *val*. If a hash-entry with key *val* is found in the hash referenced via *reghash*, it is returned in register *regdst* and the Z (Zero) condition flag is set. Otherwise a new hash-entry with *numdata* additional data-fields is created, its identifier returned in register *regdst*, and the Z condition flag is cleared.

HashIntAdd

Add a new HASHINTENTRY or return the existing one.
Synopsis: HashIntAdd(*reghash*,*regval*,*regnumdata*,*regdst*);
This instruction is identical to HashIntAddImm, except that the number of additional data-fields is not specified directly but through the register *regnumdata*.

HashIntFind

For a given key find the appropriate HASHINTENTRY.
Synopsis: HashIntFind(*reghash*,*regval*,*regdst*);
Register *regval* contains integer *val*. HashIntFind tries to find a hash-entry with key *val* in the hash referenced via register *reghash*. If such an entry is found, its identifier is stored in register *regdst* and the Z condition flags is cleared. Otherwise the Z condition flag is set and register *regdst* remains unaffected.

HashIntEntryGetKey

Return the key of a HASHINTENTRY.
Synopsis: HashIntEntryGetKey(*reghashentry,regdst*);
Retrieves the integer key from the HASHINTENTRY referenced via register *reghashentry* and stores it in register *regdst*. This instruction will rarely be required, as the hash-entry is usually retrieved with its key, which hence does not need to be read from the entry. This instruction is only of relevance if the hash-entry identifier is temporarily stored while the key gets lost.

MoveToHashIntEntry

Store a register to a HASHINTENTRY data-field.
Synopsis: MoveToHashIntEntry(*regentry,regsrc,idxdst*);
Stores the value of register *regsrc* in the $idxdst^{th}$ data-field of the hash-entry referenced via register *regentry*. For a HASHINTENTRY with n data-fields valid indices are $0, 1, \ldots, n-1$. Also see MoveFromHashIntEntry.

MoveFromHashIntEntry

Store a HASHINTENTRY data-field to a register.
Synopsis: MoveFromHashIntEntry(*regentry,idxsrc,regdst*);
Stores the $idxsrc^{th}$ data-field of the hash-entry referenced via register *regentry* in register *regdst*. For a HASHINTENTRY with n data-fields valid indices are $0, 1, \ldots, n-1$. Also see MoveTo-HashIntEntry.

HashIntNumEntries

Return a HASHINT's number of entries.
Synopsis: HashIntNumEntries(*reghash,regdst*);
Returns the number of entries (keys) of the hash referenced via register *reghash* in register *regdst*. For example, upon HASHINT-creation the number of entries is zero.

NewHashIntCol

Create a new HASHINTCOL.
Synopsis: NewHashIntCol(*regdst*);
Creates a new empty HASHINTCOL and stores its identifier in register *regdst*. Also see Discard-HashIntCol.

DiscardHashIntCol

Discard a HASHINTCOL.
Synopsis: DiscardHashIntCol(*reghash*);
Discards the HASHINTCOL referenced via register *reghash*. Also see NewHashIntCol.

HashIntColAddImm

Add a new HASHINTCOLENTRY or return the existing one.
Synopsis: HashIntColAddImm(*reghash,regval,numdata,regdst*);
Register *regval* contains integer *val*. If a hash-entry with key *val* is found in the hash referenced via *reghash*, it is returned in register *regdst* and the Z (Zero) condition flag is set. Otherwise a new hash-entry with *numdata* additional data-fields is created, its identifier returned in register *regdst*, and the Z condition flag is cleared.

HashIntColAdd

Add a new HASHINTCOLENTRY or return the existing one.
Synopsis: HashIntColAdd(*reghash,regval,regnumdata,regdst*);
This instruction is identical to HashIntColAddImm, except that the number of additional data-fields is not specified directly, but through the register *regnumdata*.

HashIntColFind

For a given key find the appropriate HASHINTCOLENTRY.
Synopsis: HashIntColFind(*reghash,regval,regdst*);
Register *regval* contains integer *val*. HashIntColFind tries to find a hash-entry with key *val* in the hash referenced via register *reghash*. If such an entry is found, its identifier is stored in register *regdst* and the Z condition flags is cleared. Otherwise the Z condition flag is set and register *regdst* remains unaffected.

HashIntColEntryGetKey

Return the key of a HASHINTCOLENTRY.
Synopsis: HashIntColEntryGetKey(*reghashentry,regdst*);
Retrieves the integer key from the HASHINTCOLENTRY referenced via register *reghashentry* and stores it in register *regdst*. This instruction will rarely be required, as the hash-entry is usually retrieved with its key, which hence does not need to be read from the entry. This instruction is only of relevance if the hash-entry identifier is temporarily stored while the key gets lost.

MoveToHashIntColEntry

Store a register to a HASHINTCOLENTRY data-field.
Synopsis: MoveToHashIntColEntry(*regentry,regsrc,idxdst*);
Stores the value of register *regsrc* in the $idxdst^{th}$ data-field of the hash-entry referenced via register *regentry*. For a HASHINTCOLENTRY with n data-fields valid indices are $0, 1, \ldots, n-1$. Also see MoveFromHashIntColEntry.

MoveFromHashIntColEntry

Store a HASHINTCOLENTRY data-field to a register.
Synopsis: MoveFromHashIntColEntry(*regentry,idxsrc,regdst*);
Stores the $idxsrc^{th}$ data-field of the hash-entry referenced via register *regentry* in register *regdst*. For a HASHINTCOLENTRY with n data-fields valid indices are $0, 1, \ldots, n-1$. Also see Move-ToHashIntColEntry.

HashIntColNumEntries

Return a HASHINTCOL's number of entries.
Synopsis: HashIntColNumEntries(*reghash,regdst*);
Returns the number of entries (keys) of the hash referenced via register *reghash* in register *regdst*. For example, upon HASHINTCOL-creation the number of entries is zero.

HashIntColBrowseInit

Get a handle for browsing through a HASHINTCOL's entries.
Synopsis: HashIntColBrowseInit(*reghash,regdst*);
Stores a handle for browsing through the entries of the hash referenced via register *reghash* in

register *regdst*. This handle can then be used with `HashIntColBrowseNext` and `HashInt-ColBrowsePrev`.

HashIntColBrowseNext

Browse to the next entry of a `HASHINTCOL`.
Synopsis: `HashIntColBrowseNext`(*reghash,regentry*);
regentry may either be a `HASHINTCOLENTRY` identifier or a browse-handle as returned by `Hash-IntColBrowseInit`. In the latter case it is attempted to return the hash's first entry, otherwise it is attempted to return the entry following the specified entry. If such a hash-entry (first or following) exists, the Z flag is cleared and the entry-identifier is returned in register *regentry*. Otherwise the Z flag is set and register *regentry* remains unaffected.

HashIntColBrowsePrev

Browse to the previous entry of a `HASHINTCOL`.
Synopsis: `HashIntColBrowsePrev`(*reghash,regentry*);
regentry may either be a `HASHINTCOLENTRY` identifier or a browse-handle as returned by `Hash-IntColBrowseInit`. In the latter case it is attempted to return the hash's last entry, otherwise it is attempted to return the entry preceding the specified entry. If such a hash-entry (last or preceding) exists, the Z flag is cleared and the entry-identifier is returned in register *regentry*. Otherwise the Z flag is set and register *regentry* remains unaffected.

NewHashIntStack

Create a new `HASHINTSTACK`.
Synopsis: `NewHashIntStack`(*regnumdata,regdst*);
Creates a new empty `HASHINTSTACK` and stores its identifier in register *regdst*. The integer in register *regnumdata* determines the number of additional data-fields with each entry (must be set to zero if no additional data-fields are required). Also see `DiscardHashIntStack`.

DiscardHashIntStack

Discard a `HASHINTSTACK`.
Synopsis: `DiscardHashIntStack`(*reghash*);
Discards the `HASHINTSTACK` referenced via register *reghash*. Also see `NewHashIntStack`.

HashIntStackAdd

Add a new `HASHINTSTACKENTRY` or return the existing one.
Synopsis: `HashIntStackAdd`(*reghash,regval,regdst*);
Register *regval* contains integer *val*. If a hash-entry with key *val* is found in the hash referenced via *reghash*, it is returned in register *regdst* and the Z (Zero) condition flag is set. Otherwise a new hash-entry is created, its identifier returned in register *regdst*, and the Z condition flag is cleared.

HashIntStackRemove

Remove the top-of-the-stack `HASHINTSTACKENTRY`.
Synopsis: `HashIntStackRemove`(*reghash*);
Removes the most recently added hash-entry from the hash referenced via register *reghash*. This hash must be nonempty.

HashIntStackFind

For a given key find the appropriate HASHINTSTACKENTRY.
Synopsis: HashIntStackFind(*reghash,regval,regdst*);
Register *regval* contains integer *val*. HashIntStackFind tries to find a hash-entry with key *val* in the hash referenced via register *reghash*. If such an entry is found, its identifier is stored in register *regdst* and the Z condition flags is cleared. Otherwise the Z condition flag is set and register *regdst* remains unaffected.

MoveToHashIntStackEntry

Store a register to a HASHINTSTACKENTRY data-field.
Synopsis: MoveToHashIntStackEntry(*regentry,regsrc,idxdst*);
Stores the value of register *regsrc* in the *idxdst*th data-field of the hash-entry referenced via register *regentry*. For a HASHINTSTACKENTRY with n data-fields valid indices are $0, 1, \ldots, n-1$. Also see MoveFromHashIntStackEntry.

MoveFromHashIntStackEntry

Store a HASHINTSTACKENTRY data-field to a register.
Synopsis: MoveFromHashIntStackEntry(*regentry,idxsrc,regdst*);
Stores the *idxsrc*th data-field of the hash-entry referenced via register *regentry* in register *regdst*. For a HASHINTSTACKENTRY with n data-fields valid indices are $0, 1, \ldots, n-1$. Also see MoveToHashIntStackEntry.

CopyCargoTree

Create a copy of a CARGOTREE.
Synopsis: CopyCargoTree(*regmem,regsrc,regdst*);
A new CARGOTREE is created and its identifier is stored in register *regdst*. All nodes are allocated from the CARGOTREEMEM specified through register *regmem*. The new CARGOTREE is identical to the one referenced via register *regsrc*.

CollectIntVal

Create a new HASHINTCOL containing selected Int-values of a CARGOTREE.
Synopsis: CollectIntVal(*regtree,regintid,regdst*);
Creates a new HASHINTCOL and stores its identifier in register *regdst*. *id* is the integer specified in register *regintid*, and *tree* the CARGOTREE referenced via register *regtree*. The resulting HASHINTCOL contains all the values of Int-nodes with id *id* from tree *tree* (these values are the keys). Each hash-entry has one additional data-field, containing the value's occurrence-index, resulting from depth-first left-to-right traversal. The occurrence-indices start with 0. The following is an example for occurrence-indices. For greater comprehensibility occurrence-indices for string-identifiers are given—note that CollectIntVal works with integer-identifiers: In the arithmetic expression

```
c*(3*a+c^2+y+a^2+d+c^3)
```

the occurrence-indices of a, c, d and y are as follows:

variable-identifier	occurrence-index
a	1
c	0
d	3
y	2

HashIntVal

Create a new HASHINT containing selected Int-values of a CARGOTREE.
Synopsis: HashIntVal(*regtree,regintid,regdst*);
Creates a new HASHINT and stores its identifier in register *regdst*. *id* is the integer specified in register *regintid*, and *tree* the CARGOTREE referenced via register *regtree*. The resulting HASH-INT contains all the values of Int-nodes with id *id* from tree *tree* (these values are the keys). Each hash-entry has one additional data-field, containing the value's occurrence-index, resulting from depth-first left-to-right traversal. Occurrence-indices start with 0. An example is given with CollectIntVal.

HashIntValCont

Add selected Int-values of a CARGOTREE to a HASHINT.
Synopsis: HashIntValCont(*regtree,regintid,reghash,regoffset*);
Let *id* be the integer specified in register *regintid*, *tree* the CARGOTREE referenced via register *regtree*, *offset* the integer in register *regoffset*, and register *reghash* contain an identifier for the HASHINT to which new hash-entries are added. All the values of Int-nodes with id *id* from tree *tree* (these values are the keys) are added to the hash. Each new entry has one additional data-field, the value stored there is as follows: For the first entry added (if there is one) it is *offset*, for the next one it is *offset* + 1, for the next one *offset* + 2, and so on. If *n* new entries are added, then register *regoffset* is set to *offset* + *n*. The most common scenario is the specification of an *offset* which is identical to the number of hash-entries upon instruction-invocation. The entry-addition order is determined by depth-first left-to-right traversal.

SubstIntAscA

Perform substitution of selected Int-values of a CARGOTREE according to a HASHINTCOL.
Synopsis: SubstIntAscA(*regtree,reghash,regintid,regadd*);
Let *id* be the integer specified in register *regintid*, *tree* the CARGOTREE referenced via register *regtree*, and *add* the integer in register *regadd*. Register *reghash* must contain a HASHINTCOL identifier where for each entry there is at least one additional data-field. For any Int-node in tree *tree* with id *id*, if the value occurs in the hash (there is an entry *e* having the value as key) it is replaced as follows: Let $s(e)$ denote the integer stored in data-field 0 of *e*. Then the replacement value is $s(e) + add$. Values not appearing as hash-keys remain unaffected.

CopySubstIntAscA

Create a copy of a CARGOTREE in which selected Int-values are replaced according to a HASH-INTCOL.
Synopsis: CopySubstIntAscA(*regmem,regtree,reghash,regintid,regadd,regdst*);
This instruction is a combination of CopyCargoTree and SubstIntAscA. Compared to using a sequence of those two instructions CopySubstIntAscA is more efficient, as the substitution can be performed during copying. The parameters are the same as in the two mentioned instructions.

CopySubstIntAscB

Create a copy of a CARGOTREE in which selected Int-values are replaced according to a HASHINT.
Synopsis: CopySubstIntAscB(*regmem,regtree,reghash,regintid,regadd,regdst*);
This instruction is identical to CopySubstIntAscA, except that instead of a HASHINTCOL a HASHINT is used.

CopyColSubstIntAscB

Create a copy of a CARGOTREE in which selected Int-values are replaced according to a HASHINT. The hash is extended if necessary.

Synopsis: CopyColSubstIntAscB(*regmem,regtree,reghash,regnumhash,*

regintid,regadd,regdst);

This instruction is very similar to CopySubstIntAscB. The only difference is that values not yet occurring as hash-keys are added. Like in HashIntValCnt there is one additional data-field for each new entry, as usual containing the occurrence-index. If the integer in register *regnumhash* is denoted n, then the first new entry has value n in data-field 0, the next one $n + 1$, etc. The entry-addition-order is determined by depth-first left-to-right traversal. The register *regnumhash* is updated with value $n + a$, where a is the number of new hash-entries added. The other parameters are identical to those of CopySubstIntAscB.

CopyColSubstIntAscBM

Create a copy of a CARGOTREE in which selected Int-values are replaced according to a HASHINT. The hash is extended if necessary.

Synopsis: CopyColSubstIntAscBM(*regmem,regtree,reghash,regnumhash,*

regintid,regadd,regmul,regdst);

This instruction is identical to CopyColSubstIntAscB, except that a slightly different substitution is performed. Let *add* be the integer in register *regadd* and *mul* be the integer in register *regmul*. Furthermore, $s(e)$ denotes data-entry 0 of hash-entry e. If e is a matching hash-entry for the Int-value, then in CopyColSubstIntAscB the value gets replaced with $s(e) + add$. Here however, the replacement value is $s(e) * mul + add$. This can be useful in cases where different arrays of corresponding identifiers get introduced. The other parameters are identical to CopyColSubstIntAscB.

WriteCargoTreeCGE

Store a CARGOTREE into a file in CARGOTREE Exchange Format.

Synopsis: WriteCargoTreeCGE(*regtree,regnumname*);

Creates a file named "tree*num*.cge", where *num* is a 4-digit decimal representation of the integer in register *regnumname*. The file contains a representation of the CARGOTREE referenced via register *regtree*, the representation is in the standardised CARGOTREE Exchange Format. Currently a CARGOTREE used with this instruction must not contain GrammarRule-, GrammarToken- or any of the Local-nodes. There are no other restrictions for the CARGOTREE.

WriteCargoTreeGDL

Store a CARGOTREE into a file in Graph Description Language.

Synopsis: WriteCargoTreeGDL(*regtree,regnumname*);

Creates a file named "tree*num*.gdl", where *num* is a 4-digit decimal representation of the integer in register *regnumname*. This file contains a description of the CARGOTREE in the Graph Description Language. Any CARGOTREE can be used with this instruction—there are no restrictions. The GDL file-format is used by graph visualisation software aiSee [1].

WriteCargoTreeGDLImm

Store a CARGOTREE into a file in Graph Description Language.

Synopsis: WriteCargoTreeGDLImm(*regtree,numname*);

Creates a file named "tree*num*.gdl", where *num* is a 4-digit decimal representation of the integer *numname*. This file contains a description of the CARGOTREE in the Graph Description

Language. Any CARGOTREE can be used with this instruction—there are no restrictions. The GDL file-format is used by graph visualisation software aiSee [1].

DevDumpReg

Dump a register.
Synopsis: DevDumpReg(*reg*);
The value in register *reg* is dumped to the developer output. It is displayed in hexadecimal notation.

DevDumpRegNote

Dump a register and mark it with a note-character.
Synopsis: DevDumpRegNote(*note*,*reg*);
The value in register *reg* is dumped to the developer output. It is displayed in hexadecimal notation. It is preceded by the 'note' character. The note character is determined by the integer *note*, which contains the ASCII-code of that character. This is useful for distinction if the same register is dumped in different locations.

DevDumpRegs

Dump subsequent registers.
Synopsis: DevDumpReg(*regfrst*,*numregs*);
The values of registers *regfrst*, *regfrst*+1, ..., *regfrst*+*numregs*-1 are dumped to the developer output. They are displayed in hexadecimal notation. *numregs* must be greater or equal to 1, and set such that the range of available registers is not exceeded.

DevDumpHashIntColImm

Dump a HASHINTCOL.
Synopsis: DevDumpHashIntColImm(*reghash*,*numname*);
Creates a file named "hash*num*.txt", where *num* is a 4-digit decimal representation of the integer *numname*. This text file contains the decimal representations of all the integer keys from the entries of the HASHINTCOL referenced via register *reghash*.

DevDumpStack

Dump entries of the main data stack.
Synopsis: DevDumpStack(*numdata*);
Dumps entries 0,1,...,*numdata*-1 of the current (top-of-the-stack) stack block to developer output. Of course *numdata* must not exceed the number of entries of that block.

DevDumpResourceSummary

Dump a summary of the number of resources in use.
Synopsis: DevDumpResourceSummary();
For each resource-type the number of resources in use gets printed to developer output. This includes CARGOTREEMEMs, ARRAYs, HASHINTs, etc. Any resource-instance which is created but not discarded by a Smute Function must be clearly documented. A Smute Function for Smute Function Users must always return with no resources in use. This developer instruction can help detecting unintended resource-loss.

WriteCargoTreeBooleRaw

Store a QBF-CARGOTREE into a file in raw 'boole' QBF-format.
Synopsis: `WriteCargoTreeBooleRaw`(*regtree,regnumname*);
Creates a file named "`qbfnum.txt`", where *num* is a 4-digit decimal representation of the integer in register *regnumname*. This file contains the Quantified Boolean Formula referenced via register *regtree* (CARGOTREE in QBF-Scheme) in the format specified by QBF-solver 'boole' [2]. It contains only the formula, without variable specifications, etc.

WriteCargoTreeBooleRawImm

Store a QBF-CARGOTREE into a file in raw 'boole' QBF-format.
Synopsis: `WriteCargoTreeBooleRawImm`(*regtree,numname*);
This instruction is identical to `WriteCargoTreeBooleRaw`, except that the name-integer is provided directly and not within a register.

WriteCargoTreeBoole

Store a QBF-CARGOTREE into a file in 'boole' QBF-format.
Synopsis: `WriteCargoTreeBoole`(*regtree,regnumname,idxtermsel*);
Creates a file named "`qbfnum.txt`", where *num* is a 4-digit decimal representation of the integer in register *regnumname*. This file contains the Quantified Boolean Formula referenced via register *regtree* (CARGOTREE in QBF-Scheme) in the format specified by QBF-solver 'boole' [2]. It also contains the variable specification and an instruction-term for the formula. Thus it is complete specification which can be passed to the 'boole'-solver. One of three 'boole' instruction-terms can be selected with the parameter *idxtermsel*: 0 for 'print', 1 for 'sop' and 2 for 'satisfy'.

WriteCargoTreeBooleImm

Store a QBF-CARGOTREE into a file in 'boole' QBF-format.
Synopsis: `WriteCargoTreeBooleImm`(*regtree,numname,idxtermsel*);
This instruction is identical to `WriteCargoTreeBoole`, except that the name-integer is provided directly and not within a register.

WriteCargoTreeGDL_QBFS

Store a QBFS-CARGOTREE into a file in Graph Description Language.
Synopsis: `WriteCargoTreeGDL_QBFS`(*regtree,regnumname*);
Creates a file named "`qbfnum.gdl`", where *num* is a 4-digit decimal representation of the integer in register *regnumname*. This file contains a description of the QBFS-CARGOTREE in the Graph Description Language. The output is QBFS-CARGOTREE-Scheme-specific.

WriteCargoTreeGDL_QBFSImm

Store a QBFS-CARGOTREE into a file in Graph Description Language.
Synopsis: `WriteCargoTreeGDL_QBFSImm`(*regtree,numname*);
This instruction is identical to `WriteCargoTreeGDL_QBFS`, except that the name-integer is provided directly and not within a register.

WriteCargoTreeGDL_QBF

Store a QBF-CARGOTREE into a file in Graph Description Language.
Synopsis: `WriteCargoTreeGDL_QBF`(*regtree,regnumname*);

Creates a file named "qbf*num*.gdl", where *num* is a 4-digit decimal representation of the integer in register *regnumname*. This file contains a description of the QBF-CARGOTREE in the Graph Description Language. The output is QBF-CARGOTREE-Scheme-specific.

WriteCargoTreeGDL_QBFImm

Store a QBF-CARGOTREE into a file in Graph Description Language.
Synopsis: WriteCargoTreeGDL_QBFImm(*regtree,numname*);
This instruction is identical to WriteCargoTreeGDL_QBF, except that the name-integer is provided directly and not within a register.

4.2 CARGOTREE-Schemes

A CARGOTREE-Scheme is a convention laying down *how* specific recursive data structures, such as arithmetic expressions, are represented with CARGOTREEs. A *uniform* representation of data is of great relevance for avoiding unnecessary conversions. Ideally, for any recursive data structure all Smute Functions working with that structure apply the same CARGOTREE-Scheme.

Example 4.1 (CARGOTREE-Scheme) In order not to stress arithmetic expressions only, the following CARGOTREE-Scheme example is for recursively structured data known as *propositional formulas*. Propositional formulas are defined as follows: $Conn = \{\wedge, \vee, \rightarrow, \neg\}$ is the set of *logical connectives*, referred to as *conjunction, disjunction, implication* and *negation* respectively. $Const = \{\top, \bot\}$ is the set of *logical constants*, referred to as *truthhood* and *falsehood*. Furthermore, let P be an arbitrary set which is disjoint from $Conn$ and $Const$, i.e., $P \cap Conn = P \cap Const = \emptyset$. Then the set of *propositional formulas* over P, $PROP(P)$, is recursively defined as follows:

1. $\top \in PROP(P)$ and $\bot \in PROP(P)$.

2. $p \in PROP(P)$ for every $p \in P$.

3. If $\phi \in PROP(P)$, then $\neg\phi \in PROP(P)$.

4. If $\phi_1 \in PROP(P)$ and $\phi_2 \in PROP(P)$, then $\phi_1 \circ \phi_2 \in PROP(P)$ for $\circ \in \{\wedge, \vee, \rightarrow\}$.

The elements of P are called the *propositional variables* of $PROP(P)$.

Note that currently there is no syntax for CARGOTREE-Schemes, instead they are informal specifications. The "propositional formula" CARGOTREE-Scheme defines integer identifiers for the logical connectives, propositional variables and logical constants. They are used as CARGO-TREE-node ids.

string alias	integer value	represents
NOT	0	logical connective '$\neg$'
OR	1	logical connective '$\vee$'
AND	2	logical connective '$\wedge$'
IMPL	3	logical connective '$\rightarrow$'
PROPVAR	4	propositional variable
CONST	5	logical constant

In particular, the representation is as follows:

- Logical constant: Int-node with id CONST, where a value of 0 encodes '$\bot$' and a value of 1 encodes '$\top$'.

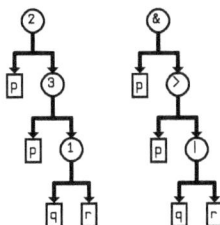

Figure 4.1: CARGOTREE visualisations

- Propositional variable: Str-node with id PROPVAR, the string value serves as variable identifier.

- Formula ¬φ: ConCls-node with id NOT, has got 1 child which represents φ.

- Formula $\phi_1 \lor \phi_2$: ConCls-node with id OR, has got 2 children, the left one (index 0) representing ϕ_1 and the right one (index 1) ϕ_2.

- Formula $\phi_1 \land \phi_2$: ConCls-node with id AND, has got 2 children, the left one (index 0) representing ϕ_1 and the right one (index 1) ϕ_2.

- Formula $\phi_1 \rightarrow \phi_2$: ConCls-node with id IMPL, has got 2 children, the left one (index 0) representing ϕ_1 and the right one (index 1) ϕ_2.

Figure 4.1 displays the CARGOTREE-representation of propositional formula $p \land (p \rightarrow (q \lor r))$, complying with the "propositional formula" CARGOTREE-Scheme. □

Node-ids for a CARGOTREE-Scheme should be picked from a small integer-range to support querying them with the JumpTab-instruction of the Smute Language.

4.3 Data I/O

For Smute Function Developers there are currently the following options for data input/output:

- Reading and writing of files in CARGOTREE Exchange Format.

- Reading of text-files in an LALR-language.

- Additional options might be provided by the respective Smute Interpreter Edition.

4.3.1 CARGOTREE Exchange Format

The CARGOTREE Exchange Format is a convention for binary storage of recursively structured data. Reading input in CARGOTREE Exchange Format, as well as output to this format is readily supported by Smute (cf. #load-instruction in the Smute Function User Manual and the "WriteCargoTreeCGE"-instruction on page 61). Hence a Smute Function Developer does not need to know about the file layout of the CARGOTREE Exchange Format.

Whether or not a Smute Function Developer supports input/output in CARGOTREE Exchange Format should be based on the following considerations:

- If Smute Function Users want to pass the output to other Smute Functions or to external applications, then output in CARGOTREE Exchange Format should be supported.

- If Smute Function Users want to use input generated by other Smute Functions or by external applications, then input in CARGOTREE Exchange Format should be supported.

By default, CARGOTREE Exchange Format input/output should be supported, because it increases a function's versatility and the implementation requires little effort, due to the handling by Smute.

4.3.2 Data Input through an LALR-language

The principle of Smute support for input data specification in arbitrary LALR-languages has already been outlined: The Smute Function Developer creates a parsing-table for the language in question. The Smute Function User specifies data in an LALR-language and references the appropriate parsing-table. This is illustrated in Example 4.3.2.

Example 4.2 (Input specification through an LALR-language) The following Smute Launch File instructs data to be LALR-parsed:

```
<formula0>      := #load("fla0000.txt","fla.cgt")
loadmodules(flamod);
flamod:Simplify(formula0);
```

Here the Smute Function **Simplify** is applied to the formula specified in file "fla0000.txt", which is parsed according to the LALR-parsing-table of file "fla.cgt". □

Currently Smute relies on parsing-tables created by the publicly available GOLD Parser [3]. From a Backus-Naur form GOLD Parser creates a Compiled Grammar Table ('.cgt'-file), i.e., an LALR-parsing table in GOLD-Parser-specific format. For Smute Function Developers this means that in order to support input specifications in a new LALR-language, they need to write a Backus-Naur form, load it with GOLD Parser Builder, and save the Compiled Grammar Table. This process is documented in the GOLD Parser documentation [3].

From specifications in LALR-languages the Smute Interpreter automatically creates CARGO-TREEs in grammar-dependent CARGOTREE-Schemes. These CARGOTREEs are composed of GrammarRule- and GrammarToken-nodes, representing the data in terms of rule-ids, token-ids and token-strings. The only difficulty in processing this information is to find the correspondence between rule-ids (token-ids) with the rules (tokens) from the Backus-Naur form. Due to using GOLD Parser there is currently no way of assigning arbitrary ids within the Backus-Naur form. Instead, these ids are auto-assigned array-indices. There are two very simple ways of finding out which rule-id (token-id) corresponds to which rule (token). The first is GOLD Parser, where—after having created the Compiled Grammar Table—the rules (tokens) can be displayed. They are automatically displayed with their id. Another one is to use a simple CARGOTREE visualisation routine like the following:

```
Label(DumpCargoTree);
WriteCargoTreeGDL(R00,R01);
Return;
```

Then data instances are specified according to the grammar's rules, and used with the DumpCargoTree function. The visualisation displays the rules' and tokens' ids.

Example 4.3 (Rule-ids and token-ids for the rules and tokens of a Backus-Naur form) The following listing shows a simple Backus-Naur form for arithmetic expressions:

```
"Start Symbol"         = <expr_add>

{id_head}              = {Letter} + [_]
{id_tail}              = {id_head} + {Digit}
```

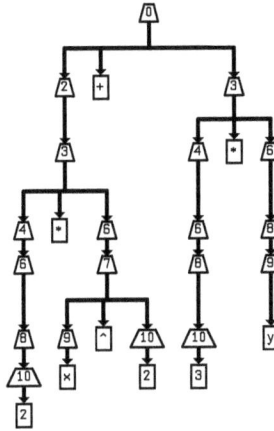

Figure 4.2: CARGOTREE in grammar-dependent CARGOTREE-Scheme

```
decliteral              = {Digit}+
id                      = {id_head}{id_tail}*

<expr_add>              ::= <expr_add> '+' <expr_mul>
                        | <expr_add> '-' <expr_mul>
                        | <expr_mul>

<expr_mul>              ::= <expr_mul> '*' <expr_div>
                        | <expr_div>

<expr_div>              ::= <expr_exp> '/' <expr_exp>
                        | <expr_exp>

<expr_exp>              ::= <expr_bot> '^' <expr_bot>
                        | <expr_bot>

<expr_bot>              ::= id
                        | decliteral
                        | '(' <expr_add> ')'
```

The visualisation of the grammar-dependent CARGOTREE-representation of arithmetic expression $2x^2 + 3y$, specified as "2*x^2+3*y", is shown in Figure 4.2. The rule-ids for CARGOTREEs created according to LALR-parsing-table expr.cgt can be concluded from this visualisation. Examples:

id	rule
3	<expr_mul> ::= <expr_mul> '*' <expr_div>
9	<expr_bot> ::= id
...	...

$\square$

67

It must be remarked that the CARGOTREE-Schemes implied by LALR-grammars are usually ill-suited for data-representation, especially if data is altered or newly created: The rules of an LALR-grammar define how to specify data-instances in a string, which is not a concise reflection of the recursive structure. The additional information (which does not relate to the recursive structure, but only to the specification in strings) is superfluous for the CARGOTREE-representation. Furthermore, Smute Functions working with grammar-dependent CARGOTREE-Schemes are of little versatility: Changes in the grammar require adaptations of the Smute Function, support of different grammars is intricate. Hence, CARGOTREEs in grammar-dependent CARGOTREE-Schemes are usually converted to grammar-independent CARGOTREE-Schemes before being further processed. Smute Functions solely performing these conversions are called *Preprocessing Functions*. For the sake of the aforementioned versatility only Preprocessing Functions should work with grammar-dependent CARGOTREE-Schemes.

The support of new LALR-languages within Smute Launch Files requires new Smute Interpreter Editions. Smute Function Developers interested in a new Smute Interpreter Edition, or in extending a existing one, should get in touch with the author of the Smute Interpreter.

4.4 Core Functions and Wrapper Functions

The following are recommendations for writing modular and versatile Smute Functions.

It is the intent of Smute Function Developers to implement a certain functionality, e.g, the simplification of arithmetic expressions. Most Smute Functions for Smute Function Users will need to read input from files and/or write output to files. The implemented functionality might however be useful as part of other Smute Functions. For example, the simplification of an arithmetic expression could be applied in a function before evaluating that expression. In this case the input does not need to be read from files, and the output does not need to be written to files. Instead, a Smute Function with CARGOTREE-input/output, but without file-access is required.

Therefore, it is recommended to write so-called *Core Functions* and *Wrapper Functions*. A Core Function is a Smute Function not accessing files, i.e., not using the input/output-related Smute Language instructions. Thus, a Core Function can be used modularly in other Smute Functions. A Wrapper Function works as follows:

1. optionally read/preprocess input;

2. call one or more Core Functions;

3. optionally post-process/write output.

In step 1 Wrapper Functions working with LALR-language input typically invoke Preprocessing Functions.

An additional advantage of the Core Function/Wrapper Function-conception is that support for new input-file-formats or new output-file-formats is extremely simple, as it only requires new Wrapper Functions. The principle of Core Functions and Wrapper Functions is depicted in Figure 4.3.

4.5 Smute Assembler Usage

Example 4.4 (Smute Assembler usage) The source code of a Smute Module is written to file "testmod.txt":

```
Label(DumpCargoTree);
WriteCargoTreeGDL(R00,R01);
Return;
```

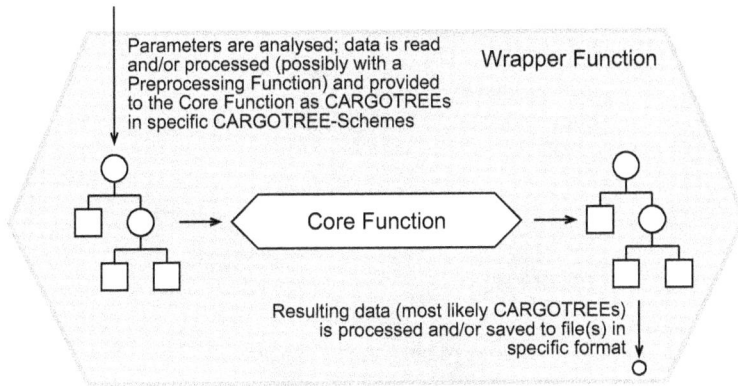

Figure 4.3: Core Functions and Wrapper Functions

```
Export(DumpCargoTree);
```

(The `Export`-declaration is used for exporting labels.)
The Smute Module `m_testmod.tmm` is created by passing the source code file to the Smute
Assembler:
```
>assemble testmod.txt                                             □
```

To date Example 4.5.4 is fictitious, as the Smute Assembler has not been implemented yet.
Currently Smute Function Developers need to work with a tentative solution, called Smute Assembler Library. As the Smute Assembler Library is less user-friendly than a Smute Assembler
would be, Smute Function Developers should check for the availability of the Smute Assembler
before starting to write Smute Functions.

The Smute Assembler Library is a static C library called "modcompile.lib" (currently for Intel
Pentium/Windows and Intel Pentium/Linux) and comes with an accompanying header-file. A C-
compiler and linker is needed. For each instruction of the Smute Language there is a function in
the Smute Assembler Library. Smute Language code is thus specified as a sequence of function-
calls in C. Example 4.5.5 shows how the Smute Module of Example 4.5.4 can be created with the
Smute Assembler Library:

Example 4.5 (Smute Assembler Library usage) The Smute Language instructions are specified in
a C-source file:

```
#include "modcompile.h"

uBOOL STDCALL WriteModule(TMMWrite* ptmmw)
{
  TMMWrite_WLabel(ptmmw, (PuCHAR)"DumpCargoTree",13);
  TMMWrite_WWriteCargoTreeGDL(ptmmw,R00,R01);
  TMMWrite_WReturn(ptmmw);

  TMMWrite_AddExport(ptmmw, (PuCHAR)"DumpCargoTree",13);
  return(TRUE);
}
```

```
void main(int argc, char** ppstrarg)
{
  compiler::CompilerData*    pdata;
  compiler::PFUNCPREPAREMOD  PPrepareMod;
  PuCHAR                     pstr0;
  uLONG                      i0;

  if ((pdata=compiler::InitCompilerData()))
  {
    pstr0="m_testmod.tmm";
    i0=13;
    PPrepareMod=WriteModule;
    compiler::ModCompiler(pdata,pstr0,i0,PPrepareMod);

    compiler::ExitCompilerData(pdata);
  }
}
```

The "main"-function is only a static frame, i.e., it is independent from the Smute Function. Compiling this file and linking it with "modcompile.lib" generates a command-line executable. Running the executable creates the desired Smute Module if successful, otherwise error-messages are issued.

A note about the number-arguments in the function-calls above: These are simply the string-lengths which have to be provided along with the character array (for example, 13 is the string-length of "DumpCargoTree"). A more convenient usage not requiring string-length parameters, but only pointers to 0-terminated strings, can be facilitated via small helper routines like the following:

```
uBOOL TMMWrite_WLabel(TMMWrite* ptmmw, PuCHAR pstrlabel)
{
  return(TMMWrite_WLabel(ptmmw,pstrlabel,StringLen(pstrlabel)));
}
```

The above WriteModule function is not fully correct as it ignores return-values. A correct version is printed below:

```
uBOOL STDCALL WriteModule(TMMWrite* ptmmw)
{
  if (!TMMWrite_WLabel(ptmmw,(PuCHAR)"DumpCargoTree",13)) goto errmem;
  if (!TMMWrite_WWriteCargoTreeGDL(ptmmw,R00,R01)) goto errmem;
  if (!TMMWrite_WReturn(ptmmw)) goto errmem;

  if (!TMMWrite_AddExport(ptmmw,(PuCHAR)"DumpCargoTree",13)) goto errmem;
  return(TRUE);
errmem:
  return(FALSE);
}
```

However, as the compiled file is usually executed only once, a Smute Function Developer might prefer to be careless and ignore the return values. □

Chapter 5

Support for the Interaction of External Applications with Smute

Currently support for the interaction of Smute with external applications is limited to the CARGO-TREE Exchange Format. There are two cases where it makes sense to apply the CARGOTREE Exchange Format:

- For an external application support of processing its output via Smute Functions is desired. This is easily achieved if the external application offers output generation in CARGOTREE Exchange Format.

- For an external application support of reading Smute Function output is desired. This is easily achieved if the external application accepts input in CARGOTREE Exchange Format.

The advantages of CARGOTREE Exchange Format over alternative solutions are obvious:

- The CARGOTREE Exchange Format is a binary format which is machine readable, without elaborate parsers that would be required for textual specifications.

- The usual advantage of standardisation: Data can be passed between applications that do not need to know about each other.

- For the Smute Function Developer there is no work to do, as CARGOTREE Exchange Format input/output is readily supported by Smute.

The file-layout of CARGOTREE Exchange Format is documented in Section 5.1. Options for advanced integration with external applications are discussed in Chapter 10.

5.1 File Layout for the **CARGOTREE** Exchange Format

In CARGOTREE Exchange Files all integers are stored in big-endian-format. Figure 5.1 depicts this storage format for BYTEs (8-bit integers), WORDs (16-bit-integers) and LONGs (32-bit-integers). The respective 2nd rows contain the bit indices. Those bit-arrays represent integers $\sum_{i=0}^{n} 2^i b_i$, where n is 7, 15, or 31 respectively.

In the following paragraphs the structure of CARGOTREE Exchange Files is presented in a bottom-up manner, i.e., starting with small sub-structures. The first is ConCls, used for storing ConCls-nodes.

```
ConCls:
BYTE            type;
BYTE            id;
WORD            numchild;
LONG            childidx[<numchild>];
```

							Byte 0
07	06	05	04	03	02	01	00

						Byte 1								Byte 0
15	14	13	12	11	10	09	08	07	06	05	04	03	02	01	00

					Byte 3						Byte 2						Byte 1						Byte 0
31	30	29	28	27	26	25	24	23	22	21	20	19	18	17	16	15	14	13	12	11	10	09	08	07	06	05	04	03	02	01	00

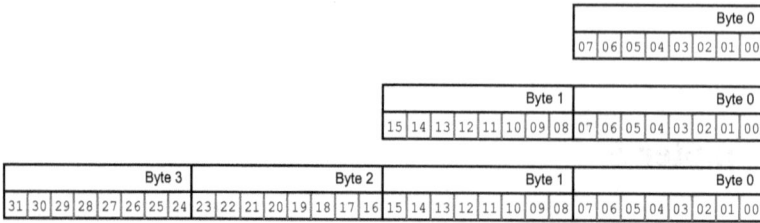

Figure 5.1: Big Endian Integer Storage

The last line states that the WORD numchild is followed by an array of LONGs, with the array-size determined by the value of numchild. Array-entries are referenced childidx[0],..., childidx[*numchild*-1].

The contents are as follows: type is the constant CNX_CONCLS (defined in a header-file) and used for distinction from other nodes. id contains the node-id. The array specified through numchild and childidx determines the child-nodes. In the childidx-array there can be integers $0,\ldots,n-1$, where n is the total number of CARGOTREE-nodes. These indices refer to the order the nodes are stored in the CARGOTREE Exchange File. For example, an entry with value 0 refers to the first node of the CARGOTREE Exchange File.

The next structure is ConArr:

```
ConArr:
BYTE              type;
BYTE              id;
WORD              numchild;
LONG              childidx[<numchild>];
```

Except for type, where CNX_CONARR is stored, the structure contents are identical to those of ConCls.

```
Int:
BYTE              type;
BYTE              id;
LONG              val;
```

Here the type-entry must contain CNX_INT, and the val-entry contains the Int-node's value.

```
Str:
BYTE              type;
BYTE              id;
WORD              lstr;
BYTE              str[<lstr>];
```

The type-entry must contain CNX_STR, and the Str-node's string-value is stored via the array specified through lstr and str.

```
Node:
ConCls|ConArr|Int|Str;
```

The `Node` specification has the following meaning: `a|b|c|`... stands for a set of options. In the place of a `Node`-structure one of the optional structures (`ConCls,ConArr,`...) is stored. For a file-format to be meaningful it must be possible to tell which of the optional structures is actually used. In the case of `Nodes`, distinction is possible via the `BYTE`-entry `type`, as each of the optional structures starts with this entry. While there is a similarity with unions from the programming language C, there is also a significant difference, namely that the size of the `Node`-entry depends on the selected structure (whereas for C-unions the size is always the size of the largest optional structure).

The next structure is already the `CGE` file format:

```
LONG            id;
LONG            chksum;
LONG            frmtver;
LONG            numnode;
LONG            sizenodearray;
Node            nodes[numnode];
```

The `id`-entry is provided for the identification of files in `CGE`-format and for distinction from files in other formats, its value is always 0x43474521. The `chksum`-entry is there to ensure the file is in valid format. It is an 32-bit-wise 'exclusive or' over the whole file, except the `chksum`-entry itself, and one additional 'exclusive or' with the constant `CGE_CHECKSUMBONNET`. The `frmtver`-entry must always be set to 0 for this version of the `CGE` file format and is there to allow distinction from potential extended future formats. `numnode` contains the number of nodes of the `CARGOTREE` stored in that file. `sizenodearray` contains the number of bytes taken up by the `nodes`-array. `nodes` is the array of `CARGOTREE`-nodes. There is a restriction for the array-order: Namely, for every inner node the children must be in front of that node. In other words: If an inner node is stored as i^{th} node in the `CARGOTREE` Exchange File, then the child-node-index-array of this node in the `CGE`-file can only contain numbers $0, 1, \ldots, i - 1$. Smute stores the nodes in the following order, which is recommended for the creation of `CGE`-files: The order is determined by 'post-order left-to-right depth-first' traversal. 'Depth-first' says that for any node with children the nodes are traversed subtree-wise, i.e., only after all nodes of a subtree have been visited can nodes of a different subtree be visited. 'Left-to-right' means that traversal starts with the 0th subtree, continues with the 1st, etc. 'Post-order' means that a node is visited after all child-nodes have already been visited.

Chapter 6

Reductions-to-QBFs Background

The background of reductions-to-QBFs is structured as follows: Propositional Logic is introduced in Section 6.1. Quantified Boolean Formulas (QBFs) are introduced in Section 6.2. Various reasoning formalisms are introduced in Section 6.3. Finally, Section 6.4 presents an exemplary reduction-to-QBF for reasoning tasks in one of the previously introduced formalisms.

The reasoning formalisms of Section 6.3 are relevant insofar, as Smute Language implementations of reductions-to-QBFs for these formalisms are presented in Chapter 8.

6.1 Propositional Logic

The syntax of propositional logic is defined as follows: $Conn = \{\wedge, \vee, \rightarrow, \neg\}$ is the set of *logical connectives*, referred to as *conjunction-*, *disjunction-*, *implication-* and *negation*-connectives respectively. $Const = \{\top, \bot\}$ is the set of *logical constants*, referred to as *truthhood* and *falsehood*. $Aux = \{`(`, `)`\}$ is the set of *auxiliary symbols*. '(' is the *left parenthesis* and ')' is the *right parenthesis*. Furthermore, let P be an arbitrary set which is disjoint from *Conn*, *Const*, and *Aux*, i.e., $P \cap Conn = P \cap Const = P \cap Aux = \emptyset$. Then the *propositional language* $PROP(P)$ over P, also called the set of *(well formed) propositional formulas* over P, is the formal language[1] over $P \cup Conn \cup Const \cup Aux$, where elements are recursively defined as follows:

1. $\top \in PROP(P)$ and $\bot \in PROP(P)$.

2. $p \in PROP(P)$ for every $p \in P$.

3. If $\phi \in PROP(P)$, then $(\neg\phi) \in PROP(P)$.

4. If $\phi_1 \in PROP(P)$ and $\phi_2 \in PROP(P)$, then $(\phi_1 \circ \phi_2) \in PROP(P)$ for $\circ \in \{\wedge, \vee, \rightarrow\}$.

For convenience, parentheses in rules 3 and 4 are usually omitted, syntactic unambiguity is maintained by assuming operator precedence (higher first) $\neg, \wedge, \vee, \rightarrow$ and left-associativity of the binary operators $\wedge, \vee, \rightarrow$. The elements of P are called the *propositional variables* of $PROP(P)$. $P \cup \{\top, \bot\}$ is called the set of *atoms* of $PROP(P)$. $\{p : p \in P\} \cup \{\neg p : p \in P\}$ is called the set of *literals*, denoted $Lit(P)$. Disjunctions of literals are called *clauses*. Binary operator symbol $\leftrightarrow$ is used as shortcut: $\phi_1 \leftrightarrow \phi_2$ stands for $(\phi_1 \rightarrow \phi_2) \wedge (\phi_2 \rightarrow \phi_1)$. For operator $\leftrightarrow$ a lower precedence than $\rightarrow$ is assumed.

Let $PROP(P)$ be a propositional language. An *interpretation* $\mathcal{I}$ of P is a function $\mathcal{I} : P \rightarrow \{t, f\}$, i.e., a function from P into the set of *truth values*. The *truth assignment* of a formula $\phi \in PROP(P)$ under interpretation $\mathcal{I}$, denoted $\bar{\mathcal{I}}(\phi)$, is recursively defined as follows:

1. If $\phi = \top$, then $\bar{\mathcal{I}}(\phi) = t$; if $\phi = \bot$, then $\bar{\mathcal{I}}(\phi) = f$.

---

[1]The term *formal language* is defined on page 12.

2. If $\phi = p \in P$, then $\bar{\mathcal{I}}(\phi) = \mathcal{I}(p)$.

3. If $\phi = \neg\phi_1$, or $(\phi_1 \circ \phi_2) \in PROP(P)$ for $\circ \in \{\wedge, \vee, \rightarrow\}$, then $\bar{\mathcal{I}}(\phi)$ is determined by $\bar{\mathcal{I}}(\phi_1)$ and $\bar{\mathcal{I}}(\phi_2)$ according to the tables below (row $\bar{\mathcal{I}}(\phi_1)$, column $\bar{\mathcal{I}}(\phi_2)$).

$\neg$	
t	f
f	t

$\wedge$	t	f
t	t	f
f	f	f

$\vee$	t	f
t	t	t
f	t	f

$\rightarrow$	t	f
t	t	f
f	t	t

If $\bar{\mathcal{I}}(\phi) = \text{t}$, then ϕ is called *true under* $\mathcal{I}$. If $\bar{\mathcal{I}}(\phi) = \text{f}$, then ϕ is called *false under* $\mathcal{I}$. ϕ is called *satisfied* by $\mathcal{I}$, or, equivalently, $\mathcal{I}$ is called a *model* of ϕ, denoted $\mathcal{I} \vDash \phi$, if ϕ is true under I. A formula ϕ is called *satisfiable* if at least one interpretation of P is a model of ϕ, otherwise it is called *unsatisfiable*. A formula ϕ is called *valid* if every interpretation of P is a model of ϕ. The truth assignment of a finite set of formulas $\{\phi_1, \phi_2, \ldots\}_{i \in I}$ is defined as the truth assignment of $\bigwedge_{i \in I} \phi_i$. If it holds that every model of a set W of formulas from $PROP(P)$ is a model of ψ, then ψ is called a *logical consequence* of W, denoted $W \vDash \psi$. Hence a formula ϕ is valid iff $\top \vDash \phi$. With $Cn(W)$ the set of logical consequences of W is denoted, i.e., $Cn(W) = \{\phi \in PROP(P) : W \vDash \phi\}$. W is called *inconsistent* if it is unsatisfiable. Otherwise, i.e., if it is satisfiable, it is called *consistent*. Two formulas ϕ_1 and ϕ_2 are called *logically equivalent* if every model of ϕ_1 is a model of ϕ_2 and every model of ϕ_2 is a model of ϕ_1. In other words: ϕ_1 and ϕ_2 are called logically equivalent if ϕ_2 is a logical consequence of ϕ_1 and ϕ_1 is a logical consequence of ϕ_2.

6.2 Quantified Boolean Formulas

For the definition of the syntax of Quantified Boolean Formulas the set $Conn = \{\wedge, \vee, \rightarrow, \neg\}$ of logical connectives, the set $Const = \{\top, \bot\}$ of logical constants, and the set $Aux = \{`(`, `)`\}$ of auxiliary symbols, get reused from the definition of the syntax of propositional languages. Additionally, a new set, the set of *quantifiers* $Quant = \{\exists, \forall\}$, called *existential quantifier* and *universal quantifier* respectively, is introduced. Let P be an arbitrary set which is disjoint from $Conn$, $Const$, Aux, and $Quant$, i.e., $P \cap Conn = P \cap Const = P \cap Aux = P \cap Quant = \emptyset$. Then $QBF(P)$, the language of *Quantified Boolean Formulas* over P, is the formal language over $P \cup Conn \cup Const \cup Aux \cup Quant$ whose elements are defined as follows:

1. $\top \in QBF(P)$ and $\bot \in QBF(P)$.

2. $p \in QBF(P)$ for every $p \in P$.

3. If $\phi \in QBF(P)$, then $(\neg\phi) \in QBF(P)$.

4. If $\phi_1 \in QBF(P)$ and $\phi_2 \in QBF(P)$, then $(\phi_1 \circ \phi_2) \in PROP(P)$ for $\circ \in \{\wedge, \vee, \rightarrow\}$.

5. If $\phi \in QBF(P)$ and $p \in P$, then $\exists p(\phi) \in QBF(P)$ and $\forall p(\phi) \in QBF(P)$.

Like in the definition of propositional languages, brackets from rules 3 and 4 are usually omitted, syntactic unambiguity is maintained by the same operator precedence and associativity assumptions as in the propositional language over P. The elements of P are called the *propositional variables* of $QBF(P)$.

A QBF ψ is called *direct subformula* of QBF ϕ over P, if one of the following conditions holds:

- $\phi = \neg\psi$;

- $\phi = \phi_1 \circ \psi$ for any QBF ϕ_1 and any $\circ \in \{\wedge, \vee, \rightarrow\}$;

- $\phi = \psi \circ \phi_2$ for any QBF ϕ_2 and any $\circ \in \{\wedge, \vee, \rightarrow\}$;

- $\phi = \exists p(\psi)$ for any $p \in P$;

- $\phi = \forall p(\psi)$ for any $p \in P$.

A QBF ψ is called *subformula* of QBF ϕ if one of the following conditions holds:

- $\phi = \psi$;

- ψ is a direct subformula of ϕ;

- there is a direct subformula χ of ϕ and ψ is a subformula of χ.

For a QBF ϕ over P, let $N(\phi)$ be defined as follows:

- If $\phi = \top$, then $N(\phi) = 1$; if $\phi = \bot$, then $N(\phi) = 1$;

- If $\phi = p \in P$ then $N(\phi) = 1$;

- If $\phi = \neg\phi_1$ then $N(\phi) = N(\phi_1) + 1$;

- If $\phi = \phi_1 \circ \phi_2$ for any $\circ \in \{\wedge, \vee, \rightarrow\}$, then $N(\phi) = N(\phi_1) + N(\phi_2) + 1$;

- If $\phi = Qp(\phi_1)$ for any $Q \in \{\exists, \forall\}$ and any $p \in P$, then $N(\phi) = N(\phi_1) + 1$;

Let ϕ be a QBF over P, and $i \in \{0, 1, \ldots, N(\phi) - 1\}$. Then $S(i, \phi)$ is defined as follows:

- If $\phi = \top$, then $S(i, \phi) = \top$; if $\phi = \bot$, then $S(i, \phi) = \bot$;

- If $\phi = p \in P$, then $S(i, \phi) = p$;

- If $\phi = \neg\phi_1$, then

    - $S(i, \phi) = \phi$ if $i = N(\phi_1)$, and
    - $S(i, \phi) = S(i, \phi_1)$ otherwise;

- If $\phi = \phi_1 \circ \phi_2$ for any $\circ \in \{\wedge, \vee, \rightarrow\}$, then

    - $S(i, \phi) = \phi$ if $i = N(\phi_1) + N(\phi_2)$,
    - $S(i, \phi) = S(i, \phi_1)$ if $i < N(\phi_1)$, and
    - $S(i, \phi) = S(i - N(\phi_1), \phi_2)$ otherwise;

- If $\phi = Qp(\phi_1)$ for any $Q \in \{\exists, \forall\}$ and any $p \in P$, then

    - $S(i, \phi) = \phi$ if $i = N(\phi_1)$, and
    - $S(i, \phi) = S(i, \phi_1)$ otherwise.

For a QBF ϕ and $i \in \{0, 1, \ldots, N(\phi) - 1\}$ it follows from the definition that $S(i, \phi)$ is a subformula of ϕ.

Let ϕ and ψ be QBFs, and $i \in \{0, 1, \ldots, N(\phi) - 1\}$. Then ψ is said to *occur* in ϕ at position i if $S(i, \phi) = \psi$. Obviously, for any subformula ψ of QBF ϕ there is at least one position $i \in \{0, 1, \ldots, N(\phi) - 1\}$ where ψ occurs in ϕ.

Example 6.1 (Occurrence of a subformula in a formula) Let $\phi = (p \rightarrow q) \wedge (p \rightarrow q)$. Then subformula $p \rightarrow q$ occurs at positions 2 and 5 in ϕ. Subformula p occurs at positions 0 and 3 in ϕ, and subformula q occurs at positions 1 and 4 in ϕ. $N(\phi)$ is 7. $\qquad\square$

Let ϕ be a QBF, and a denote an occurrence of QBF ψ in ϕ (at an arbitrary position), and b denote an occurrence of QBF χ in ψ (at an arbitrary position). Then obviously the position of an occurrence c of χ in ϕ is determined by the position of a (in ϕ) and b (in ψ), and c is called a *descendant* of b. Conversely, b is called an *ancestor* of c. The ancestor and descendant relationships define partial orders on the set of occurrences of subformulas in a formula.

Example 6.2 (Ancestor of a subformula occurrence) Let $\phi = (p \rightarrow q) \wedge (p \rightarrow q)$. Then the occurrence of subformula $p \rightarrow q$ at position 2 is an ancestor of the occurrence of subformula p at position 0. □

An occurrence a of a propositional variable p in a QBF ϕ is said to be *in the scope of a quantification*, if for any QBF ψ there is an occurrence b of $\exists p(\psi)$ or $\forall p(\psi)$ in ϕ which is an ancestor of a. An occurrence of a propositional variable in a QBF is called *bound* if it is in the scope of a quantification, otherwise it is called *free*.

A QBF ϕ is called *closed* if all occurrences of propositional variables in ϕ are bound. Otherwise it is called *open*.

The semantics of QBFs is based on interpretations of the propositional variables. For an interpretation $\mathcal{I}$ of P the truth value assignment $\hat{\mathcal{I}} : \mathrm{QBF}(P) \rightarrow \{\mathrm{t}, \mathrm{f}\}$ is defined as follows:

1. If $\phi = \top$, then $\hat{\mathcal{I}}(\phi) = \mathrm{t}$; if $\phi = \bot$, then $\hat{\mathcal{I}}(\phi) = \mathrm{f}$.

2. If $\phi = p \in P$, then $\hat{\mathcal{I}}(\phi) = \mathcal{I}(p)$.

3. If $\phi = \neg\phi_1$, or $\phi = \phi_1 \circ \phi_2$ for any $\circ \in \{\wedge, \vee, \rightarrow\}$, then $\hat{\mathcal{I}}(\phi)$ is determined by $\hat{\mathcal{I}}(\phi_1)$ and $\hat{\mathcal{I}}(\phi_2)$ according to the tables on page 75 (row $\hat{\mathcal{I}}(\phi_1)$, column $\hat{\mathcal{I}}(\phi_2)$).

4. If $\phi = \forall p(\phi_1)$, then $\hat{\mathcal{I}}(\phi) = \hat{\mathcal{I}}(\phi_1[p/\top] \wedge \phi_1[p/\bot])$ [2].

5. If $\phi = \exists p(\phi_1)$, then $\hat{\mathcal{I}}(\phi) = \hat{\mathcal{I}}(\phi_1[p/\top] \vee \phi_1[p/\bot])$.

If $\hat{\mathcal{I}}(\phi) = \mathrm{t}$, then QBF ϕ is said to be *true under* $\mathcal{I}$. If $\hat{\mathcal{I}}(\phi) = \mathrm{f}$, then ϕ is said to be *false under* $\mathcal{I}$. A QBF ϕ is called *satisfied* by interpretation $\mathcal{I}$, and, equivalently, $\mathcal{I}$ is called a *model* of ϕ, denoted $\mathcal{I} \vDash \phi$, if ϕ is true under $\mathcal{I}$. A QBF ϕ is called *satisfiable* if at least one interpretation of P is a model of ϕ, otherwise it is called *unsatisfiable*. A QBF ϕ is called *valid* if every interpretation of P is a model of ϕ. Observe that a closed QBF is always either valid or unsatisfiable. A finite set $\{\phi_i\}_{i \in I}$ of QBFs is identified with the QBF $\bigwedge_{i \in I} \phi_i$.

6.3 Nonmonotonic Reasoning Formalisms

This section presents five nonmonotonic reasoning formalisms. For classical abduction, equilibrium logic, paraconsistent reasoning via signed systems, and paraconsistent reasoning via three-valued logic this thesis presents implementations of reductions-to-QBFs in the Smute Language, which are documented in Chapter 8. Default logic is introduced because it is used in the definition of paraconsistent reasoning via signed systems.

6.3.1 Default Logic

Default Logic has been introduced in [27]. Let P be a set of propositional variables. Then a *default* δ over P is a triple of propositional formulas $\alpha, \beta, \gamma \in PROP(P)$, denoted $\delta = \frac{\alpha : \beta}{\gamma}$, where α is called the *prerequisite* of δ, β is called the *justification* of δ, and γ is called the *consequent* of δ. $\frac{:\beta}{\gamma}$, i.e., a default rule with "empty" prerequisite, is used as notational shortcut for the default rule $\frac{\top : \beta}{\gamma}$.

A *default theory* over a set of propositional variables P is a pair (W, Δ) of a set $W \subseteq PROP(P)$ of propositional formulas and a set Δ of defaults over P.

---

[2] $\phi[p_1/q_1, \ldots p_n/q_n]$ denotes the substitution of free occurrences of propositional variables p_i in QBF ϕ with q_i, for all $i = 1, \ldots, n$.

Let Δ be a set of defaults over P and $S \subseteq PROP(P)$ a set of propositional formulas. Then $pc(\Delta, S)$ is defined as follows: $pc(\Delta, S) := \{\frac{\alpha}{\gamma} : \frac{\alpha : \beta}{\gamma} \in \Delta \text{ and } \neg\beta \notin S\}$.

Let (W, Δ) be a default theory over P and $S \subseteq PROP(P)$ a set of propositional formulas. Then $Cn_d(W, \Delta, S)$ is defined as follows:

- $Cn_d(W, \Delta, S) := Cn(W \cup \bigcup_{i \geq 0} E_i)$ where

- $E_0 := \{\gamma : \frac{\alpha}{\gamma} \in pc(\Delta, S) \text{ and } W \vDash \alpha\}$ and

- $E_i := \{\gamma : \frac{\alpha}{\gamma} \in pc(\Delta, S) \text{ and } (W \cup E_{i-1}) \vDash \alpha\}$ for all $i \geq 1$.

A set $E \subseteq PROP(P)$ is called an *extension* of default theory (W, Δ) over P if $E = Cn_d(W, \Delta, E)$. For a default theory (W, Δ) over P and a propositional formula $\phi \in PROP(P)$

- ϕ is called a *brave consequence* of (W, Δ) if there is at least one extension E of (W, Δ) with $\phi \in E$;

- ϕ is called a *skeptical consequence* of (W, Δ) if $\phi \in E$ for every extension E of (W, Δ).

6.3.2 Classical Abduction

Abduction has first been studied in [23], the logic-based abduction has been introduced in [24].

Let $W \subseteq PROP(P)$ be a theory, $H \subseteq P$ a set of propositional variables, which is called the set of *hypotheses*, and let $p \in P$ be a designated propositional variable. Then a subset $E \subseteq H$ is called an *abductive explanation* for p from W and H if the following two conditions hold:

1. $T \cup E$ is consistent; and

2. $T \cup E \vDash p$.

An abductive explanation E for p from W and H is *minimal* if no proper subset $E' \subset E$ of hypotheses is an abductive explanation for p from W and H.

The following are typical reasoning tasks:

- Given $W \subseteq PROP(P)$, $H \subseteq P$ and $p \in P$, find out whether there is an abductive explanation for p from W and H.

- *Relevance Problem*: Given $W \subseteq PROP(P)$, $H \subseteq P$, $p \in P$, and a hypothesis $h \in H$, find out whether there is a (minimal) abductive explanation for p from W and H containing h.

- *Necessity Problem*: Given $W \subseteq PROP(P)$, $H \subseteq P$, $p \in P$, and a hypothesis $h \in H$, find out whether every (minimal) abductive explanation for p from W and H contains h.

6.3.3 Equilibrium Logic

Equilibrium Logic has been introduced in [21].

The following definitions are required: As usual, P denotes a set of propositional variables. An *HT-interpretation*[3] $\mathcal{I}$ of P is an ordered pair $(\mathcal{I}_H, \mathcal{I}_T)$ of interpretations $\mathcal{I}_H$ and $\mathcal{I}_T$ with

$$\{p \in P : \mathcal{I}_H(p) = \mathrm{t}\} \subseteq \{p \in P : \mathcal{I}_T(p) = \mathrm{t}\}.$$

Let $\mathcal{I} = (\mathcal{I}_H, \mathcal{I}_T)$ be an HT-interpretation of P. Then a truth value assignment $\bar{\mathcal{I}} : \{H, T\} \times PROP(P) \to \{\mathrm{t}, \mathrm{f}\}$ is defined as follows ($V_{\neg} : \{\mathrm{t}, \mathrm{f}\} \to \{\mathrm{t}, \mathrm{f}\}$ and $V_{\wedge}, V_{\vee}, V_{\to} : \{\mathrm{t}, \mathrm{f}\} \times \{\mathrm{t}, \mathrm{f}\} \to \{\mathrm{t}, \mathrm{f}\}$ are defined according to the tables on page 75):

---

[3] 'H' stands for "Here" and 'T' stands for "There". The logic of here-and-there is also commonly known as Gödel's three-valued logic [15]. It was first presented in the form of truth matrices by Heyting [17] and first axiomatised by Łukasiewicz [19].

- If $\phi = \top$ then

  - $\bar{\mathcal{I}}(H, \phi) = \mathrm{t}$;
  - $\bar{\mathcal{I}}(T, \phi) = \mathrm{t}$;

  if $\phi = \bot$ then

  - $\bar{\mathcal{I}}(H, \phi) = \mathrm{f}$;
  - $\bar{\mathcal{I}}(T, \phi) = \mathrm{f}$;

- If $\phi = p \in P$ then

  - $\bar{\mathcal{I}}(H, \phi) = \mathcal{I}_H(p)$;
  - $\bar{\mathcal{I}}(T, \phi) = \mathcal{I}_T(p)$;

- If $\phi = \neg \phi_1$ then

  - $\bar{\mathcal{I}}(H, \phi) = V_\wedge(V_\neg(\bar{\mathcal{I}}(H, \phi_1)), V_\neg(\bar{\mathcal{I}}(T, \phi_1)))$;
  - $\bar{\mathcal{I}}(T, \phi) = V_\neg(\bar{\mathcal{I}}(T, \phi_1))$;

- If $\phi = \phi_1 \wedge \phi_2$ then

  - $\bar{\mathcal{I}}(H, \phi) = V_\wedge(\bar{\mathcal{I}}(H, \phi_1), \bar{\mathcal{I}}(H, \phi_2))$;
  - $\bar{\mathcal{I}}(T, \phi) = V_\wedge(\bar{\mathcal{I}}(T, \phi_1), \bar{\mathcal{I}}(T, \phi_2))$;

- If $\phi = \phi_1 \vee \phi_2$ then

  - $\bar{\mathcal{I}}(H, \phi) = V_\vee(\bar{\mathcal{I}}(H, \phi_1), \bar{\mathcal{I}}(H, \phi_2))$;
  - $\bar{\mathcal{I}}(T, \phi) = V_\vee(\bar{\mathcal{I}}(T, \phi_1), \bar{\mathcal{I}}(T, \phi_2))$;

- If $\phi = \phi_1 \rightarrow \phi_2$ then

  - $\bar{\mathcal{I}}(H, \phi) = V_\wedge(V_\rightarrow(\bar{\mathcal{I}}(H, \phi_1), \bar{\mathcal{I}}(H, \phi_2)), V_\rightarrow(\bar{\mathcal{I}}(T, \phi_1), \bar{\mathcal{I}}(T, \phi_2)))$;
  - $\bar{\mathcal{I}}(T, \phi) = V_\rightarrow(\bar{\mathcal{I}}(T, \phi_1), \bar{\mathcal{I}}(T, \phi_2))$.

Let $\mathcal{I} = (\mathcal{I}_H, \mathcal{I}_T)$ be an HT-interpretation of P and $\phi \in PROP(P)$. Then ϕ is said to be *true under I* if $\bar{\mathcal{I}}(H, \phi) = \mathrm{t}$. ϕ is said to be *false under I* if $\bar{\mathcal{I}}(H, \phi) = \mathrm{f}$. An HT-interpretation $\mathcal{I}$ is said to *statisfy* propositional formula ϕ or, equivalently, $\mathcal{I}$ is called a *HT-model* of ϕ, if ϕ is true under $\mathcal{I}$. If all HT-interpretations of P are HT-models of ϕ, then ϕ is *HT-valid*.

An interpretation $\mathcal{I}$ is an *equilibrium model* of a formula ϕ if both of the following conditions hold:

1. $(\mathcal{I}, \mathcal{I})$ is an HT-model of ϕ; and

2. for every interpretation $\mathcal{I}_s$ with

$$\{p \in P : \mathcal{I}_s(p) = \mathrm{t}\} \subset \{p \in P : \mathcal{I}(p) = \mathrm{t}\},$$

$(\mathcal{I}_s, \mathcal{I})$ is not an HT-model of ϕ.

Let $W = \{\phi_i\}_{i \in I} \subseteq PROP(P)$ be a set of propositional formulas and $\phi \in PROP(P)$ a propositional formula. Then ϕ is an *equilibrium consequence* of W if every equilibrium model of W (i.e., every equilibrium model of $\bigwedge_{i \in I} \phi_i$) is a model of ϕ.

6.3.4 Paraconsistent Reasoning via Signed Systems

Paraconsistent Reasoning via Signed Systems has been introduced in [5].

The section starts with a few definitions. The *polarity* of an occurrence[4] of a subformula in a formula is defined as follows:

- The occurrence of ψ in ψ (note that there is only one such occurrence) is positive.

- If a is a positive (negative) occurrence of ψ in ϕ, then the corresponding occurrences of ψ in $\neg\phi$ and in $\phi \rightarrow \chi$ are negative (positive).

- If a is a positive (negative) occurrence of ψ in ϕ, then the corresponding occurrences of ψ in $\chi \vee \phi$, $\phi \vee \chi$, $\chi \wedge \phi$, $\phi \wedge \chi$, and $\chi \rightarrow \phi$ are positive (negative).

Let $(p_i)_{i \in I}$ be a sequence of pairwise distinct propositional variables, and $P = \{p_i : i \in I\}$. Furthermore, let $(p_i^+)_{i \in I}$ and $(p_i^-)_{i \in I}$ be sequences of pairwise distinct propositional variables with the same index set I and such that for $P^+ = \{p_i^+ : i \in I\}$ and $P^- = \{p_i^- : i \in I\}$ the three sets are disjoint, i.e., $P \cap P^+ = P \cap P^- = P^+ \cap P^- = \emptyset$. Let $\phi \in PROP(P)$ be a propositional formula. Then $pm((p_i)_{i \in I}, (p_i^+)_{i \in I}, (p_i^-)_{i \in I}, \phi)$ denotes a propositional formula over $P^+ \cup P^-$ which is constructed from ϕ as follows: For all $i \in I$, every positive occurrence of propositional variable p_i in ϕ gets replaced with p_i^+, and every negative occurrence gets replaced with p_i^-. For a set $W \subseteq PROP(P)$ of propositional formulas,

$$pm((p_i)_{i \in I}, (p_i^+)_{i \in I}, (p_i^-)_{i \in I}, W) := \{pm((p_i)_{i \in I}, (p_i^+)_{i \in I}, (p_i^-)_{i \in I}, \phi) : \phi \in W\}.$$

With $(p_i)_{i \in I}$, $(p_i^+)_{i \in I}$, and $(p_i^-)_{i \in I}$ as defined above, for every $i \in I$ the following default is defined:

$$\delta((p_i)_{i \in I}, (p_i^+)_{i \in I}, (p_i^-)_{i \in I}, i) := \frac{: p_i^+ \leftrightarrow \neg p_i^-}{(p_i \leftrightarrow p_i^+) \wedge (\neg p_i \leftrightarrow p_i^-)}.$$

Let Δ be a set of defaults over P and $S \subseteq PROP(P)$ a set of propositional formulas. Then $c(\Delta, S)$ is defined as follows:

$$c(\Delta, S) := \{\gamma : \frac{\alpha : \beta}{\gamma} \in \Delta \text{ and } \neg\beta \notin S\}.$$

Let $W \subseteq PROP(P)$ be a set of propositional formulas and $\phi \in PROP(P)$ a propositional formula. Then with the above definitions three new consequence relations can be defined as follows: Let $(p_i)_{i \in I}$ be a sequence of pairwise distinct propositional variables such that $P = \{p_i : i \in I\}$, and let $(p_i^+)_{i \in I}$ and $(p_i^-)_{i \in I}$ be arbitrary sequences of pairwise distinct propositional variables such that for $P^+ = \{p_i^+ : i \in I\}$ and $P^- = \{p_i^- : i \in I\}$ the three sets are disjoint, i.e., $P \cap P^+ = P \cap P^- = P^+ \cap P^- = \emptyset$. Furthermore, let $W^\pm$ denote $pm((p_i)_{i \in I}, (p_i^+)_{i \in I}, (p_i^-)_{i \in I}, W)$, and let Δ denote $\{\delta((p_i)_{i \in I}, (p_i^+)_{i \in I}, (p_i^-)_{i \in I}, i) : i \in I\}$, and let $Ext((W^\pm, \Delta))$ denote the set of extensions of default theory $(W^\pm, \Delta)$. Then

- $W \models_c \phi$ (ϕ is a *credulous unsigned consequence* of W) if

$$\phi \in \bigcup_{E \in Ext(W^\pm, \Delta)} Cn(W^\pm \cup c(\Delta, E));$$

- $W \models_s \phi$ (ϕ is a *skeptical unsigned consequence* of W) if

$$\phi \in \bigcap_{E \in Ext(W^\pm, \Delta)} Cn(W^\pm \cup c(\Delta, E));$$

---

[4]The *occurrence* of a subformula in a formula is defined on page 76.

- $W \vDash_p \phi$ (ϕ is a *prudent unsigned consequence* of W) if

$$\phi \in Cn\left(W^{\pm} \cup \bigcap_{E \in Ext(W^{\pm}, \Delta)} c(\Delta, E)\right).$$

Numerous additional consequence relations are defined in [5].

6.3.5 Paraconsistent Reasoning via Three-Valued Logic

The reasoning formalisms of Paraconsistent Reasoning via Three-valued Logic have been introduced in [5, 25, 26].

The following definitions are required: For a set P of propositional variables a *three-valued-interpretation* is defined as function $\mathcal{I} : P \to \{t, f, o\}$. The name three-valued-interpretation is used for distinction from interpretations $\mathcal{I} : P \to \{t, f\}$. For a three-valued-interpretation $\mathcal{I}$ the truth value assignment function $\bar{\mathcal{I}} : PROP(P) \to \{t, f, o\}$ is defined as follows:

1. If $\phi = \top$, then $\bar{\mathcal{I}}(\phi) = t$, if $\phi = \bot$ then $\bar{\mathcal{I}}(\phi) = f$.

2. If $\phi = p \in P$, then $\bar{\mathcal{I}}(\phi) = \mathcal{I}(p)$.

3. If $\phi = \neg\phi_1$, or $\phi = \phi_1 \circ \phi_2$ for any $\circ \in \{\wedge, \vee, \to\}$, then $\bar{\mathcal{I}}(\phi)$ is determined by $\bar{\mathcal{I}}(\phi_1)$ and $\bar{\mathcal{I}}(\phi_2)$ according to the tables below (row $\bar{\mathcal{I}}(\phi_1)$, column $\bar{\mathcal{I}}(\phi_2)$).

$\neg$	
t	f
f	t
o	o

$\wedge$	t	f	o
t	t	f	o
f	f	f	f
o	o	f	o

$\vee$	t	f	o
t	t	t	t
f	t	f	o
o	t	o	o

$\to$	t	f	o
t	t	f	o
f	t	t	t
o	t	f	o

A three-valued-interpretation $\mathcal{I}$ is said to be a *three-valued-model* of a formula $\phi \in PROP(P)$ if $\bar{\mathcal{I}}(\phi) = t$ or $\bar{\mathcal{I}}(\phi) = o$.

For three-valued-interpretations of P the following partial orderings are defined, the second one depending on a set $W \subseteq PROP(P)$ of formulas.

- $\mathcal{I}_0 \leq_m \mathcal{I}_1$ if $\{p \in P : \mathcal{I}_0(p) = o\} \subseteq \{p \in P : \mathcal{I}_1(p) = o\}$;

- $\mathcal{I}_0 \leq_n \mathcal{I}_1$ if $\{\phi \in W : \bar{\mathcal{I}}_0(\phi) = o\} \subseteq \{\phi \in W : \bar{\mathcal{I}}_1(\phi) = o\}$.

Three new consequence operators are defined as follows:

- $W \vDash_3 \phi$ if every three-valued-model of W is a three-valued-model of ϕ.

- $W \vDash_m \phi$ if every three-valued-model of W which is minimal with respect to $\leq_m$ is a three-valued-model of ϕ.

- $W \vDash_n \phi$ if every three-valued-model of W which is minimal with respect to $\leq_n$ is a three-valued-model of ϕ (the partial ordering $\leq_n$ is constructed from W).

The reasoning formalisms based on consequence relations $\vDash_3$, $\vDash_m$, and $\vDash_n$ are referred to as LP, LP_m, and LP_n respectively. LP and LP_m have been introduced by Priest in in [25] and [26], LP_n by Philippe Besnard and Torsten Schaub in [5].

6.4 An Example Reduction-to-QBF

This section presents reductions-to-QBFs for paraconsistent reasoning via three-valued logic. The reductions are taken from [7], though represented here in a slightly modified way. They serve as example for the reductions-to-QBFs which have been implemented in the Smute Language. The other implemented reductions-to-QBFs can be found in [6, 9, 10, 22]. For the following reductions-to-QBFs a detailed description of its implementations, including the Smute Language code, is given in Chapter 9.

The following notions are required in the specification of the reductions-to-QBFs. Let S be a set. An *array* a over S is a (possibly empty) finite sequence of elements of S, the length of the sequence is called the *size* of array a. An array $[a_0, \ldots, a_n]$ is called *pairwise distinct* if $a_i \neq a_j$ holds for all $i, j = 0, \ldots, n$ with $i \neq j$. Two arrays $[a_0, \ldots, a_n]$ and $[b_0, \ldots, b_n]$ are called *distinct* if $a_i \neq b_j$ holds for all $i, j = 0, \ldots, n$. For arrays $A = [a_0, \ldots, a_n]$ and $B = [b_0, \ldots, b_n]$, $A \circ B$ denotes array $[a_0, \ldots, a_n, b_0, \ldots, b_n]$, the *concatenation* of A and B. For an array $A = [a_0, \ldots, a_n]$ the *set of array-elements* from A, denoted $A_{\{\}}$, is defined as $\bigcup_{i=0,\ldots,n} \{a_i\}$. An array A is said to *represent* a set S if $A_{\{\}} = S$.

For an array of propositional variables $P = [p_0, \ldots, p_n]$ and a QBF ϕ, the QBF $\forall P \phi$ is defined as $\forall p_0 \forall p_1 \ldots \forall p_n \phi$ and $\exists P \phi$ is defined as $\exists p_0 \exists p_1 \ldots \exists p_n \phi$.

For an array of QBFs $\Phi = [\phi_0, \ldots, \phi_n]$ and a propositional variable p, p is said to *occur* in Φ if there is at least one $i \in \{0, 1, \ldots, n\}$ such that p occurs in ϕ_i (at an arbitrary position).

For two arrays of QBFs $\Phi = [\phi_0, \ldots, \phi_n]$ and $\Psi = [\psi_0, \ldots, \psi_n]$, $\Phi \leq \Psi$ denotes QBF $\bigwedge_{i=0,\ldots,n} (\phi_i \to \psi_i)$. $\Phi < \Psi$ denotes QBF $\bigwedge_{i=0,\ldots,n} (\phi_i \to \psi_i) \wedge \neg \bigwedge_{i=0,\ldots,n} (\psi_i \to \phi_i)$.

For a QBF ϕ and two equally sized arrays of propositional variables $P = [p_0, \ldots, p_m]$ and $Q = [q_0, \ldots, q_m]$, $\phi[P/Q]$ is constructed from ϕ by replacing all free occurrences of propositional variable p_i with q_i, for $i = 0, \ldots, m$. For an array of QBFs $\Phi = [\phi_0, \ldots, \phi_n]$ and two equally sized arrays of propositional variables $P = [p_0, \ldots, p_m]$ and $Q = [q_0, \ldots, q_m]$, $\Phi[P/Q]$ is defined as the array of QBFs $[\phi_0[P/Q], \ldots, \phi_n[P/Q]]$.

For the next definition the following is assumed: $P = [p_0, \ldots, p_n]$ is an array of pairwise distinct propositional variables, $P' = [p'_0, \ldots, p'_n]$ is an array of pairwise distinct propositional variables distinct from P, $\mathcal{I}_o$ is a three-valued interpretation of $P_{\{\}}$, and $\mathcal{I}$ is an interpretation of $P_{\{\}} \cup P'_{\{\}}$. Then $\mathcal{I}_o$ and $\mathcal{I}$ are called *associated* with respect to P and P' if all of the following conditions are true:

- for every p_i with $\mathcal{I}_o(p_i) = \text{t}$, $\mathcal{I}(p_i) = \text{t}$ and $\mathcal{I}(p'_i) = \text{t}$;

- for every p_i with $\mathcal{I}_o(p_i) = \text{f}$, $\mathcal{I}(p_i) = \text{f}$ and $\mathcal{I}(p'_i) = \text{f}$;

- for every p_i with $\mathcal{I}_o(p_i) = \text{o}$, $\mathcal{I}(p_i) = \text{f}$ and $\mathcal{I}(p'_i) = \text{t}$.

Note that an interpretation $\mathcal{I}$ of $P_{\{\}} \cup P'_{\{\}}$ has an associated three-valued interpretation iff $\bar{\mathcal{I}}(P \leq P') = \text{t}$.

Let Q denote a set of variables, and $n \in \mathbb{N}$, $n > 0$. Then in the definition of translations the expression

$$P := \textit{nvar}(Q, n)$$

states that P is a new array of pairwise distinct propositional variables with array-size n such that $P_{\{\}} \cap Q = \emptyset$. For an array Φ of propositional formulas, the expression

$$P := \textit{var}(\Phi)$$

states that P is assigned an array of pairwise distinct propositional variables such that $P_{\{\}} = \{p : p \text{ occurs in } \Phi\}$. For an array P, the expression $\textit{size}(P)$ is used to denote the array-size of P.

With these notions and definitions the translations are specified as follows: The specifications are "bottom-up", i.e., starting with smaller sub-translations.

The first function is called τ and expects the following parameters: An arbitrary propositional formula ϕ, an array of pairwise distinct propositional variables $P = [p_0, \ldots, p_n]$ representing the variables occurring in ϕ (or a superset of those), an array of pairwise distinct propositional variables $P' = [p'_0, \ldots, p'_n]$ which is distinct from P, plus a fourth parameter which is one of t,f, or o.

τ is defined as follows:

1. (a) $\tau(P, P', p_i, t) := p_i$;
   (b) $\tau(P, P', p_i, f) := \neg p'_i$;
   (c) $\tau(P, P', p_i, t) := \neg p_i \wedge p'_i$;

2. (a) $\tau(P, P', \neg \phi_1, t) := \tau(P, P', \phi_1, f)$;
   (b) $\tau(P, P', \neg \phi_1, f) := \tau(P, P', \phi_1, t)$;
   (c) $\tau(P, P', \neg \phi_1, o) := \tau(P, P', \phi_1, o)$;

3. (a) $\tau(P, P', \phi_1 \wedge \phi_2, t) := \tau(P, P', \phi_1, t) \wedge \tau(P, P', \phi_2, t)$;
   (b) $\tau(P, P', \phi_1 \wedge \phi_2, f) := \tau(P, P', \phi_1, f) \vee \tau(P, P', \phi_2, f)$;
   (c) $\tau(P, P', \phi_1 \wedge \phi_2, o) := \neg \tau(P, P', \phi_1 \wedge \phi_2, t) \wedge \neg \tau(P, P', \phi_1 \wedge \phi_2, f)$;

4. (a) $\tau(P, P', \phi_1 \vee \phi_2, t) := \tau(P, P', \phi_1, t) \vee \tau(P, P', \phi_2, t)$;
   (b) $\tau(P, P', \phi_1 \vee \phi_2, f) := \tau(P, P', \phi_1, f) \wedge \tau(P, P', \phi_2, f)$;
   (c) $\tau(P, P', \phi_1 \vee \phi_2, o) := \neg \tau(P, P', \phi_1 \vee \phi_2, t) \wedge \neg \tau(P, P', \phi_1 \vee \phi_2, f)$;

5. (a) $\tau(P, P', \phi_1 \rightarrow \phi_2, t) := \tau(P, P', \phi_1, f) \vee \tau(P, P', \phi_2, t)$;
   (b) $\tau(P, P', \phi_1 \rightarrow \phi_2, f) := \neg \tau(P, P', \phi_1, f) \wedge \tau(P, P', \phi_2, f)$;
   (c) $\tau(P, P', \phi_1 \rightarrow \phi_2, o) := \neg \tau(P, P', \phi_1, f) \wedge \tau(P, P', \phi_2, o)$.

The models of $\tau(P, P', \phi, x)$ ($x \in \{t, f, o\}$) correspond to three-valued interpretations in the following way:

- For any model $\mathcal{I} : P_{\{\}} \cup P'_{\{\}} \rightarrow \{t, f\}$ of $\tau(P, P', \phi, x)$ either

  - $\bar{\mathcal{I}}(P \leq P') = f$ or
  - $\mathcal{I}$ has an associated three-valued interpretation $\mathcal{I}_o : P \rightarrow \{t, f, o\}$ with $\bar{\mathcal{I}}_o(\phi) = x$.

- Conversely, if $\mathcal{I}_o$ is a three-valued interpretation with $\bar{\mathcal{I}}_o(\phi) = x$, then the associated interpretation $\mathcal{I} : P_{\{\}} \cup P'_{\{\}} \rightarrow \{t, f\}$ is a model of $\tau(P, P', \phi, x)$.

The parameters of the next translation, called $m3$, are as follows: There is an array $W = [\phi_0, \ldots, \phi_n]$ of propositional formulas, an array $P = [p_0, \ldots, p_m]$ of pairwise distinct propositional variables representing the variables occurring in W (or a superset of those), and there is an array $P' = [p'_0, \ldots, p'_m]$ of pairwise distinct propositional variables distinct from P. $m3(P, P', W)$ is defined as:

$$m3(P, P', W) := \bigwedge_{i=0}^{n} \neg \tau(P, P', \phi_i, f).$$

The models of $m3(P, P', W)$ correspond to three-valued models of W as follows:

- For any model $\mathcal{I} : P_{\{\}} \cup P'_{\{\}} \rightarrow \{t, f\}$ of $m3(P, P', W)$ either

  - $\bar{\mathcal{I}}(P \leq P') = f$ or
  - $\mathcal{I}$ has an associated three-valued interpretation which is a three-valued model of W.

- Conversely, if $\mathcal{I}_o$ is a three-valued model of W, then the associated interpretation $\mathcal{I} : P_{\{\}} \cup P'_{\{\}} \to \{t, f\}$ is a model of $m3(P, P', W)$.

Translation *ConsLP* takes two parameters. The first, $W = [\phi_0, \ldots, \phi_n]$, is an array of propositional formulas and the second, ψ, is a propositional formula. $ConsLP(W, \psi)$ is defined as follows:

1. $P := var(W \circ [\psi])$;

2. $P' := nvar(P_{\{\}}, size(P))$;

3. $ConsLP(W, \psi) := \forall P \forall P' \big(((P \leq P') \wedge m3(P, P', W)) \to m3(P, P', \psi) \big)$.

$ConsLP(W, \psi)$ is a closed QBF, establishing the following correspondence:

$$W \vDash_3 \psi \text{ iff } ConsLP(W, \psi) \text{ is valid.}$$

For the next function, *min_m*, there are 3 parameters: An array $W = [\phi_0, \ldots, \phi_n]$ of propositional formulas, an array $P = [p_0, \ldots, p_m]$ of pairwise distinct propositional variables, representing the variables occurring in W or a superset of these variables, plus an array of pairwise distinct propositional variables $P' = [p'_0, \ldots, p'_m]$ which is distinct from P. The function is defined as follows:

1. $Q = [q_0, \ldots, q_m] := nvar(P_{\{\}} \cup P'_{\{\}}, size(P))$;

2. $Q' := nvar(P_{\{\}} \cup P'_{\{\}} \cup Q_{\{\}}, size(P))$;

3. $O_P := [\tau(P, P', p_0, o), \ldots, \tau(P, P', p_m, o)]$;

4. $O_Q := [\tau(P, P', q_0, o), \ldots, \tau(P, P', q_m, o)]$;

5. $min\_m(P, P', W)$ is given by

$$(P \leq P') \wedge \neg \exists Q \exists Q' \big((O_Q < O_P) \wedge (Q \leq Q') \wedge m3(Q, Q', W[P/Q]) \big).$$

Let $\mathcal{I}$ be an interpretation of $P_{\{\}} \cup P'_{\{\}}$. The models of $min\_m(P, P', W)$ correspond to certain three-valued interpretations of $P_{\{\}}$, as given by the equivalence of the following two statements:

1. $\mathcal{I} \vDash min\_m(P, P', W)$.

2. $\mathcal{I}$ has an associated three-valued interpretation $\mathcal{I}_o$ and for every three-valued model $\mathcal{I}_o^i$ of W the following is true: $\mathcal{I}_o^i \not\prec_m \mathcal{I}_o$ ($\leq_m$ is defined with respect to the variables of P, and "$a < b$" stands for "$a \leq b$ and $a \neq b$").

For the next translation, *min_n*, the set of parameters is the same as with *min_m*: An array $W = [\phi_0, \ldots, \phi_n]$ of propositional formulas, an array $P = [p_0, \ldots, p_m]$ of pairwise distinct propositional variables, representing the variables occurring in W or a superset of these variables, plus an array of pairwise distinct propositional variables $P' = [p'_0, \ldots, p'_m]$ which is distinct from P. The function is defined as follows:

1. $Q = [q_0, \ldots, q_m] := nvar(P_{\{\}} \cup P'_{\{\}}, size(P))$;

2. $Q' := nvar(P_{\{\}} \cup P'_{\{\}} \cup Q_{\{\}}, size(P))$;

3. $O_P := [\tau(P, P', \phi_0, o), \ldots, \tau(P, P', \phi_n, o)]$;

4. $O_Q := [\tau(P, P', \phi_0[P/Q], o), \ldots, \tau(P, P', \phi_n[P/Q], o)]$;

5. $min\_n(P, P', W)$ is given by

$$(P \leq P') \wedge \neg \exists Q \exists Q' \Big((O_Q < O_P) \wedge (Q \leq Q') \wedge m3(Q, Q', W[P/Q]) \Big).$$

Let $\mathcal{I}$ be an interpretation of $P_{\{\}} \cup P'_{\{\}}$. The models of $min\_n(P, P', W)$ correspond to certain three-valued interpretations of $P_{\{\}}$, as given by the equivalence of the following two statements:

1. $\mathcal{I} \models min\_n(P, P', W)$.

2. $\mathcal{I}$ has an associated three-valued interpretation $\mathcal{I}_o$ and for every three-valued model $\mathcal{I}_o^i$ of W the following is true: $\mathcal{I}_o^i \not<_n \mathcal{I}_o$ ($\leq_n$ is defined with respect to W).

For the next translation, $ConsLPm$, there are two parameters: An array $W = [\phi_0, \ldots, \phi_n]$ of propositional formulas and a propositional formula ψ. $ConsLPm(W, \psi)$ is defined as follows:

1. $P := var(W \circ [\psi])$;

2. $P' := nvar(P_{\{\}}, size(P))$;

3. $ConsLPm(W, \psi) := \forall P \forall P' \Big((min\_m(P, P', W) \wedge m3(P, P', W)) \rightarrow m3(P, P', \psi) \Big)$.

Another translation, $ConsLPn$, has exactly the same parameters and is defined with these steps:

1. $P := var(W \circ [\psi])$;

2. $P' := nvar(P_{\{\}}, size(P))$;

3. $ConsLPn(W, \psi) := \forall P \forall P' \Big((min\_n(P, P', W) \wedge m3(P, P', W)) \rightarrow m3(P, P', \psi) \Big)$.

Both translations create closed QBFs, establishing the following correspondences:

- $W \models_m \psi$ iff $ConsLPm(W, \psi)$ is valid.

- $W \models_n \psi$ iff $ConsLPn(W, \psi)$ is valid.

Chapter 7

Smute Interpreter Logic Edition

There are two important aspects of Smute Interpreter Logic Edition:

- It introduces CARGOTREE-Schemes for several logic-related data structures.

- It introduces a syntax according to which logic-related data instances can be specified within Smute Launch Files. Preprocessing Functions for the respective grammar-dependent CARGOTREEs are included.

The topics of Smute Interpreter Logic Edition which are relevant for Smute Function Users, namely how to specify logic-related data instances in Smute Launch Files, are documented in Section 7.1. The topics which are relevant for Smute Function Developers, namely which CARGO-TREE-Schemes and which Preprocessing Functions there are, follow in Section 7.2.

7.1 Logic Edition Launch File Syntax

Currently the following data-instances can be specified within the Smute Launch File for Smute Interpreter Logic Edition:

- "formula": Propositional formula;

- "vararray": Array of propositional variables.

Additional grammars for data like defaults (from default logic), formula arrays (for the specification of theories), etc., are likely to be implemented in coming versions.

The Backus-Naur form of "formula":

```
<formula>          ::= <fla_or> '>' <fla_or>
                   | <fla_or>

<fla_or>           ::= <fla_or> '|' <fla_and>
                   | <fla_or> '+' <fla_and>
                   | <fla_and>

<fla_and>          ::= <fla_and> '^' <fla_not>
                   | <fla_and> '&' <fla_not>
                   | <fla_and> '*' <fla_not>
                   | <fla_not>

<fla_not>          ::= '~' <fla_not>
                   | '!' <fla_not>
                   | <fla_bot>
```

```
<fla_const>              ::= '$T'
                          | '$F'

<fla_bot>                ::= id  !propositional variable identifier
                          | <fla_const>
                          | '(' <formula> ')'
```

Example specifications:

```
~p & p & (p > q) & (r > q)
((a&(b|c))>b)&(!a|!c>$F)
```

The Backus-Naur form of "vararray" (start symbol is idarraydef):

```
<idarraydef>             ::= '<' <idarray> '>'

<idarray>                ::= id ',' <idarray>
                          | id
```

Example specification:

```
<a,b,p,d,z,g>
```

7.2 Logic Edition Preprocessing Functions and **CARGOTREE**-Schemes

With Smute Interpreter Logic Edition it is possible to specify data-instances with the following structures in Smute Launch Files:

- Propositional Formula;

- Variable Array.

Smute Interpreter Logic Edition also defines grammar-independent CARGOTREE-Schemes for these data structures and comes with a Smute Module called "precorelogic" containing the respective Preprocessing Functions.

Here is an overview of the CARGOTREE-Schemes:

QBFS : For the representation of Quantified Boolean Formulas (QBFs). There are string identifiers for propositional variables. Note that propositional formulas are QBFs without quantifiers. There is no separate CARGOTREE-Scheme for propositional formulas.

QBF : Identical to QBFS, except that there are integer identifiers for propositional variables.

VARARRAYS : For the representation of propositional variable arrays. There are string identifiers for propositional variables.

VARARRAY : Identical to VARARRAYS, except that there are integer identifiers for propositional variables.

For the sake of better comprehensibility node-ids for these CARGOTREE-Schemes are referenced with string aliases. These are the ids for the *QBFS-Scheme*:

String alias	Integer value
QBF_NOT	0
QBF_OR	1
QBF_AND	2
QBF_IMPL	3
QBF_EXISTS	4
QBF_FORALL	5
QBF_PROPVAR	6
QBF_CONST	7

With the QBFS-Scheme Quantified Boolean Formulas are encoded as follows:

- A ConCls-node with 1 child and id QBF_NOT is used to represent a QBF $\neg\phi$. The sub-CARGOTREE represents ϕ.

- A ConCls-node with 2 children and id QBF_OR is used to represent a QBF $\phi_0 \vee \phi_1$. The 0th sub-CARGOTREE represents ϕ_0, the 1st sub-CARGOTREE represents ϕ_1.

- A ConCls-node with 2 children and id QBF_AND is used to represent a QBF $\phi_0 \wedge \phi_1$. The 0th sub-CARGOTREE represents ϕ_0, the 1st sub-CARGOTREE represents ϕ_1.

- A ConCls-node with 2 children and id QBF_IMPL is used to represent a QBF $\phi_0 \rightarrow \phi_1$. The 0th sub-CARGOTREE represents ϕ_0, the 1st sub-CARGOTREE represents ϕ_1.

- An Int-node with id QBF_CONST is used to represent the logical constants $\bot$ and $\top$. A value of 0 is used for the representation of $\bot$, a value of 1 for the representation of $\top$.

- A Str-node with id QBF_PROPVAR is used to represent a logical variable. The string-value serves as variable identifier.

- A ConCls-node with 2 children and id QBF_EXISTS is used to represent a QBF $\exists p(\phi)$. The 0th sub-CARGOTREE represents propositional variable p (and hence is always a Str-node with id QBF_PROPVAR), the 1st sub-CARGOTREE represents ϕ.

- A ConCls-node with 2 children and id QBF_FORALL is used to represent a QBF $\forall p(\phi)$. The 0th sub-CARGOTREE represents propositional variable p (and hence is always a Str-node with id QBF_PROPVAR), the 1st sub-CARGOTREE represents ϕ.

The *QBF-Scheme* is identical to the QBFS-Scheme, except that Int-nodes with id QBF_PROP-VAR are used for the representation of propositional variables instead of Str-nodes. The integer-value serves as variable identifier.

These are the node-ids for CARGOTREE-Scheme *VARARRAYS*:

String alias	Integer value
VARARRAY_LINK	0
VARARRAY_PROPVAR	1

Propositional variable arrays are encoded as follows:

- A Str-node with id VARARRAY_PROPVAR is used to represent a propositional variable. The string-value serves as variable identifier.

- A ConCls-node with 2 children and id VARARRAY_LINK is used to represent a variable-array with more than 1 entry. The 0th sub-CARGOTREE represents the array's 0th entry (and hence is always a Str-node with id VARARRAY_PROPVAR). The 1st sub-CARGOTREE represents the sub-array consisting of all entries except the 0th.

The *VARARRAY-Scheme* is identical to the VARARRAYS-Scheme, except that Int-nodes with id `VARARRAY_PROPVAR` are used for the representation of propositional variables instead of Str-nodes. The integer-value serves as variable identifier.

The Preprocessing Functions for Smute Interpreter Logic Edition are contained in Smute Module `precorelogic`. Recall that data specified in Smute Launch Files for Smute Interpreter Logic Edition *must* be preprocessed with the Preprocessing Functions of `precorelogic`. Smute Functions not obeying this rule are rendered useless with changes in the Smute Launch File grammar for Smute Interpreter Logic Edition.

Module	**precorelogic**
Version	0.00 (27/08/2003)
Author	Norbert Pfaffinger
Description	Preprocessing Functions which from grammar-dependent CARGOTREEs created by Smute Interpreter Logic Edition build new `CARGOTREE` representations complying with certain grammar-independent `CARGOTREE`-Schemes.

Overview

PreFLA (0.00), p.90	Preprocesses a `CARGOTREE` generated by the Smute Interpreter Logic Edition according to the "formula"-syntax of the Logic Edition Launch File Grammar, creating a `CARGOTREE` representing the same formula and complying with the QBFS-Scheme.
PreQBF (0.00), p.90	Preprocesses a `CARGOTREE` generated by the Smute Interpreter Logic Edition according to the "qbfdef"-syntax of the Logic Edition Launch File Grammar, creating a `CARGOTREE` representing the same QBF and complying with the QBFS-Scheme.
PreVarArray (0.00), p.91	Preprocesses a `CARGOTREE` generated by the Smute Interpreter Logic Edition according to the "idarraydef"-syntax of the Logic Edition Launch File Grammar, creating a `CARGOTREE` representing the same variable array and complying with the VARARRAYS-Scheme.
IdxSubstC (0.00), p.91	From a single input-QBF in QBFS-Scheme creates a logically equivalent QBF in QBF-Scheme (string identifiers are replaced with `INTEGER` identifiers of a range starting at 0).
IdxSubst2C (0.00), p.92	From two input-QBFs in QBFS-Scheme creates logically equivalent QBFs in QBF-Scheme (string identifiers are replaced with `INTEGER` identifiers of a range starting at 0).
IdxSubst (0.00), p.92	From a single input-QBF in QBFS-Scheme creates a logically equivalent QBF in QBF-Scheme. Integer-identifiers are determined by a `HASHSTRCOL`.
IdxSubstVarArray (0.00), p.93	From a variable-array in VARARRAYS-Scheme creates an `INTEGER-ARRAY` which re-identifies the original string variables.

PreFLA (0.00)

Synopsis

```
(R00 = CARGOTREEMEM ctmem  =Pr.(R00 = CARGOTREEMEM ctmem
 R01 = CARGOTREE      fla  )      R01 = CARGOTREE      fla  );
```

Description

Preprocesses a CARGOTREE generated by the Smute Interpreter Logic Edition according to the "formula"-syntax of the Logic Edition Launch File Grammar, creating a CARGOTREE representing the same formula and complying with the QBFS-Scheme.

Parameters

ctmem	Memory used to create the resulting formula within.
fla	In accordance to the "formula"-syntax of the Logic Edition Launch File Grammar.

Return Values

ctmem	Passed through.
fla	Resulting formula in QBFS-Scheme. Completely allocated in ctmem. The string-values are only referenced from the input CARGOTREE though.

PreQBF (0.00)

Synopsis

```
(R00 = CARGOTREEMEM ctmem  =Pr.(R00 = CARGOTREEMEM ctmem
 R01 = CARGOTREE      fla  )      R01 = CARGOTREE      fla  );
```

Description

Preprocesses a CARGOTREE generated by the Smute Interpreter Logic Edition according to the "qbfdef"-syntax of the Logic Edition Launch File Grammar, creating a CARGOTREE representing the same QBF and complying with the QBFS-Scheme.

Parameters

ctmem	Memory used to create the resulting QBF within.
fla	In accordance to the "qbfdef"-syntax of the Logic Edition Launch File Grammar.

Return Values

ctmem	Passed through.
fla	Resulting QBF in QBFS-Scheme. Completely allocated in ctmem. The string-values are only referenced from the input CARGOTREE though.

PreVarArray (0.00)

Synopsis

(R00 = CARGOTREEMEM *ctmem* =**Pr.** (R00 = CARGOTREEMEM *ctmem*

  R01 = CARGOTREE   *varray*)   R01 = CARGOTREE   *varray*);

Description

Preprocesses a CARGOTREE generated by the Smute Interpreter Logic Edition according to the "idarraydef"-syntax of the Logic Edition Launch File Grammar, creating a CARGOTREE representing the same variable array and complying with the VARARRAYS-Scheme.

Parameters

ctmem	Memory used to create the resulting variable array within.
varray	In accordance to the "idarraydef"-syntax of the Logic Edition Launch File Grammar.

Return Values

ctmem	Passed through.
varray	Resulting variable array in VARARRAYS-Scheme. Completely allocated in *ctmem*. The string-values are only referenced from the input CARGOTREE though.

IdxSubstC (0.00)

Synopsis

(R00 = CARGOTREEMEM *ctmem* =**Id.** (R00 = CARGOTREEMEM *ctmem*

  R01 = CARGOTREE   *qbf*)   R01 = CARGOTREE   *qbfs*);

Description

From a single input-QBF in QBFS-Scheme creates a logically equivalent QBF in QBF-Scheme (string identifiers are replaced with INTEGER identifiers of a range starting at 0).

The replacement-method is replacement-by-occurrence. (For example, the first string encountered is replaced with '0').

Parameters

ctmem	Memory used to create the resulting QBF within. Note that not an entirely new QBF is created, instead the input-QBFS gets modified.
qbfs	QBF in QBFS-Scheme. Gets modified.

Return Values

ctmem	Passed through.
qbf	Resulting QBF in QBF-Scheme. Is a modification of the input-QBF.

IdxSubst2C (0.00)

Synopsis

```
( R00 = CARGOTREEMEM  ctmem  = Id. ( R00 = CARGOTREEMEM  ctmem
  R01 = CARGOTREE      qbf0           R01 = CARGOTREE        qbfs0
  R02 = CARGOTREE      qbf1 )         R02 = CARGOTREE        qbfs1 );
```

Description

From two input-QBFs in QBFS-Scheme creates logically equivalent QBFs in QBF-Scheme (string identifiers are replaced with INTEGER identifiers of a range starting at 0).

Identity across the two QBFs remains of course intact. The replacement-method is replacement-by-occurrence. New nodes for both the resulting QBFs are allocated from *ctmem*.

Parameters

ctmem	Memory used to create the resulting QBFs within. Note that not entirely new QBFs are created, instead the input-QBFs get modified.
qbfs0	QBF in QBFS-Scheme. Gets modified.
qbfs1	QBF in QBFS-Scheme. Gets modified.

Return Values

ctmem	Passed through.
qbf0	Resulting QBF in QBF-Scheme. Is a modification of the input-QBF *qbfs0*.
qbf1	Resulting QBF in QBF-Scheme. Is a modification of the input-QBF *qbfs1*.

IdxSubst (0.00)

Synopsis

```
( R00 = CARGOTREEMEM  ctmem  = Id. ( R00 = CARGOTREEMEM  ctmem
  R01 = CARGOTREE      qbf            R01 = CARGOTREE        qbfs
  R02 = HASHSTRCOL     hash           R02 = HASHSTRCOL       hash
  R03 = INTEGER        idxstrt )      R03 = INTEGER          idxstrt );
```

Description

From a single input-QBF in QBFS-Scheme creates a logically equivalent QBF in QBF-Scheme. Integer-identifiers are determined by a HASHSTRCOL.

Parameters

ctmem	Memory used to create the resulting QBF within. Note that not an entirely new QBF is created, instead the input-QBF gets modified.
qbfs	QBF in QBFS-Scheme. Gets modified.
hash	This hash may be empty or already contain strings with their occurrence-index in data-field 0.
idxstrt	The next new string is replaced with *idxstrt*. Is usually set to the number of entries already stored in *hash*.

Return Values

ctmem	Passed through.
qbf	Resulting QBF in QBF-Scheme. Is a modification of the input-QBF *qbfs*.
hash	Passed through and possibly altered.
idxstrt	Updated.

IdxSubstVarArray (0.00)

Synopsis

```
( R00 = CARGOTREE  vararray  =Id. ( R00 = CARGOTREE  vararray
  R01 = HASHSTRCOL hash            R01 = HASHSTRCOL hash
  R02 = INTEGER    idxstrt          R02 = INTEGER    idxstrt  );
  R03 = ARRAY      idxarray )
```

Description

From a variable-array in VARARRAYS-Scheme creates an INTEGER-ARRAY which re-identifies the original string variables.

Parameters

vararray	Variable array in VARARRAYS-Scheme.
hash	This hash may be empty or already contain strings with their occurrence-index in data-field 0.
idxstrt	The next new string is replaced with *idxstrt*. Is usually set to the number of entries already stored in *hash*.

Return Values

vararray	Passed through.
hash	Passed through and possibly altered.
idxstrt	Updated.
idxarray	Contains the replacement-INTEGER-array for the *vararray*-identifiers.

Chapter 8

Reduction-to-QBF Smute Package Documentation

The Reduction-to-QBF Smute Package implements several reductions-to-QBFs. An overview of the Smute Package is given in Section 8.1. An example for the invocation of a reduction-to-QBF Smute Function is provided in Section 8.2. Finally, Section 8.3 lists the interfaces to all Smute Functions of the Reduction-to-QBF Smute Package.

8.1 Overview

Currently reductions for reasoning tasks from the following propositional nonmonotonic reasoning formalisms are implemented:

- Classical Abduction;
- Equilibrium Logic;
- Paraconsistent Reasoning via Signed Systems;
- Paraconsistent Reasoning via Three-Valued Logic.

The reduction-to-QBF Smute Functions in this Smute Package are based on the reductions-to-QBFs presented in [6, 7, 10, 22]. The reductions-to-QBFs for Paraconsistent Reasoning via Three-Valued Logic are presented on pages 82ff. in Chapter 6. For a description of the other implemented reductions-to-QBFs refer to the aforementioned papers.

This Smute Package requires Smute Interpreter Logic Edition. Currently all reasoning tasks have to be specified in a Smute Launch File, i.e., the Smute Package does not include Wrapper Functions for reading data specified externally.

It is intended to extend this Smute Package with further reductions-to-QBFs for coming releases.

Currently the package contains the following Smute Modules:

1.	cabduction	(p.96ff.)
2.	equilib	(p.103ff.)
3.	parasigned	(p.107ff.)
4.	para3val	(p.113ff.)
5.	cabductionlaunch	(p.119ff.)
6.	equiliblaunch	(p.123ff.)
7.	parasignedlaunch	(p.124ff.)
8.	para3vallaunch	(p.125ff.)
9.	qbf	(p.126ff.)

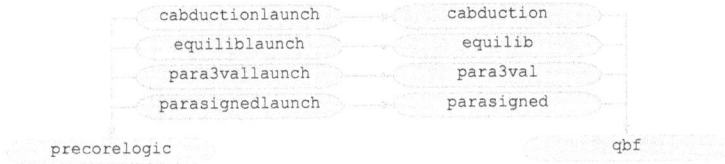

cabductionlaunch	⟶	cabduction
equiliblaunch	⟶	equilib
para3vallaunch	⟶	para3val
parasignedlaunch	⟶	parasigned
precorelogic		qbf

Figure 8.1: Smute Module dependencies

Smute Modules 1–4 contain the actual reductions-to-QBFs (Core Functions), for the respective propositional nonmonotonic reasoning formalisms. Smute Function Users never invoke them directly. Smute Modules 5–8 contain Wrapper Functions for Smute Modules 1–4, providing interfaces to Smute Function Users. These functions store resulting QBFs in two formats: In so-called 'boole'-format, and in GDL-format. The former is a format defined by QBF-solver boole [2], the latter is defined by graph visualisation software aiSee [1]. With these two programs it is hence possible to solve (find models) and to visualise resulting QBFs. The last Smute Module, qbf, contains various utility Smute Functions for Quantified Boolean Formulas. The reductions-to-QBFs depend on those Smute Functions. Currently the qbf Smute Module is developed and distributed as part of the Reduction-to-QBF Smute Package. As it could be useful for other Smute Functions as well, it might be distributed separately in coming releases. The dependencies between the Smute Modules are depicted in Figure 8.1 (note that Smute Module precorelogic comes with Smute Interpreter Logic Edition).

8.2 Smute Function Invocation Example

Example 8.1 (Invocation of a reduction-to-QBF Smute Function) In this example a reduction-to-QBF for to the consequence relation of LP_m gets invoked (see [7] for a description). In particular, for propositional formulas $\phi = \neg p \wedge p \wedge (p \rightarrow q) \wedge (r \rightarrow q)$ and $\psi = r$ it is assumed a Smute Function User wants to know whether $\phi \models_m \psi$, i.e., whether ψ is a consequence of ϕ according to the logic of LP_m. The respective Smute Function for this reasoning task is called **ConsLPm** and resides in Smute Module para3vallaunch. This function possesses three parameters, *flaleft*, *flaright*, and *storenum*. The two formulas *flaleft* and *flaright* have to be specified directly in the Smute Launch File according to the Logic Edition's 'formula'-syntax. The QBF created by function **ConsLPm** has the property that it is satisfiable iff *flaleft* $\models_m$ *flaright*. The parameter *storenum* is an integer, which determines the filename of the output-files. If, for example, a value of 27 is passed, then the resulting files are named "qbf0027.gdl" and "qbf0027.txt". These files are created in the 'current directory', i.e., the directory the Smute Interpreter is called from.

The appropriate Smute Launch File for the reasoning task is as follows:

```
<phi> := ~p & p & (p > q) & (r > q)
<psi> := r
loadmodules(precorelogic,qbf,para3val,para3vallaunch);
para3vallaunch:ConsLPm(phi,psi,20);
```

Of course any text-editor can be used to write and edit a Smute Launch File. It is recommended to store Smute Launch Files to the "working directory" of Smute (the directory where the Smute Interpreter is located). For this example the Smute Launch File is assumed to be named "1.txt".

The Smute Function can now be invoked as follows:

```
>smute 1.txt
```

95

If execution is successful the two files 'qbf0020.gdl' and 'qbf0020.txt' are created. The '.gdl'-file is the graph description which can be loaded with aiSee [1] in order to visualise the resulting QBF. The '.txt'-file is the resulting QBF represented in 'boole'-syntax. If boole is available the reasoning task can be solved by passing the file to boole:

```
>boole <qbf0020.txt
```

The output of boole is a simple '0', which stands for 'false' ('true' would be represented by '1'). The answer 'false' means the QBF is not valid, i.e., unsatisfiable. Accordingly, the answer to the reasoning task is 'no': In the logic of LP_m, ψ is not a consequence of ϕ. Below is a listing of the QBF in file "qbf0020.txt":

```
forall [P0] (forall [P1] (forall [P2] (forall [P3] (forall [P4] (forall
[P5] (~((~P0|P1)&(~P2|P3)&(~P4|P5)&forall [P6] (forall [P7] (forall [P8]
(forall [P9] (forall [P10] (forall [P11] (~(((~(~P6&P7)|~P0&P1)&(~(~P8&P9)|
~P2&P3)&(~(~P10&P11)|~P4&P5)&~(((~(~P0&P1)|~P6&P7)&(~(~P2&P3)|~P8&P9)&
(~(~P4&P5)|~P10&P11))&(~P6|P7)&(~P8|P9)&(~P10|P11))&
~(P6|~P7|~~P7&~P9|~~P11&~P9)))))))))&~(P0|~P1|~~P1&~P3|~~P5&~P3))|~~P5))))));
```

□

8.3 The Smute Function Interfaces

Module	cabduction
Version	0.00 (06/10/2003)
Author	Norbert Pfaffinger
Description	Translations of reasoning-task instances from classical abduction into QBFs.
	Any QBF generated by a function from this module is normalised. Normalised means that (a) no variable occurs both free and bound in the QBF and (b) any quantification of a variable occurs at most once as subformula in the QBF and (c) for any subformula which is a quantification, the quantified variable occurs in the quantification-subformula ("no empty quantifications").
	The functions in this module generally use INTEGER identifier-ranges. (An INTEGER identifier range is a set of identifiers {n,n+1,...,n+k-1}.) The start of the desired range is specified as function parameter. The size of the range is either known at the time of the function-call or it is returned by the function.
	The functions are based on the translations presented in [10].

Overview

AbductiveExplanation (0.00), p.97	Creates an open QBF where models correspond to abductive explanations.
ExistsAbductiveExplanation (0.00), p.98	Creates a closed QBF which is valid iff there is an abductive explanation.
NoSubIsAbductiveExplanation (0.00), p.99	Creates an open QBF where models correspond to selections of hypotheses such that no proper sub-selection is an abductive explanation.
NecessaryHypothesis (0.00), p.100	Creates a closed QBF which is valid iff the specified hypothesis is necessary for the abductive explanations.
RelevantHypothesis (0.00), p.101	Creates a closed QBF which is valid iff the specified hypothesis is relevant for the abductive explanations.

NecessaryHypothesis.Min   Creates a closed QBF which is valid iff the specified hypothesis is
   (0.00), p.102   necessary for the minimal abductive explanations.
RelevantHypothesis.Min   Creates a closed QBF which is valid iff the specified hypothesis is
   (0.00), p.103   relevant for the minimal abductive explanations.

AbductiveExplanation (0.00)

Synopsis

(R00 = CARGOTREEMEM	ctmem	=**Ab.** (R00 = CARGOTREEMEM	ctmem
R01 = CARGOTREE	fla	R01 = CARGOTREE	fla
R02 = ARRAY	hypotheses	R02 = ARRAY	hypotheses
R03 = CARGOTREE	flacons	R03 = CARGOTREE	flacons
R04 = INTEGER	varstrtfree	R04 = INTEGER	varstrtfree
R05 = INTEGER	varstrtbound	R05 = INTEGER	varstrtbound);
R06 = CARGOTREE	qbf)		

Description

Creates an open QBF where models correspond to abductive explanations.
The abductive explanations in question are those for *flacons* from *fla* and *hypotheses*.
The number of free variables in the resulting QBF equals the array-size of
hypotheses. An interpretation corresponds to a hypotheses-subarray by selecting
those hypotheses for which the interpretation of the corresponding variable is TRUE.
The first free variable in the specified range corresponds to the first hypothesis, the
second free variable to the second hypothesis and so forth.

Parameters

ctmem	Memory used to create the resulting QBF within.
fla	Formula in QBF-Scheme. Is NOT utilised.
hypotheses	Array of formulas, each in QBF-Scheme. Formulas are NOT utilised.
flacons	Formula in QBF-Scheme. Is NOT utilised.
varstrtfree	First element of the free-variables identifier range. Range-size is given by the array-size of *hypotheses*.
varstrtbound	First element of the bound-variables range. Range-size via updated return-value.

Return Values

ctmem	Passed through.
fla	Passed through.
hypotheses	Passed through.
flacons	Passed through.
varstrtfree	Passed through.
varstrtbound	Updated.
qbf	Resulting QBF.

ExistsAbductiveExplanation (0.00)

Synopsis

(R00 = CARGOTREEMEM	*ctmem*	=**Ex.** (R00 = CARGOTREEMEM	*ctmem*	
R01 = CARGOTREE	*qbf*	R01 = CARGOTREE	*fla*	
R02 = INTEGER	*varstrt*)	R02 = ARRAY	*hypotheses*	
		R03 = CARGOTREE	*flacons*	
		R04 = INTEGER	*varstrt*	);

Description

Creates a closed QBF which is valid iff there is an abductive explanation.

The abductive explanations in question are those for *flacons* from *fla* and *hypotheses*.

Parameters

ctmem	Memory used to create the resulting QBF within.
fla	Formula in QBF-Scheme. Is NOT utilised.
hypotheses	Array of formulas, each in QBF-Scheme. Formulas are NOT utilised.
flacons	Formula in QBF-Scheme. Is NOT utilised.
varstrt	First element of the (bound-)variables range. Range-size via updated return-value.

Return Values

ctmem	Passed through.
qbf	Resulting QBF.
varstrt	Updated.

NoSubIsAbductiveExplanation (0.00)

Synopsis

(R00 = CARGOTREEMEM	*ctmem*	=**No**. (R00 = CARGOTREEMEM	*ctmem*	
R01 = CARGOTREE	*fla*	R01 = CARGOTREE	*fla*	
R02 = ARRAY	*hypotheses*	R02 = ARRAY	*hypotheses*	
R03 = CARGOTREE	*flacons*	R03 = CARGOTREE	*flacons*	
R04 = INTEGER	*varstrtfree*	R04 = INTEGER	*varstrtfree*	
R05 = INTEGER	*varstrtbound*	R05 = INTEGER	*varstrtbound*);	
R06 = CARGOTREE	*qbfr*	)		

Description

Creates an open QBF where models correspond to selections of hypotheses such that no proper sub-selection is an abductive explanation.

In other words: An interpretation of the QBF's free variables is a model iff no subarray (no interpretation evaluating a subarray to TRUE) corresponds to an abductive explanation (by selecting those hypotheses for which the corresponding variable is evaluated to TRUE).

The abductive explanations in question are those for *flacons* from *fla* and *hypotheses*.

Parameters

ctmem	Memory used to create the resulting QBF within.
fla	Formula in QBF-Scheme. Is NOT utilised.
hypotheses	Array of formulas, each in QBF-Scheme. Formulas are NOT utilised. The array-size must be greater or equal to 1.
flacons	Formula in QBF-Scheme. Is NOT utilised.
varstrtfree	First element of the free-variables identifier range. Range-size is given by the array-size of *hypotheses*.
varstrtbound	First element of the bound-variables range. Range-size via updated return-value.

Return Values

ctmem	Passed through.
fla	Passed through.
hypotheses	Passed through.
flacons	Passed through.
varstrtfree	Passed through.
varstrtbound	Updated.
qbfr	Resulting QBF.

NecessaryHypothesis (0.00)

Synopsis

(R00 = CARGOTREEMEM *ctmem*   =**Ne**. (R00 = CARGOTREEMEM *ctmem*
  R01 = CARGOTREE   *qbf*   R01 = CARGOTREE   *fla*
  R02 = INTEGER   *varstrt*)   R02 = ARRAY   *hypotheses*
                                R03 = CARGOTREE   *flacons*
                                R04 = INTEGER   *varstrt*
                                R05 = INTEGER   *idxhyp*   );

Description

Creates a closed QBF which is valid iff the specified hypothesis is necessary for the abductive explanations.

The abductive explanations in question are those for *flacons* from *fla* and *hypotheses*.

Parameters

ctmem	Memory used to create the resulting QBF within.
fla	Formula in QBF-Scheme. Is NOT utilised.
hypotheses	Array of formulas, each in QBF-Scheme. Formulas are NOT utilised.
flacons	Formula in QBF-Scheme. Is NOT utilised.
varstrt	First element of the (bound-)variables range. Range-size via updated return-value.
idxhyp	Index of the hypothesis to check necessity for. Valid indices are 0,...,arraysize(*hypotheses*)-1.

Return Values

ctmem	Passed through.
qbf	Resulting QBF.
varstrt	Updated.

RelevantHypothesis (0.00)

Synopsis

(R00 = CARGOTREEMEM	*ctmem*	=**Re.** (R00 = CARGOTREEMEM	*ctmem*		
R01 = CARGOTREE	*qbf*	R01 = CARGOTREE	*fla*		
R02 = INTEGER	*varstrt*)	R02 = ARRAY	*hypotheses*		
		R03 = CARGOTREE	*flacons*		
		R04 = INTEGER	*varstrt*		
		R05 = INTEGER	*idxhyp*	);	

Description

Creates a closed QBF which is valid iff the specified hypothesis is relevant for the abductive explanations.

The abductive explanations in question are those for *flacons* from *fla* and *hypotheses*.

Parameters

ctmem	Memory used to create the resulting QBF within.
fla	Formula in QBF-Scheme. Is NOT utilised.
hypotheses	Array of formulas, each in QBF-Scheme. Formulas are NOT utilised.
flacons	Formula in QBF-Scheme. Is NOT utilised.
varstrt	First element of the (bound-)variables range. Range-size via updated return-value.
idxhyp	Index of the hypothesis to check relevance for. Valid indices are 0,...,arraysize(*hypotheses*)-1.

Return Values

ctmem	Passed through.
qbf	Resulting QBF.
varstrt	Updated.

NecessaryHypothesis_Min (0.00)

(R00 = CARGOTREEMEM	*ctmem*	=**Ne.** (R00 = CARGOTREEMEM	*ctmem*		
R01 = CARGOTREE	*qbf*	R01 = CARGOTREE	*fla*		
R02 = INTEGER	*varstrt*)	R02 = ARRAY	*hypotheses*		
		R03 = CARGOTREE	*flacons*		
		R04 = INTEGER	*varstrt*		
		R05 = INTEGER	*idxhyp*	);	

Description

Creates a closed QBF which is valid iff the specified hypothesis is necessary for the minimal abductive explanations.

The minimal abductive explanations in question are those for *flacons* from *fla* and *hypotheses*.

Parameters

ctmem	Memory used to create the resulting QBF within.
fla	Formula in QBF-Scheme. Is NOT utilised.
hypotheses	Array of formulas, each in QBF-Scheme. Formulas are NOT utilised.
flacons	Formula in QBF-Scheme. Is NOT utilised.
varstrt	First element of the (bound-)variables range. Range-size via updated return-value.
idxhyp	Index of the hypothesis to check necessity for. Valid indices are 0,...,arraysize(*hypotheses*)-1.

Return Values

ctmem	Passed through.
qbf	Resulting QBF.
varstrt	Updated.

RelevantHypothesis_Min (0.00)

Synopsis

(R00 = CARGOTREEMEM *ctmem* =**Re.** (R00 = CARGOTREEMEM *ctmem*

  R01 = CARGOTREE   *qbf*   R01 = CARGOTREE   *fla*

  R02 = INTEGER   *varstrt*)   R02 = ARRAY   *hypotheses*

                                R03 = CARGOTREE   *flacons*

                                  R04 = INTEGER   *varstrt*

                                  R05 = INTEGER   *idxhyp*   );

Description

Creates a closed QBF which is valid iff the specified hypothesis is relevant for the minimal abductive explanations.

The minimal abductive explanations in question are those for *flacons* from *fla* and *hypotheses*.

Parameters

ctmem	Memory used to create the resulting QBF within.
fla	Formula in QBF-Scheme. Is NOT utilised.
hypotheses	Array of formulas, each in QBF-Scheme. Formulas are NOT utilised.
flacons	Formula in QBF-Scheme. Is NOT utilised.
varstrt	First element of the (bound-)variables range. Range-size via updated return-value.
idxhyp	Index of the hypothesis to check relevance for. Valid indices are 0,...,arraysize(*hypotheses*)-1.

Return Values

ctmem	Passed through.
qbf	Resulting QBF.
varstrt	Updated.

Module	equilib
Version	0.00 (02/10/2003)
Author	Norbert Pfaffinger
Description	Translations of reasoning-task instances from equilibrium logic into QBFs.

Any QBF generated by a function from this module is normalised. Normalised means that (a) no variable occurs both free and bound in the QBF and (b) any quantification of a variable occurs at most once as subformula in the QBF and (c) for any subformula which is a quantification, the quantified variable occurs in the quantification-subformula ("no empty quantifications").

The functions in this module generally use INTEGER identifier-ranges. (An INTEGER identifier range is a set of identifiers {n,n+1,...,n+k-1}.) The start of the desired range is specified as function parameter. The size of the range is either known at the time of the function-call or it is returned by the function.

The functions are based on the translations presented in [22].

Overview

HereThere
    (0.00), p.104

Translates a formula to the logic of "Here-and-There".

HereThereB
    (0.00), p.105

Translates a formula to the logic of "Here-and-There". (Different identifier-assignment than **HereThere**).

HTModel
    (0.00), p.106

Creates a propositional formula where the models correspond to the HT-models of the input formula.

EquiModel
    (0.00), p.107

Creates an open QBF where the models correspond to the equilibrium models of the input formula.

HereThere (0.00)

Synopsis

(R00 = CARGOTREEMEM	ctmem	=**He.** (R00 = CARGOTREEMEM	ctmem
R01 = CARGOTREE	flar	R01 = CARGOTREE	fla
R02 = HASHINT	hash	R02 = HASHINT	hash
R03 = INTEGER	numhash	R03 = INTEGER	numhash
R04 = INTEGER	varstrt)	R04 = INTEGER	varstrt);

Description

Translates a formula to the logic of "Here-and-There".

Variables for "Here" are $varstrt, varstrt+2,...$, and variables for "There" are $varstrt+1, varstrt+3,...$ in the resulting formula. As usual the correspondence to the original set of variables from the input formula is given by occurrence (for example, $varstrt$ (here) and $varstrt+1$ (there) correspond to the first variable occurrence in fla, $varstrt+2$ (here) and $varstrt+3$ (there) to the second occurrence and so forth).

There is a one-to-one correspondence between (a) the models of the resulting formula which satisfy $(varstrt > varstrt+1)\&(varstrt+2 > varstrt+3)\&...$ and (b) the HT-models of the input formula.

Parameters

ctmem	Memory used to create the resulting QBF within.
fla	QBF-Scheme. No quantifiers. Is NOT utilised.
hash	Variables with occurrence-index. Gets extended if necessary.
numhash	Number of entries in *hash*.
varstrt	See description.

Return Values

ctmem	Passed through.
flar	Resulting formula. QBF-Scheme. No quantifiers.
hash	Passed through and altered if necessary.
numhash	Passed through or updated if necessary.
varstrt	Passed through.

HereThereB (0.00)

Synopsis

(R00 = CARGOTREEMEM	*ctmem*	=**He**. (R00 = CARGOTREEMEM	*ctmem*
R01 = CARGOTREE	*flar*	R01 = CARGOTREE	*fla*
R02 = HASHINT	*hash*	R02 = HASHINT	*hash*
R03 = INTEGER	*numhash*	R03 = INTEGER	*numhash*
R04 = INTEGER	*varstrta*	R04 = INTEGER	*varstrta*
R05 = INTEGER	*varstrtb*)	R05 = INTEGER	*varstrtb*);

Description

Translates a formula to the logic of "Here-and-There". (Different identifier-assignment than **HereThere**).

Variables for "Here" are *varstrtb*,*varstrtb*+1,..., variables for "There" are *varstrta*,*varstrta*+1,... in the resulting formula.

There is a one-to-one correspondence between (a) the models of the resulting formula which satisfy (*varstrtb*>*varstrta*)&(*varstrtb*+1>*varstrta*+1)&... and (b) the HT-models of the input formula.

Parameters

ctmem	Memory used to create the resulting QBF within.
fla	QBF-Scheme. No quantifiers. Is NOT utilised.
hash	Variables with occurrence-index. Must contain all *fla* variables.
numhash	Number of entries in *hash*.
varstrta	See description.
varstrtb	See description.

Return Values

ctmem	Passed through.
flar	Resulting formula. QBF-Scheme. No quantifiers.
hash	Passed through.
numhash	Passed through.
varstrta	Passed through.
varstrtb	Passed through.

HTModel (0.00)

Synopsis

```
( R00 = CARGOTREEMEM ctmem      =HT.( R00 = CARGOTREEMEM ctmem
  R01 = CARGOTREE      flar          R01 = CARGOTREE      fla
  R02 = HASHINT        hash          R02 = HASHINT        hash
  R03 = INTEGER        numhash       R03 = INTEGER        numhash
  R04 = INTEGER        varstrt )      R04 = INTEGER        varstrt );
```

Description

Creates a propositional formula where the models correspond to the HT-models of
the input formula.

The variables in the resulting formula should be seen grouped to tuples
($varstrt, varstrt+1$), ($varstrt+2, varstrt+3$), ... A model of the resulting formula
corresponds to the following HT-model: The "Here"-interpretation is given by the
assignments to $varstrt, varstrt+2, varstrt+4$,... The "There"-interpretation is given by
the assignments to $varstrt+1, varstrt+3, varstrt+5$,....

Parameters

ctmem	Memory used to create the resulting QBF within.
fla	QBF-Scheme. No quantifiers. Is NOT utilised.
hash	Variables with occurrence-index. Gets extended if necessary.
numhash	Number of entries in hash.
varstrt	See description.

Return Values

ctmem	Passed through.
flar	Resulting formula. QBF-Scheme. No quantifiers.
hash	Passed through and altered if necessary.
numhash	Passed through or updated if necessary.
varstrt	Passed through.

EquiModel (0.00)

Synopsis

(R00 = CARGOTREEMEM	*ctmem*	=**Eq.** (R00 = CARGOTREEMEM	*ctmem*
R01 = CARGOTREE	*qbfr*	R01 = CARGOTREE	*fla*
R02 = HASHINT	*hash*	R02 = HASHINT	*hash*
R03 = INTEGER	*numhash*	R03 = INTEGER	*numhash*
R04 = INTEGER	*varstrt*	R04 = INTEGER	*varstrtfree*
R05 = INTEGER	*varstrtbound*)	R05 = INTEGER	*varstrtbound*);

Description

Creates an open QBF where the models correspond to the equilibrium models of the input formula.

The models are given by interpretations of $varstrtfree, varstrtfree+1, ..., varstrtfree+numhash-1$. The propositional variable identifiers $varstrtbound, varstrtbound+1, ..., varstrtbound+numhash-1$ are used quantified in the resulting QBF.

Parameters

ctmem	Memory used to create the resulting QBF within.
fla	QBF-Scheme. No quantifiers. Is NOT utilised.
hash	Variables with occurrence-index. Must contain exactly the variables of the *fla*-formula (but not a superset).
numhash	Number of entries in *hash*.
varstrtfree	See description.
varstrtbound	See description.

Return Values

ctmem	Passed through.
qbfr	Resulting QBF. QBF-Scheme.
hash	Passed through.
numhash	Passed through.
varstrt	Passed through.
varstrtbound	Passed through.

Module	parasigned
Version	0.00 (09/09/2003)
Author	Norbert Pfaffinger
Description	Translations of reasoning-task instances from paraconsistent reasoning via signed systems into QBFs.

Any QBF generated by a function from this module is normalised. Normalised means that (a) no variable occurs both free and bound in the QBF and (b) any quantification of a variable occurs at most once as subformula in the QBF and (c) for any subformula which is a quantification, the quantified variable occurs in the quantification-subformula ("no empty quantifications").

The functions in this module generally use INTEGER identifier-ranges. (An INTEGER identifier range is a set of identifiers $\{n,n+1,...,n+k-1\}$.) The start of the desired range is specified as function parameter. The size of the range is either known at the time of the function-call or it is returned by the function.

The functions are based on the translations presented in [6].

Overview

FLACollectPolarity (0.00), p.108	Gathers polarity occurrence information of the formulas' propositional variables.
FLACollectPlus (0.00), p.109	Collects variables into a HASHINTCOL with data-entries like in **FLACollectPolarity**, but ignores polarity information.
PolaritySubstCopyA (0.00), p.110	Copies the input formula and at the same time performs polarity related substitutions. Only those variables from the premise formula get polarity-replaced which occur both positive and negative.
PolaritySubstCopyB (0.00), p.111	Copies the input formula and at the same time performs polarity related substitutions. Works exactly like **PolaritySubstCopyA**, except that all variables from the premise input formula get polarity-replaced, even those that occur positive or negative only.
ConsUnsignedCredulous (0.00), p.112	Creates a closed QBF which is valid iff the second input formula is a credulous unsigned consequence of the first input formula.
ConsUnsignedSkeptical (0.00), p.112	Creates a closed QBF which is valid iff the second input formula is a sceptical unsigned consequence of the first input formula.
ConsUnsignedPrudent (0.00), p.113	Creates a closed QBF which is valid iff the second input formula is a prudent unsigned consequence of the first input formula.

FLACollectPolarity (0.00)

Synopsis

```
( R00 = HASHINTCOL hash      =FL. ( R00 = HASHINTCOL hash
  R01 = CARGOTREE   fla            R01 = CARGOTREE   fla
  R02 = INTEGER     numhash        R02 = INTEGER     numhash
  R03 = INTEGER     numposneg )    R03 = INTEGER     numposneg );
```

Description

Gathers polarity occurrence information of the formulas' propositional variables. Collects all occurring variables in a HASHINTCOL, where for each entry there are 2 additional data-fields, namely (a) the occurrence-index in the input formula, and (b) the polarity occurrence information: A value of 1 means the variable occurs positive only, 2 means the variable occurs negative only and 3 means the variable occurs both positive and negative.

Parameters

hash	Usually empty.
fla	QBF-Scheme. No quantifiers.
numhash	Number of entries already in *hash*. Usually 0.
numposneg	Number of pos/neg-occurrences so far. Usually 0.

Return Values

hash	Altered. See description.
fla	Passed through.
numhash	Updated.
numposneg	Updated.

108

FLACollectPlus (0.00)

Synopsis

(R00 = HASHINTCOL *hash*   =**FL.** (R00 = HASHINTCOL *hash*

  R01 = CARGOTREE *fla*   R01 = CARGOTREE *fla*

  R02 = INTEGER   *numhash*)   R02 = INTEGER   *numhash*);

Description

Collects variables into a HASHINTCOL with data-entries like in **FLACollectPolarity**, but ignores polarity information.

New variables (if there are any) have their polarity occurrence data-field set to 0.

Parameters

hash	See description.
fla	QBF-Scheme. No quantifiers.
numhash	Number of entries already in *hash*.

Return Values

hash	Altered. See description.
fla	Passed through.
numhash	Updated.

PolaritySubstCopyA (0.00)

Synopsis

(R00 = CARGOTREEMEM	*ctmem*	**=Po.** (R00 = CARGOTREEMEM	*ctmem*		
R01 = CARGOTREE	*flalr*	R01 = CARGOTREE	*flal*		
R02 = CARGOTREE	*flarr*	R02 = CARGOTREE	*flar*		
R03 = INTEGER	*varstrt*	R03 = INTEGER	*varstrt*);		
R04 = INTEGER	*numvar*				
R05 = INTEGER	*numposneg*)				

Description

Copies the input formula and at the same time performs polarity related substitutions. Only those variables from the premise formula get polarity-replaced which occur both positive and negative.

A re-sorting such that positive/negative occurrences come first, and positive or negative only occurrences come second is performed.

In the resulting formula there are variable triples

($varstrt+k, varstrt+numvar+2k, varstrt+numvar+2k+1$) for k=0,...,$numposneg$-1 (there are no such triples if $numposneg$ is 0). $varstrt+k$ identifies the original variable, occurring both positive and negative in the input formula. As all such occurrences get replaced this identifier does not actually occur in the resulting formula.

$varstrt+numvar+2k$ identifies the replacement for positive occurrences of $varstrt+k$ in the input formula, while $varstrt+numvar+2k+1$ identifies the replacement for negative occurrences of $varstrt+k$ in the input formula.

Parameters

ctmem	Memory used to create the resulting formulas within.
flal	QBF-Scheme. No quantifiers. Is NOT utilised.
flar	QBF-Scheme. No quantifiers. Is NOT utilised.
varstrt	For the variable range to use. See description. The range-size is $numvar+numposneg*2$.

Return Values

ctmem	Passed through.
flalr	Resulting transformation of formula *flal*.
flarr	Resulting transformation of formula *flar*.
varstrt	Passed through.
numvar	Number of variables.
numposneg	Number of pos/neg occurring variables.

PolaritySubstCopyB (0.00)

Synopsis

(R00 = CARGOTREEMEM	*ctmem*	=**Po.** (R00 = CARGOTREEMEM	*ctmem*
R01 = CARGOTREE	*flalr*	R01 = CARGOTREE	*flal*
R02 = CARGOTREE	*flarr*	R02 = CARGOTREE	*flar*
R03 = INTEGER	*varstrt*	R03 = INTEGER	*varstrt*);
R04 = INTEGER	*numvar*		
R05 = INTEGER	*numposneg*)		

Description

Copies the input formula and at the same time performs polarity related substitutions. Works exactly like **PolaritySubstCopyA**, except that all variables from the premise input formula get polarity-replaced, even those that occur positive or negative only. Again, as in **PolaritySubstCopyA**, the variables are reordered such that those occurring both positive and negative come first, those occurring positive or negative only come second.

Parameters

ctmem	Memory used to create the resulting formulas within.
flal	QBF-Scheme. No quantifiers. Is NOT utilised.
flar	QBF-Scheme. No quantifiers. Is NOT utilised.
varstrt	For the variable range to use. The range-size is *numvar+numvar*2 (i.e., *numvar*3).

Return Values

ctmem	Passed through.
flalr	Resulting transformation of formula *flal*.
flarr	Resulting transformation of formula *flar*.
varstrt	Passed through.
numvar	Number of variables.
numposneg	Number of pos/neg occurring variables.

ConsUnsignedCredulous (0.00)

Synopsis

(R00 = CARGOTREEMEM	*ctmem*	=**Co.** (R00 = CARGOTREEMEM	*ctmem*
R01 = CARGOTREE	*qbfr*	R01 = CARGOTREE	*flal*
R02 = INTEGER	*varstrtnew*)	R02 = CARGOTREE	*flar*
		R03 = INTEGER	*varstrt*);

Description

Creates a closed QBF which is valid iff the second input formula is a credulous unsigned consequence of the first input formula.

In other words: *flal* is the premise formula, and *flar* the formula tested for being a consequence.

The consequence relation considered here is based on non-indexed polarity substitutions (W+-) and on the defaults " : (p+ <-> p-) / (p <-> p+) & (p <-> p-)".

Parameters

ctmem	Memory used to create the resulting QBF within.
flal	QBF-Scheme. No quantifiers. Is NOT utilised.
flar	QBF-Scheme. No quantifiers. Is NOT utilised.
varstrt	For the variable range of the resulting QBF.

Return Values

ctmem	Passed through.
qbfr	Resulting QBF. QBF-Scheme.
varstrtnew	Updated *varstrt*.

ConsUnsignedSkeptical (0.00)

Synopsis

(R00 = CARGOTREEMEM	*ctmem*	=**Co.** (R00 = CARGOTREEMEM	*ctmem*
R01 = CARGOTREE	*qbfr*	R01 = CARGOTREE	*flal*
R02 = INTEGER	*varstrtnew*)	R02 = CARGOTREE	*flar*
		R03 = INTEGER	*varstrt*);

Description

Creates a closed QBF which is valid iff the second input formula is a sceptical unsigned consequence of the first input formula.

In other words: *flal* is the premise formula, and *flar* the formula tested for being a consequence.

The consequence relation considered here is based on non-indexed polarity substitutions (W+-) and on the defaults " : (p+ <-> p-) / (p <-> p+) & (p <-> p-)".

Parameters

ctmem	Memory used to create the resulting QBF within.
flal	QBF-Scheme. No quantifiers. Is NOT utilised.
flar	QBF-Scheme. No quantifiers. Is NOT utilised.
varstrt	For the variable range of the resulting QBF.

Return Values

ctmem	Passed through.
qbfr	Resulting QBF. QBF-Scheme.
varstrtnew	Updated *varstrt*.

ConsUnsignedPrudent (0.00)

Synopsis

(R00 = CARGOTREEMEM	*ctmem*	=**Co.** (R00 = CARGOTREEMEM	*ctmem*
R01 = CARGOTREE	*qbfr*	R01 = CARGOTREE	*flal*
R02 = INTEGER	*varstrtnew*)	R02 = CARGOTREE	*flar*
		R03 = INTEGER	*varstrt*);

Description

Creates a closed QBF which is valid iff the second input formula is a prudent unsigned consequence of the first input formula.

In other words: *flal* is the premise formula, and *flar* the formula tested for being a consequence.

The consequence relation considered here is based on non-indexed polarity substitutions (W+-) and on the defaults " : (p+ <-> p-) / (p <-> p+) & (p <-> p-)".

Parameters

ctmem	Memory used to create the resulting QBF within.
flal	QBF-Scheme. No quantifiers. Is NOT utilised.
flar	QBF-Scheme. No quantifiers. Is NOT utilised.
varstrt	For the variable range of the resulting QBF.

Return Values

ctmem	Passed through.
qbfr	Resulting QBF. QBF-Scheme.
varstrtnew	Updated *varstrt*.

Module	para3val
Version	0.00 (29/09/2003)
Author	Norbert Pfaffinger
Description	Translations of reasoning-task instances from paraconsistent reasoning via three-valued logic into QBFs.

Any QBF generated by a function from this module is normalised. Normalised means that (a) no variable occurs both free and bound in the QBF and (b) any quantification of a variable occurs at most once as subformula in the QBF and (c) for any subformula which is a quantification, the quantified variable occurs in the quantification-subformula ("no empty quantifications").

The functions in this module generally use INTEGER identifier-ranges. (An INTEGER identifier range is a set of identifiers {n,n+1,...,n+k-1}.) The start of the desired range is specified as function parameter. The size of the range is either known at the time of the function-call or it is returned by the function.

The functions are based on the translations presented in [7].

113

Overview

ThreeValT
(0.00), p.114

Creates a formula with a correspondence between its models and those three-valued interpretations which evaluate the input formula to 'T' ('true').

ThreeValF
(0.00), p.115

Creates a formula with a correspondence between its models and those three-valued interpretations which evaluate the input formula to 'F' ('false').

ThreeValO
(0.00), p.116

Creates a formula with a correspondence between its models and those three-valued interpretations which evaluate the input formula to 'O'.

Model3
(0.00), p.117

Creates a formula with a correspondence between its models and the three-valued models of the input formula.

ConsLP
(0.00), p.118

Creates a closed QBF which is valid iff the second input formula is a consequence of the first one under the inference relation in the logic "LP".

ConsLPm
(0.00), p.118

Creates a closed QBF which is valid iff the second input formula is a consequence of the first one under the inference relation in the logic "LP_m".

ThreeValT (0.00)

Synopsis

(R00 = CARGOTREEMEM	*ctmem*	=**Th.** (R00 = CARGOTREEMEM	*ctmem*
R01 = CARGOTREE	*flar*	R01 = CARGOTREE	*fla*
R02 = HASHINT	*hash*	R02 = HASHINT	*hash*
R03 = INTEGER	*numhashr*	R03 = INTEGER	*numhash*
R04 = INTEGER	*varstrt*)	R04 = INTEGER	*varstrt*);

Description

Creates a formula with a correspondence between its models and those three-valued interpretations which evaluate the input formula to 'T' ('true').

In the resulting formula *varstrt*, *varstrt*+2, *varstrt*+4, ... correspond to the original formula's variables (correspondence by occurrence), while *varstrt*+1, *varstrt*+3, ... correspond to the "associated" ones.

An interpretation of the resulting formula's variables corresponds to a three-valued interpretation evaluating the input-formula to 'T' iff (a) it is a model of the resulting formula and (b) there is no tuple (*varstrt*+2k, *varstrt*+2k+1) interpreted to (true,false). The associated three-valued interpretation to any such interpretation is given by tuples (*varstrt*+2k, *varstrt*+2k+1): (true,true) corresponds to 'T', (false,false) corresponds to 'F', and (false,true) corresponds to 'O'.

Parameters

ctmem	Memory used to create the resulting formula within.
fla	QBF-Scheme. No quantifiers. Is NOT utilised.
hash	Hash with occurrence-indices. May be empty.
numhash	Number of entries in the occurrence-index hash.
varstrt	See description. The range-size is *numhashr**2.

Return Values

ctmem	Passed through.
flar	Resulting formula. QBF-Scheme.
hash	Passed through and altered.
numhashr	Updated.
varstrt	Passed through.

ThreeValF (0.00)

Synopsis

(R00 = CARGOTREEMEM	*ctmem*	**=Th.** (R00 = CARGOTREEMEM	*ctmem*
R01 = CARGOTREE	*flar*	R01 = CARGOTREE	*fla*
R02 = HASHINT	*hash*	R02 = HASHINT	*hash*
R03 = INTEGER	*numhashr*	R03 = INTEGER	*numhash*
R04 = INTEGER	*varstrt*)	R04 = INTEGER	*varstrt*);

Description

Creates a formula with a correspondence between its models and those three-valued interpretations which evaluate the input formula to 'F' ('false').

The calling interface of this function is exactly like the one of **ThreeValT**.

In the resulting formula *varstrt*, *varstrt*+2, *varstrt*+4, ... correspond to the original formula's variables (correspondence by occurrence), while *varstrt*+1, *varstrt*+3, ... correspond to the "associated" ones.

An interpretation of the resulting formula's variables corresponds to a three-valued interpretation evaluating the input-formula to 'F' iff (a) it is a model of the resulting formula and (b) there is no tuple (*varstrt*+2k,*varstrt*+2k+1) interpreted to (true,false). The associated three-valued interpretation to any such interpretation is given by tuples (*varstrt*+2k,*varstrt*+2k+1): (true,true) corresponds to 'T', (false,false) corresponds to 'F', and (false,true) corresponds to 'O'.

Parameters

ctmem	Memory used to create the resulting formula within.
fla	QBF-Scheme. No quantifiers. Is NOT utilised.
hash	Hash with occurrence-indices. May be empty.
numhash	Number of entries in the occurrence-index hash.
varstrt	See description. The range-size is *numhashr**2.

Return Values

ctmem	Passed through.
flar	Resulting formula. QBF-Scheme.
hash	Passed through and altered.
numhashr	Updated.
varstrt	Passed through.

ThreeValO (0.00)

Synopsis

(R00 = CARGOTREEMEM	*ctmem*	=**Th**. (R00 = CARGOTREEMEM	*ctmem*
R01 = CARGOTREE	*flar*	R01 = CARGOTREE	*fla*
R02 = HASHINT	*hash*	R02 = HASHINT	*hash*
R03 = INTEGER	*numhashr*	R03 = INTEGER	*numhash*
R04 = INTEGER	*varstrt*)	R04 = INTEGER	*varstrt*);

Description

Creates a formula with a correspondence between its models and those three-valued interpretations which evaluate the input formula to 'O'.

The calling interface of this function is exactly like the one of **ThreeValT**.

In the resulting formula *varstrt*, *varstrt*+2, *varstrt*+4, ... correspond to the original formula's variables (correspondence by occurrence), while *varstrt*+1, *varstrt*+3, ... correspond to the "associated" ones.

An interpretation of the resulting formula's variables corresponds to a three-valued interpretation evaluating the input-formula to 'O' iff (a) it is a model of the resulting formula and (b) there is no tuple (*varstrt*+2k,*varstrt*+2k+1) interpreted to (true,false). The associated three-valued interpretation to any such interpretation is given by tuples (*varstrt*+2k,*varstrt*+2k+1): (true,true) corresponds to 'T', (false,false) corresponds to 'F', and (false,true) corresponds to 'O'.

Parameters

ctmem	Memory used to create the resulting formula within.
fla	QBF-Scheme. No quantifiers. Is NOT utilised.
hash	Hash with occurrence-indices. May be empty.
numhash	Number of entries in the occurrence-index hash.
varstrt	See description. The range-size is *numhashr**2.

Return Values

ctmem	Passed through.
flar	Resulting formula. QBF-Scheme.
hash	Passed through and altered.
numhashr	Updated.
varstrt	Passed through.

Model3 (0.00)

Synopsis

(R00 = CARGOTREEMEM	*ctmem*	=**Mo.** (	R00 = CARGOTREEMEM	*ctmem*	
R01 = CARGOTREE	*flar*		R01 = CARGOTREE	*fla*	
R02 = HASHINT	*hash*		R02 = HASHINT	*hash*	
R03 = INTEGER	*numhashr*		R03 = INTEGER	*numhash*	
R04 = INTEGER	*varstrt*	)	R04 = INTEGER	*varstrt*	);

Description

Creates a formula with a correspondence between its models and the three-valued models of the input formula.

In the resulting formula *varstrt*, *varstrt*+2, *varstrt*+4, ... correspond to the original formula's variables (correspondence by occurrence), while *varstrt*+1, *varstrt*+3, ... correspond to the "associated" ones.

An interpretation of the resulting formula's variables corresponds to a three-valued model of the input-formula iff (a) it is a model of the resulting formula and (b) there is no tuple (*varstrt*+2k,*varstrt*+2k+1) interpreted to (true,false).

The associated three-valued model to any such interpretation is given by tuples (*varstrt*+2k,*varstrt*+2k+1): (true,true) corresponds to 'T', (false,false) corresponds to 'F', and (false,true) corresponds to 'O'.

Parameters

ctmem	Memory used to create the resulting formula within.
fla	QBF-Scheme. No quantifiers. Is NOT utilised.
hash	Hash with occurrence-indices. May be empty.
numhash	Number of entries in the occurrence-index hash.
varstrt	See description. The range-size is *numhashr**2.

Return Values

ctmem	Passed through.
flar	Resulting formula, QBF-Scheme.
hash	Passed through and altered.
numhashr	Updated.
varstrt	Passed through.

117

ConsLP (0.00)

Synopsis

(R00 = CARGOTREEMEM	*ctmem*	=**Co.** (R00 = CARGOTREEMEM	*ctmem*
R01 = CARGOTREE	*qbfres*	R01 = CARGOTREE	*flal*
R02 = INTEGER	*varstrtnew*)	R02 = CARGOTREE	*flar*
		R03 = INTEGER	*varstrt*);

Description

Creates a closed QBF which is valid iff the second input formula is a consequence of the first one under the inference relation in the logic "LP".

flal is the premise formula, *flar* the formula tested for being a consequence. In other words: The QBF is valid iff every three-valued model of *flal* is a three-valued model of *flar*.

Parameters

ctmem	Memory used to create the resulting QBF within.
flal	QBF-Scheme. No quantifiers. Is NOT utilised.
flar	QBF-Scheme. No quantifiers. Is NOT utilised.
varstrt	For the variable-range to use.

Return Values

ctmem	Passed through.
qbfres	Resulting QBF.
varstrtnew	Updated *varstrt*.

ConsLPm (0.00)

Synopsis

(R00 = CARGOTREEMEM	*ctmem*	=**Co.** (R00 = CARGOTREEMEM	*ctmem*
R01 = CARGOTREE	*qbfres*	R01 = CARGOTREE	*flal*
R02 = INTEGER	*varstrtnew*)	R02 = CARGOTREE	*flar*
		R03 = INTEGER	*varstrt*);

Description

Creates a closed QBF which is valid iff the second input formula is a consequence of the first one under the inference relation in the logic "LP_m".

flal is the premise formula, *flar* the formula tested for being a consequence.

Parameters

ctmem	Memory used to create the resulting QBF within.
flal	QBF-Scheme. No quantifiers. Is NOT utilised.
flar	QBF-Scheme. No quantifiers. Is NOT utilised.
varstrt	For the variable-range to use.

Return Values

ctmem	Passed through.
qbfres	Resulting QBF.
varstrtnew	Updated *varstrt*.

Module	cabductionlaunch
Version	0.00 (06/10/2003)
Author	Norbert Pfaffinger
Description	Wrapper Functions for calling translations related to classical abduction of Smute Module "cabduction" from within a Smute Launch File. Detailed descriptions of what is encoded with the resulting QBFs can be found in the documentation to Smute Module "cabduction".

All the routines in this Smute Module take a parameter *storenum*. The resulting QBFs are saved to files "qbf*storenum*.txt" and "qbf*storenum*.gdl". The first is a representation of the QBF according to the syntax of QBF-solver "boole", the second is a description of the QBF in the so-called "graph description language" (gdl). The gdl-file can be loaded with "aiSee" ((c) 2000-2004 AbsInt Angewandte Informatik GmbH, see http://www.aisee.com) in order to view/print a tree-representation of the resulting QBF.

The parameters must be specified in Smute Launch Files according to the grammar of Smute Interpreter Logic Edition. The grammar's elements are only referenced throughout this Smute Module documentation, for a description see Smute Interpreter Logic Edition.

Overview

AbductiveExplanation
    (0.00), p.120
        Wrapper Function for cabduction:**AbductiveExplanation**.

ExistsAbductiveExplanation
    (0.00), p.120
        Wrapper Function for cabduction:**ExistsAbductiveExplanation**.

NecessaryHypothesis
    (0.00), p.121
        Wrapper Function for cabduction:**NecessaryHypothesis**.

RelevantHypothesis
    (0.00), p.121
        Wrapper Function for cabduction:**RelevantHypothesis**.

NecessaryHypothesis_Min
    (0.00), p.122
        Wrapper Function for cabduction:**NecessaryHypothesis_Min**.

RelevantHypothesis_Min
    (0.00), p.122
        Wrapper Function for cabduction:**RelevantHypothesis_Min**.

AbductiveExplanation (0.00)

Synopsis

Ab. (R00 = CARGOTREE *flaleft*

R01 = CARGOTREE *hypotheses*

R02 = CARGOTREE *flaright*

R03 = INTEGER *storenum*);

Description

Wrapper Function for cabduction:**AbductiveExplanation**.

The abductive explanations in question are those for *flaright* from *flaleft* and *hypotheses*.

Parameters

flaleft	Propositional formula. Must be specified according to the Logic Edition Launch File "formula" syntax.
hypotheses	Variable array. Must be specified according to the Logic Edition Launch File "idarraydef" syntax.
flaright	Propositional formula. Must be specified according to the Logic Edition Launch File "formula" syntax.
storenum	See module description.

ExistsAbductiveExplanation (0.00)

Synopsis

Ex. (R00 = CARGOTREE *flaleft*

R01 = CARGOTREE *hypotheses*

R02 = CARGOTREE *flaright*

R03 = INTEGER *storenum*);

Description

Wrapper Function for cabduction:**ExistsAbductiveExplanation**.

The abductive explanations in question are those for *flaright* from *flaleft* and *hypotheses*.

Parameters

flaleft	Propositional formula. Must be specified according to the Logic Edition Launch File "formula" syntax.
hypotheses	Variable array. Must be specified according to the Logic Edition Launch File "idarraydef" syntax.
flaright	Propositional formula. Must be specified according to the Logic Edition Launch File "formula" syntax.
storenum	See module description.

NecessaryHypothesis (0.00)
Synopsis

Ne. (R00 = CARGOTREE *flaleft*

    R01 = CARGOTREE *hypotheses*

    R02 = INTEGER   *idxhyp*

    R03 = CARGOTREE *flaright*

    R04 = INTEGER   *storenum*);

Description

Wrapper Function for cabduction:**NecessaryHypothesis**.

The abductive explanations in question are those for *flaright* from *flaleft* and *hypotheses*.

Parameters

flaleft	Propositional formula. Must be specified according to the Logic Edition Launch File "formula" syntax.
hypotheses	Variable array. Must be specified according to the Logic Edition Launch File "idarraydef" syntax.
idxhyp	Index of the hypothesis to check necessity for. Must be in the range 0,...,numberofhypotheses-1.
flaright	Propositional formula. Must be specified according to the Logic Edition Launch File "formula" syntax.
storenum	See module description.

RelevantHypothesis (0.00)
Synopsis

Re. (R00 = CARGOTREE *flaleft*

    R01 = CARGOTREE *hypotheses*

    R02 = INTEGER   *idxhyp*

    R03 = CARGOTREE *flaright*

    R04 = INTEGER   *storenum*);

Description

Wrapper Function for cabduction:**RelevantHypothesis**.

The abductive explanations in question are those for *flaright* from *flaleft* and *hypotheses*.

Parameters

flaleft	Propositional formula. Must be specified according to the Logic Edition Launch File "formula" syntax.
hypotheses	Variable array. Must be specified according to the Logic Edition Launch File "idarraydef" syntax.
idxhyp	Index of the hypothesis to check relevance for. Must be in the range 0,...,numberofhypotheses-1.
flaright	Propositional formula. Must be specified according to the Logic Edition Launch File "formula" syntax.
storenum	See module description.

NecessaryHypothesis_Min (0.00)
Synopsis

Ne. (R00 = CARGOTREE *flaleft*

    R01 = CARGOTREE *hypotheses*

    R02 = INTEGER   *idxhyp*

    R03 = CARGOTREE *flaright*

    R04 = INTEGER   *storenum*   );

Description

Wrapper Function for cabduction:**NecessaryHypothesis_Min**.

The minimal abductive explanations in question are those for *flaright* from *flaleft* and *hypotheses*.

Parameters

flaleft	Propositional formula. Must be specified according to the Logic Edition Launch File "formula" syntax.
hypotheses	Variable array. Must be specified according to the Logic Edition Launch File "idarraydef" syntax.
idxhyp	Index of the hypothesis to check necessity for. Must be in the range 0,...,numberofhypotheses-1.
flaright	Propositional formula. Must be specified according to the Logic Edition Launch File "formula" syntax.
storenum	See module description.

RelevantHypothesis_Min (0.00)
Synopsis

Re. (R00 = CARGOTREE *flaleft*

    R01 = CARGOTREE *hypotheses*

    R02 = INTEGER   *idxhyp*

    R03 = CARGOTREE *flaright*

    R04 = INTEGER   *storenum*   );

Description

Wrapper Function for cabduction:**RelevantHypothesis_Min**.

The minimal abductive explanations in question are those for *flaright* from *flaleft* and *hypotheses*.

Parameters

flaleft	Propositional formula. Must be specified according to the Logic Edition Launch File "formula" syntax.
hypotheses	Variable array. Must be specified according to the Logic Edition Launch File "idarraydef" syntax.
idxhyp	Index of the hypothesis to check relevance for. Must be in the range 0,...,numberofhypotheses-1.
flaright	Propositional formula. Must be specified according to the Logic Edition Launch File "formula" syntax.
storenum	See module description.

Module	equiblaunch
Version	0.00 (08/10/2003)
Author	Norbert Pfaffinger
Description	Wrapper Functions for calling translations related to equilibrium logic of Smute Module "equilib" from within a Smute Launch File.

Detailed descriptions of what is encoded with the resulting QBFs can be found in the documentation to Smute Module "equilib".

All the routines in this Smute Module take a parameter *storenum*. The resulting QBFs are saved to files "qbf*storenum*.txt" and "qbf*storenum*.gdl". The first is a representation of the QBF according to the syntax of QBF-solver "boole", the second is a description of the QBF in the so-called "graph description language" (gdl). The gdl-file can be loaded with "aiSee" ((c) 2000-2004 AbsInt Angewandte Informatik GmbH, see http://www.aisee.com) in order to view/print a tree-representation of the resulting QBF.

The parameters must be specified in Smute Launch Files according to the grammar of Smute Interpreter Logic Edition. The grammar's elements are only referenced throughout this Smute Module documentation, for a description see Smute Interpreter Logic Edition.

Overview

HTModel   Wrapper Function for equlib:**HTModel**.
   (0.00), p.123

EquiModel   Wrapper Function for equlib:**EquiModel**.
   (0.00), p.123

HTModel (0.00)
Synopsis
HT. (R00 = CARGOTREE *fla*
    R01 = INTEGER   *storenum*);
Description
Wrapper Function for equlib:**HTModel**.
Parameters
fla   Propositional formula. Must be specified according to the Logic Edition Launch File "formula" syntax.
storenum   See module description.

EquiModel (0.00)
Synopsis
Eq. (R00 = CARGOTREE *fla*
    R01 = INTEGER   *storenum*);
Description
Wrapper Function for equlib:**EquiModel**.
Parameters
fla   Propositional formula. Must be specified according to the Logic Edition Launch File "formula" syntax.
storenum   See module description.

Module	parasignedlaunch
Version	0.00 (08/10/2003)
Author	Norbert Pfaffinger
Description	Wrapper Functions for calling translations related to paraconsistent reasoning via signed systems of Smute Module "parasigned" from within a Smute Launch File.
	Detailed descriptions of what is encoded with the resulting QBFs can be found in the documentation to Smute Module "parasigned".
	All the routines in this Smute Module take a parameter *storenum*. The resulting QBFs are saved to files "qbf*storenum*.txt" and "qbf*storenum*.gdl". The first is a representation of the QBF according to the syntax of QBF-solver "boole", the second is a description of the QBF in the so-called "graph description language" (gdl). The gdl-file can be loaded with "aiSee" ((c) 2000-2004 AbsInt Angewandte Informatik GmbH, see http://www.aisee.com) in order to view/print a tree-representation of the resulting QBF.
	The parameters must be specified in Smute Launch Files according to the grammar of Smute Interpreter Logic Edition. The grammar's elements are only referenced throughout this Smute Module documentation, for a description see Smute Interpreter Logic Edition.

Overview

ConsUnsignedCredulous   Wrapper Function for parasigned:**ConsUnsignedCredulous**.
(0.00), p.124

ConsUnsignedSkeptical   Wrapper Function for parasigned:**ConsUnsignedSkeptical**.
(0.00), p.125

ConsUnsignedPrudent   Wrapper Function for parasigned:**ConsUnsignedPrudent**.
(0.00), p.125

ConsUnsignedCredulous (0.00)

Synopsis

Co. (R00 = CARGOTREE *flaleft*
    R01 = CARGOTREE *flaright*
    R02 = INTEGER   *storenum*);

Description

Wrapper Function for parasigned:**ConsUnsignedCredulous**.

Parameters

flaleft	Propositional formula representing the premise. Must be specified according to the Logic Edition Launch File "formula" syntax.
flaright	Propositional formula which is tested for being a consequence. Must be specified according to the Logic Edition Launch File "formula" syntax.
storenum	See module description.

ConsUnsignedSkeptical (0.00)

Synopsis

Co.(R00 = CARGOTREE *flaleft*

    R01 = CARGOTREE *flaright*

    R02 = INTEGER   *storenum*);

Description

Wrapper Function for parasigned:**ConsUnsignedSkeptical**.

Parameters

flaleft	Propositional formula representing the premise. Must be specified according to the Logic Edition Launch File "formula" syntax.
flaright	Propositional formula which is tested for being a consequence. Must be specified according to the Logic Edition Launch File "formula" syntax.
storenum	See module description.

ConsUnsignedPrudent (0.00)

Synopsis

Co.(R00 = CARGOTREE *flaleft*

    R01 = CARGOTREE *flaright*

    R02 = INTEGER   *storenum*);

Description

Wrapper Function for parasigned:**ConsUnsignedPrudent**.

Parameters

flaleft	Propositional formula representing the premise. Must be specified according to the Logic Edition Launch File "formula" syntax.
flaright	Propositional formula which is tested for being a consequence. Must be specified according to the Logic Edition Launch File "formula" syntax.
storenum	See module description.

Module	para3vallaunch
Version	0.00 (08/10/2003)
Author	Norbert Pfaffinger
Description	Wrapper Functions for calling translations related to paraconsistent reasoning via three-valued logic of Smute Module "para3val" from within a Smute Launch File.
	Detailed descriptions of what is encoded with the resulting QBFs can be found in the documentation to Smute Module "para3val".
	All the routines in this Smute Module take a parameter *storenum*. The resulting QBFs are saved to files "qbf*storenum*.txt" and "qbf*storenum*.gdl". The first is a representation of the QBF according to the syntax of QBF-solver "boole", the second is a description of the QBF in the so-called "graph description language" (gdl). The gdl-file can be loaded with "aiSee" ((c) 2000-2004 AbsInt Angewandte Informatik GmbH, see http://www.aisee.com) in order to view/print a tree-representation of the resulting QBF.
	The parameters must be specified in Smute Launch Files according to the grammar of Smute Interpreter Logic Edition. The grammar's elements are only referenced throughout this Smute Module documentation, for a description see Smute Interpreter Logic Edition.

Overview

ConsLP   Wrapper Function for para3val:**ConsLP**.
   (0.00), p.126

ConsLPm   Wrapper Function for para3val:**ConsLPm**.
   (0.00), p.126

ConsLP (0.00)

Synopsis

Co. (R00 = CARGOTREE *flaleft*
    R01 = CARGOTREE *flaright*
    R02 = INTEGER   *storenum*);

Description

Wrapper Function for para3val:**ConsLP**.

Parameters

flaleft	Propositional formula representing the premise. Must be specified according to the Logic Edition Launch File "formula" syntax.
flaright	Propositional formula which is tested for being a consequence. Must be specified according to the Logic Edition Launch File "formula" syntax.
storenum	See module description.

ConsLPm (0.00)

Synopsis

Co. (R00 = CARGOTREE *flaleft*
    R01 = CARGOTREE *flaright*
    R02 = INTEGER   *storenum*);

Description

Wrapper Function for para3val:**ConsLPm**.

Parameters

flaleft	Propositional formula representing the premise. Must be specified according to the Logic Edition Launch File "formula" syntax.
flaright	Propositional formula which is tested for being a consequence. Must be specified according to the Logic Edition Launch File "formula" syntax.
storenum	See module description.

Module	qbf
Version	0.00 (03/09/2003)
Author	Norbert Pfaffinger
Description	Utility functions for CARGOTREE-s in QBF-Scheme.

Overview

FLACollectVar   Collects the variables occurring in a propositional formula.
   (0.00), p.128

CollectFreeVar   Collects the variables occurring free in the specified QBF.
   (0.00), p.128

Not   Prefixes the input QBF with "NOT".
   (0.00), p.129

And   Connects the two input QBFs with "AND".
  (0.00), p.129
Or   Connects the two input QBFs with "OR".
  (0.00), p.129
Impl   Connects the two input QBFs with "IMPL".
  (0.00), p.130
EquivVarA   Creates a propositional formula expressing equivalence between
  (0.00), p.130   two variables.
EquivVarB   Creates a propositional formula expressing equivalence between
  (0.00), p.130   two variables.
BigExistsA   Prefixes the input QBF with existential quantifiers for all the propo-
  (0.00), p.131   sitional variables collected in the specified HASHINTCOL.
BigForAllA   Prefixes the input QBF with universal quantifiers for all the proposi-
  (0.00), p.131   tional variables collected in the specified HASHINTCOL.
BigExistsB   Prefixes the input QBF with existential quantifiers for all the propo-
  (0.00), p.132   sitional variables in the specified range.
BigForAllB   Prefixes the input QBF with universal quantifiers for all the proposi-
  (0.00), p.132   tional variables in the specified range.
FLAValid   Creates a closed QBF which is valid iff the propositional input for-
  (0.00), p.133   mula is valid.
FLASat   Creates a closed QBF which is valid iff the propositional input for-
  (0.00), p.133   mula is satisfiable.
FLAUnSat   Creates a closed QBF which is valid iff the propositional input for-
  (0.00), p.133   mula is unsatisfiable.
FLACons   Creates a closed QBF which is valid iff the second of the specified
  (0.00), p.134   input formulas is a consequence of the first one in propositional
                                       logic.
FLANotCons   Creates a closed QBF which is valid iff the second of the specified
  (0.00), p.134   input formulas is a not a consequence of the first one in proposi-
                                       tional logic.
ArrayIdToFLA   From an array of INTEGER identifiers creates an array of QBF-
  (0.00), p.135   Scheme CARGOTREE-s representing those propositional variables.
SubSelectionVarA   Creates a propositional formula which expresses a "subselection"
  (0.00), p.135   condition between two ranges of propositional variables.
SubSelectionVarB   Creates a propositional formula which expresses a "subselection"
  (0.00), p.136   condition between two arrays of propositional variables.
ProperSubSelectionVarA   Creates a propositional formula which expresses a "proper subse-
  (0.00), p.137   lection" condition between two ranges of propositional variables.
SubSelection   Creates a propositional formula which expresses a "subselection"
  (0.00), p.138   condition between two arrays of propositional formulas.
ProperSubSelection   Creates a propositional formula which expresses a "proper subse-
  (0.00), p.139   lection" condition between two arrays of propositional formulas.
Trigger   Creates a propositional formula which is a conjunction of trigger
  (0.00), p.140   variables triggering (i.e., implicating) formulas of an array of formu-
                                       las (correspondence between formula selection and trigger variable
                                       models).
TriggerOmit   Identical to **Trigger**, except that one formula of the passed array is
  (0.00), p.141   omitted.
ConsistentSelections   Creates an open QBF where the models correspond to selections
  (0.00), p.142   of formulas that are consistent with the specified 'theory' formula.

MaxConsistentSelections	Creates an open QBF where the models correspond to selections
(0.00), p.143	of formulas that are consistent with the input formula and that are
	maximal with this property, i.e., for each such selection no proper
	super-selection is consistent with the input formula.
ModellingSelections	Creates an open QBF where the models correspond to selections
(0.00), p.144	of propositional formulas which together with the first input formula
	model the second input formula (in propositional logic).

FLACollectVar (0.00)

Synopsis

```
(R00 = INTEGER    numdata  =FL.(R00 = INTEGER    numdata
 R01 = CARGOTREE   qbf          R01 = CARGOTREE   qbf
 R02 = HASHINTCOL hash    )      R02 = HASHINTCOL hash    );
```

Description

Collects the variables occurring in a propositional formula.

Note that instead of **FLACollectVar** the Smute Language instruction 'CollectIntVal' can be used.

Parameters

numdata	Number of data-fields in each HASHINTCOLENTRY.
qbf	QBF-Scheme. No quantifiers.
hash	Used to collect variables. Does not need to be empty.

Return Values

numdata	Passed through.
qbf	Passed through.
hash	Passed through and possibly altered.

CollectFreeVar (0.00)

Synopsis

```
(R00 = INTEGER    numdata  =Co.(R00 = INTEGER    numdata
 R01 = CARGOTREE   qbf          R01 = CARGOTREE   qbf
 R02 = HASHINTCOL hash    )      R02 = HASHINTCOL hash    );
```

Description

Collects the variables occurring free in the specified QBF.

Parameters

numdata	Number of data-fields in each HASHINTCOLENTRY.
qbf	QBF-Scheme.
hash	Used to collect variables. Does not need to be empty.

Return Values

numdata	Passed through.
qbf	Passed through.
hash	Passed through and possibly altered.

Not (0.00)

Synopsis

(R00 = CARGOTREEMEM *ctmem* =**No**. (R00 = CARGOTREEMEM *ctmem*
  R01 = CARGOTREE   *qbf*   )   R01 = CARGOTREE   *qbf*   );

Description

Prefixes the input QBF with "NOT".

This is a low-level routine guaranteed not to modify registers R03++

Parameters

ctmem   Memory used to create the resulting QBF within.
qbf   QBF-Scheme. Gets utilised as "not" child.

Return Values

ctmem   Passed through.
qbf   Resulting QBF.

And (0.00)

Synopsis

(R00 = CARGOTREEMEM *ctmem* =**An**. (R00 = CARGOTREEMEM *ctmem*
  R01 = CARGOTREE   *qbf*   )   R01 = CARGOTREE   *qbfl*
                             R02 = CARGOTREE   *qbfr*   );

Description

Connects the two input QBFs with "AND".

This is a low-level routine guaranteed not to modify registers R04++

Parameters

ctmem   Memory used to create the resulting QBF within.
qbfl   QBF-Scheme. Gets utilised as left child in "and".
qbfr   QBF-Scheme. Gets utilised as right child in "and".

Return Values

ctmem   Passed through.
qbf   Resulting QBF.

Or (0.00)

Synopsis

(R00 = CARGOTREEMEM *ctmem* =**Or**(R00 = CARGOTREEMEM *ctmem*
  R01 = CARGOTREE   *qbf*   )   R01 = CARGOTREE   *qbfl*
                             R02 = CARGOTREE   *qbfr*   );

Description

Connects the two input QBFs with "OR".

This is a low-level routine guaranteed not to modify registers R04++

Parameters

ctmem   Memory used to create the resulting QBF within.
qbfl   QBF-Scheme. Gets utilised as left child in "or".
qbfr   QBF-Scheme. Gets utilised as right child in "or".

Return Values

ctmem   Passed through.
qbf   Resulting QBF.

Impl (0.00)

Synopsis

(R00 = CARGOTREEMEM *ctmem* =**Im**. (R00 = CARGOTREEMEM *ctmem*
  R01 = CARGOTREE   *qbf*)   R01 = CARGOTREE   *qbfl*
                                     R02 = CARGOTREE   *qbfr*);

Description

Connects the two input QBFs with "IMPL".
This is a low-level routine guaranteed not to modify registers R04++

Parameters

ctmem	Memory used to create the resulting QBF within.
qbfl	QBF-Scheme. Gets utilised as left child in "impl".
qbfr	QBF-Scheme. Gets utilised as right child in "impl".

Return Values

ctmem	Passed through.
qbf	Resulting QBF.

EquivVarA (0.00)

Synopsis

(R00 = CARGOTREEMEM *ctmem* =**Eq**. (R00 = CARGOTREEMEM *ctmem*
  R01 = CARGOTREE   *qbf*)   R01 = INTEGER   *var0*
                                     R02 = INTEGER   *var1*);

Description

Creates a propositional formula expressing equivalence between two variables.
The resulting formula is $(\sim var0 | var1) \& (var0 | \sim var1)$.
This is a low-level routine guaranteed not to modify registers R08++.

Parameters

ctmem	Memory used to create the resulting QBF within.
var0	Variable identifier.
var1	Variable identifier.

Return Values

ctmem	Passed through.
qbf	Resulting QBF.

EquivVarB (0.00)

Synopsis

(R00 = CARGOTREEMEM *ctmem* =**Eq**. (R00 = CARGOTREEMEM *ctmem*
  R01 = CARGOTREE   *qbf*)   R01 = INTEGER   *var0*
                                     R02 = INTEGER   *var1*);

Description

Creates a propositional formula expressing equivalence between two variables.
The resulting formula is $(var0 > var1) \& (var1 > var0)$.
This is a low-level routine guaranteed not to modify registers R08++.

Parameters

ctmem	Memory used to create the resulting QBF within.
var0	Variable identifier.
var1	Variable identifier.

Return Values

ctmem	Passed through.
qbf	Resulting QBF.

BigExistsA (0.00)
Synopsis

```
( R00 = CARGOTREEMEM ctmem  = Bi. ( R00 = CARGOTREEMEM ctmem
  R01 = CARGOTREE      qbfout       R01 = CARGOTREE      qbf
  R02 = HASHINTCOL     hash )       R02 = HASHINTCOL     hash );
```

Description

Prefixes the input QBF with existential quantifiers for all the propositional variables collected in the specified HASHINTCOL.

Parameters

ctmem	Memory used to create the resulting QBF within.
qbf	QBF-Scheme. Gets utilised.
hash	For each of the INTEGERs collected in *hash* an existential quantification is created.

Return Values

ctmem	Passed through.
qbfout	Resulting existential-quantified QBF. QBF-Scheme.
hash	Passed through.

BigForAllA (0.00)
Synopsis

```
( R00 = CARGOTREEMEM ctmem  = Bi. ( R00 = CARGOTREEMEM ctmem
  R01 = CARGOTREE      qbfout       R01 = CARGOTREE      qbf
  R02 = HASHINTCOL     hash )       R02 = HASHINTCOL     hash );
```

Description

Prefixes the input QBF with universal quantifiers for all the propositional variables collected in the specified HASHINTCOL.

Parameters

ctmem	Memory used to create the resulting QBF within.
qbf	QBF-Scheme. Gets utilised.
hash	For each of the INTEGERs collected in *hash* a universal quantification is created.

Return Values

ctmem	Passed through.
qbfout	Resulting universal-quantified QBF. QBF-Scheme.
hash	Passed through.

BigExistsB (0.00)

Synopsis

(R00 = CARGOTREEMEM *ctmem* =**Bi.** (R00 = CARGOTREEMEM *ctmem*

R01 = CARGOTREE	*qbfout*		R01 = CARGOTREE	*qbf*
R02 = INTEGER	*strt*		R02 = INTEGER	*strt*
R03 = INTEGER	*num*)		R03 = INTEGER	*num*);

Description

Prefixes the input QBF with existential quantifiers for all the propositional variables in the specified range.

Parameters

ctmem	Memory used to create the resulting QBF within.
qbf	QBF-Scheme. Gets utilised.
strt	Start of the variable-range.
num	Number of variables, i.e., size of the variable-range.

Return Values

ctmem	Passed through.
qbfout	Resulting existential-quantified qbf. QBF-Scheme.
strt	Passed through.
num	Passed through.

BigForAllB (0.00)

Synopsis

(R00 = CARGOTREEMEM *ctmem* =**Bi.** (R00 = CARGOTREEMEM *ctmem*

R01 = CARGOTREE	*qbfout*		R01 = CARGOTREE	*qbf*
R02 = INTEGER	*strt*		R02 = INTEGER	*strt*
R03 = INTEGER	*num*)		R03 = INTEGER	*num*);

Description

Prefixes the input QBF with universal quantifiers for all the propositional variables in the specified range.

Parameters

ctmem	Memory used to create the resulting QBF within.
qbf	QBF-Scheme. Gets utilised.
strt	Start of the variable-range.
num	Number of variables, i.e., size of the variable-range.

Return Values

ctmem	Passed through.
qbfout	Resulting universal-quantified qbf. QBF-Scheme.
strt	Passed through.
num	Passed through.

FLAValid (0.00)
Synopsis
(R00 = CARGOTREEMEM *ctmem* =**FL**. (R00 = CARGOTREEMEM *ctmem*

  R01 = CARGOTREE *qbfout*)   R01 = CARGOTREE *fla*);
Description
Creates a closed QBF which is valid iff the propositional input formula is valid.
Parameters
ctmem   Memory used to create the resulting QBF within.

fla   QBF-Scheme. No quantifiers. Gets utilised.
Return Values
ctmem   Passed through.

qbfout   Resulting QBF.

FLASat (0.00)
Synopsis
(R00 = CARGOTREEMEM *ctmem* =**FL**. (R00 = CARGOTREEMEM *ctmem*

  R01 = CARGOTREE *qbfout*)   R01 = CARGOTREE *fla*);
Description
Creates a closed QBF which is valid iff the propositional input formula is satisfiable.
Parameters
ctmem   Memory used to create the resulting QBF within.

fla   QBF-Scheme. No quantifiers. Gets utilised.
Return Values
ctmem   Passed through.

qbfout   Resulting QBF.

FLAUnSat (0.00)
Synopsis
(R00 = CARGOTREEMEM *ctmem* =**FL**. (R00 = CARGOTREEMEM *ctmem*

  R01 = CARGOTREE *qbfout*)   R01 = CARGOTREE *fla*);
Description
Creates a closed QBF which is valid iff the propositional input formula is unsatisfiable.
Parameters
ctmem   Memory used to create the resulting QBF within.

fla   QBF-Scheme. No quantifiers. Gets utilised.
Return Values
ctmem   Passed through.

qbfout   Resulting QBF.

FLACons (0.00)

Synopsis

```
( R00 = CARGOTREEMEM ctmem  =FL. ( R00 = CARGOTREEMEM ctmem
  R01 = CARGOTREE    qbfout )     R01 = CARGOTREE    fla0
                                  R02 = CARGOTREE    fla1   );
```

Description

Creates a closed QBF which is valid iff the second of the specified input formulas is a consequence of the first one in propositional logic.

In other words: *fla0* is the premise formula, *fla1* the formula tested for being a consequence.

Parameters

ctmem	Memory used to create the resulting QBF within.
fla0	QBF-Scheme. No quantifiers. Gets utilised.
fla1	QBF-Scheme. No quantifiers. Gets utilised.

Return Values

ctmem	Passed through.
qbfout	Resulting QBF. Is normalised.

FLANotCons (0.00)

Synopsis

```
( R00 = CARGOTREEMEM ctmem  =FL. ( R00 = CARGOTREEMEM ctmem
  R01 = CARGOTREE    qbfout )     R01 = CARGOTREE    fla0
                                  R02 = CARGOTREE    fla1   );
```

Description

Creates a closed QBF which is valid iff the second of the specified input formulas is a not a consequence of the first one in propositional logic.

In other words: *fla0* is the premise formula, *fla1* the formula tested for not being a consequence.

Parameters

ctmem	Memory used to create the resulting QBF within.
fla0	QBF-Scheme. No quantifiers. Gets utilised.
fla1	QBF-Scheme. No quantifiers. Gets utilised.

Return Values

ctmem	Passed through.
qbfout	Resulting QBF. Is normalised.

ArrayIdToFLA (0.00)

Synopsis

```
( R00 = CARGOTREEMEM ctmem   =Ar. ( R00 = CARGOTREEMEM ctmem
  R01 = ARRAY          arrid        R01 = ARRAY           arrid  );
  R02 = ARRAY          arrfla )
```

Description

From an array of INTEGER identifiers creates an array of QBF-Scheme
CARGOTREE-s representing those propositional variables.
Useful for passing a variable-array to functions which expect a formula-array.

Parameters

ctmem	Memory used to create the resulting formulas within.
arrid	See description.

Return Values

ctmem	Passed through.
arrid	Passed through.
arrfla	The resulting formula array.

SubSelectionVarA (0.00)

Synopsis

```
( R00 = CARGOTREEMEM ctmem    =Su. ( R00 = CARGOTREEMEM ctmem
  R01 = INTEGER       varstrta       R01 = INTEGER        varstrta
  R02 = INTEGER       varstrtb       R02 = INTEGER        varstrtb
  R03 = INTEGER       numtuples      R03 = INTEGER        numtuples);
  R04 = CARGOTREE     flar    )
```

Description

Creates a propositional formula which expresses a "subselection" condition between
two ranges of propositional variables.
The tuple identifiers are ($varstrta$+k,$varstrtb$+k) for k=0,...,$numtuples$-1, the resulting
formula is the conjunction of implications $varstrta$+k > $varstrtb$+k.
Consequently an interpretation of this range of variables is a model of the resulting
formula iff no tuple is evaluated to (T,F). This is also refered to as "subselection"
condition, because for any $varstrta$+k which is "selected" (evaluated to TRUE)
$varstrtb$+k is selected too.

Parameters

ctmem	Memory used to create the resulting formula within.
varstrta	See description.
varstrtb	See description.
numtuples	See description. Must be greater or equal to 1.

Return Values

ctmem	Passed through.
varstrta	Passed through.
varstrtb	Passed through.
numtuples	Passed through.
flar	Resulting formula. QBF-Scheme. No quantifiers.

135

SubSelectionVarB (0.00)

Synopsis

(R00 = CARGOTREEMEM	*ctmem*	=**Su**. (R00 = CARGOTREEMEM	*ctmem*
R01 = INTEGER	*varstrt*	R01 = INTEGER	*varstrt*
R02 = INTEGER	*numtuples*	R02 = INTEGER	*numtuples*);
R03 = CARGOTREE	*flar*)		

Description

Creates a propositional formula which expresses a "subselection" condition between two arrays of propositional variables.

The tuple identifiers are (*varstrt*+2k,*varstrt*+2k+1) for k=0,...,*numtuples*-1, the resulting formula is the conjunction of implications *varstrt*+2k > *varstrt*+2k+1. Consequently an interpretation of this range of variables is a model of the resulting formula iff no tuple is evaluated to (T,F). This is also refered to as "subselection" condition, because for any *varstrt*+2k which is "selected" (evaluated to TRUE) *varstrt*+2k+1 is selected too.

Parameters

ctmem	Memory used to create the resulting formula within.
varstrt	See description.
numtuples	See description. Must be greater or equal to 1.

Return Values

ctmem	Passed through.
varstrt	Passed through.
numtuples	Passed through.
flar	Resulting formula. QBF-Scheme. No quantifiers.

ProperSubSelectionVarA (0.00)

(R00 = CARGOTREEMEM *ctmem*		=**Pr.** (R00 = CARGOTREEMEM *ctmem*	
R01 = INTEGER	*varstrta*	R01 = INTEGER	*varstrta*
R02 = INTEGER	*varstrtb*	R02 = INTEGER	*varstrtb*
R03 = INTEGER	*numtuples*	R03 = INTEGER	*numtuples*);
R04 = CARGOTREE	*flar*)		

Description

Creates a propositional formula which expresses a "proper subselection" condition between two ranges of propositional variables.

One variable range is given by *varstrta*+k, the other one by *varstrtb*+k, for k=0,...,*numtuples*-1. The resulting formula is (*varstrta*+0 > *varstrtb*+0) & ... & (*varstrta*+*numtuples*-1 > *varstrtb*+*numtuples*-1) & ~((*varstrtb*+0 > *varstrta*+0) & ... & (*varstrtb*+*numtuples*-1 > *varstrta*+*numtuples*-1)).

Consequently an interpretation of the ranges of variables is a model of the resulting formula iff the selection of variables from range *varstrta*+k is a proper subselection of variables from range *varstrtb*+k. (As usual "selected" corresponds to "evaluated to TRUE"). In other words: If *varstrta*+k is selected, then *varstrtb*+k is selected too, and the selections are unequal, i.e., there is at least one k0 such that *varstrta*+k0 is not selected but *varstrtb*+k0 is.

Parameters

ctmem	Memory used to create the resulting formula within.
varstrta	See description.
varstrtb	See description.
numtuples	See description. Must be greater or equal to 1.

Return Values

ctmem	Passed through.
varstrta	Passed through.
varstrtb	Passed through.
numtuples	Passed through.
flar	Resulting formula. QBF-Scheme. No quantifiers.

SubSelection (0.00)

Synopsis

(R00 = CARGOTREEMEM *ctmem*   **=Su.** (R00 = CARGOTREEMEM *ctmem*

  R01 = ARRAY   *flaarray0*   R01 = ARRAY   *flaarray0*

  R02 = ARRAY   *flaarray1*   R02 = ARRAY   *flaarray1*);

  R03 = CARGOTREE   *fla*   )

Description

Creates a propositional formula which expresses a "subselection" condition between two arrays of propositional formulas.

The two input arrays *flaarray0* and *flaarray1* are of course required to be of the same size, which is refered to as 'n'. The resulting formula is *flaarray0*[0] > *flaarray1*[0] & ... & *flaarray0*[n-1] > *flaarray1*[n-1].

This extends the principle of subselections as applied in **SubSelectionVarA** and **SubSelectionVarB** to arbitrary propositional formulas. See there for comments on the principle of "subselection".

Parameters

ctmem	Memory used to create the resulting formula within. Note that the input formulas get utilised.
flaarray0	Each entry in QBF-Scheme and without quantifiers. Entries get utilised.
flaarray1	Each entry in QBF-Scheme and without quantifiers. Entries get utilised.

Return Values

ctmem	Passed through.
flaarray0	Passed through.
flaarray1	Passed through.
fla	Resulting formula. QBF-Scheme. No quantifiers.

ProperSubSelection (0.00)

Synopsis

(R00 = CARGOTREEMEM *ctmem*   =**Pr.** (R00 = CARGOTREEMEM *ctmem*

  R01 = ARRAY   *flaarray0*   R01 = ARRAY   *flaarray0*

  R02 = ARRAY   *flaarray1*   R02 = ARRAY   *flaarray1*);

  R03 = CARGOTREE   *fla*   )

Description

Creates a propositional formula which expresses a "proper subselection" condition between two arrays of propositional formulas.

The two input arrays *flaarray0* and *flaarray1* are of course required to be of the same size, refered to as 'n'. The resulting formula is (*flaarray0*[0] > *flaarray1*[0] & ... & *flaarray0*[n-1] > *flaarray1*[n-1]) & ~(*flaarray1*[0] > *flaarray0*[0] & ... & *flaarray1*[n-1] > *flaarray0*[n-1])

This extends the principle of proper subselections as applied in **ProperSubSelectionVarA** to arbitrary propositional formulas. See there for comments on the principle of "proper subselection".

Parameters

ctmem	Memory used to create the resulting formula within. Note that the input formulas get utilised.
flaarray0	Each entry in QBF-Scheme and without quantifiers. Entries get utilised.
flaarray1	Each entry in QBF-Scheme and without quantifiers. Entries get utilised.

Return Values

ctmem	Passed through.
flaarray0	Passed through.
flaarray1	Passed through.
fla	Resulting formula. QBF-Scheme. No quantifiers.

Trigger (0.00)

Synopsis

(R00 = CARGOTREEMEM	*ctmem*	=**Tr.** (R00 = CARGOTREEMEM	*ctmem*
R01 = HASHINT	*hash*	R01 = HASHINT	*hash*
R02 = INTEGER	*numhash*	R02 = INTEGER	*numhash*
R03 = ARRAY	*flaarray*	R03 = ARRAY	*flaarray*
R04 = INTEGER	*trigstrt*	R04 = INTEGER	*trigstrt*
R05 = INTEGER	*varstrt*	R05 = INTEGER	*varstrt*);
R06 = CARGOTREE	*flatrig*)		

Description

Creates a propositional formula which is a conjunction of trigger variables triggering (i.e., implicating) formulas of an array of formulas (correspondence between formula selection and trigger variable models).

The trigger variable array is *trigstrt*+k for k=0,...,arraysize(*flaarray*)-1.

The formula's variables are mapped to a new range starting at *varstrt*.

The resulting formula is (*trigstrt* > fla[0]) & ... & (*trigstrt*+n-1 > fla[n-1]), where fla[k] results from the kth formula in *flaarray* through variable mapping and n is the size of array *flaarray*.

This can, for example, be used to create correspondences between selections of formulas and models (of the trigger variables).

Parameters

ctmem	Memory used to create the resulting formula within.
hash	Occurrence hash for the formula array. Does not need to contain variables.
numhash	Number of entries already in *hash*.
flaarray	Each entry in QBF-Scheme and without quantifiers. The formulas do not get utilised.
trigstrt	Start of the range of trigger-variables. Range-size is the size of array *flaarray*.
varstrt	Start of the range of new variables to use. The range-size is returned via the *numhash* return-value.

Return Values

ctmem	Passed through.
hash	Passed through and possibly altered.
numhash	Updated.
flaarray	Passed through.
trigstrt	Passed through.
varstrt	Passed through.
flatrig	Resulting trigger-formula. QBF-Scheme.

TriggerOmit (0.00)

Synopsis

(R00 = CARGOTREEMEM	ctmem	=**Tr.** (R00 = CARGOTREEMEM	ctmem
R01 = HASHINT	hash	R01 = HASHINT	hash
R02 = INTEGER	numhash	R02 = INTEGER	numhash
R03 = ARRAY	flaarray	R03 = ARRAY	flaarray
R04 = INTEGER	trigstrt	R04 = INTEGER	trigstrt
R05 = INTEGER	varstrt	R05 = INTEGER	varstrt
R06 = INTEGER	idxomit	R06 = INTEGER	idxomit);
R07 = CARGOTREE	flatrig)		

Description

Identical to **Trigger**, except that one formula of the passed array is omitted.

If the size of array *flaarray* is 1, and hence everything is omitted, this function returns the propositional formula 'T' (constant 'true').

Parameters

ctmem	Memory used to create the resulting formula within.
hash	Occurrence hash for the formula array. Does not need to contain variables.
numhash	Number of entries already in *hash*.
flaarray	Each entry in QBF-Scheme and without quantifiers. The formulas do not get utilised.
trigstrt	Start of the range of trigger-variables. Range-size is size of array *flaarray*. *trigstrt+idxomit* is omitted.
varstrt	Start of the range of new variables to use. The range-size is returned via the *numhash* return-value.
idxomit	Selects which array-entry to omit. Must be in the range [0,*arraysize*-1].

Return Values

ctmem	Passed through.
hash	Passed through and possibly altered.
numhash	Updated.
flaarray	Passed through.
trigstrt	Passed through.
varstrt	Passed through.
idxomit	Passed through.
flatrig	Resulting trigger-formula. QBF-Scheme.

ConsistentSelections (0.00)

Synopsis

(R00 = CARGOTREEMEM	*ctmem*	**=Co.** (R00 = CARGOTREEMEM	*ctmem*
R01 = CARGOTREE	*fla*	R01 = CARGOTREE	*fla*
R02 = ARRAY	*flaarray*	R02 = ARRAY	*flaarray*
R03 = INTEGER	*trigstrt*	R03 = INTEGER	*trigstrt*
R04 = INTEGER	*varstrtnew*	R04 = INTEGER	*varstrt*);
R05 = CARGOTREE	*qbf*		
R06 = INTEGER	*varstrt*)		

Description

Creates an open QBF where the models correspond to selections of formulas that are consistent with the specified 'theory' formula.

The variables occurring free in the resulting QBF are
$trigstrt, trigstrt+1,...,trigstrt+$arraysize($flaarray$)$-1$. A model evaluating
$trigstrt+k0, trigstrt+k1,...,trigstrt+km$ to TRUE and the other variables to FALSE
corresponds to the selection of formulas $flarray[k0],...,flaarray[km]$.

A selection $flaarray[k0],...,flaarray[km]$ is called consistent with the input formula fla
iff fla & $flaarray[k0]$ & ... & $flaarray[km]$ is satisfiable.

Parameters

ctmem	Memory used to create the resulting QBF within.
fla	QBF-Scheme. No quantifiers. Does not get utilised.
flaarray	Each entry in QBF-Scheme and without quantifiers. The formulas do not get utilised.
trigstrt	Start of the range of trigger-variables.
varstrt	Start of the range of new variables to use. Range-size via return-value.

Return Values

ctmem	Passed through.
fla	Passed through.
flaarray	Passed through.
trigstrt	Passed through.
varstrtnew	Updated varstrt.
qbf	Resulting QBF.
varstrt	Passed through.

MaxConsistentSelections (0.00)

Synopsis

(R00 = CARGOTREEMEM	*ctmem*		=**Ma.** (R00 = CARGOTREEMEM	*ctmem*
R01 = CARGOTREE	*fla*		R01 = CARGOTREE	*fla*
R02 = ARRAY	*flaarray*		R02 = ARRAY	*flaarray*
R03 = INTEGER	*trigstrt*		R03 = INTEGER	*trigstrt*
R04 = INTEGER	*varstrtnew*		R04 = INTEGER	*varstrt*);
R05 = CARGOTREE	*qbf*			
R06 = INTEGER	*varstrt*	)		

Description

Creates an open QBF where the models correspond to selections of formulas that are consistent with the input formula and that are maximal with this property, i.e., for each such selection no proper super-selection is consistent with the input formula. This function is identical to **ConsistentSelections**, except for the maximality property. See there for a more detailed description.

Parameters

ctmem	Memory used to create the resulting QBF within.
fla	QBF-Scheme. No quantifiers. Does not get utilised.
flaarray	Each entry in QBF-Scheme and without quantifiers. The formulas do not get utilised.
trigstrt	Start of the range of trigger-variables.
varstrt	Start of the range of new variables to use. Range-size via return-value.

Return Values

ctmem	Passed through.
fla	Passed through.
flaarray	Passed through.
trigstrt	Passed through.
varstrtnew	Updated *varstrt*.
qbf	Resulting QBF.
varstrt	Passed through.

ModellingSelections (0.00)

(R00 = CARGOTREEMEM	*ctmem*	=**Mo.** (R00 = CARGOTREEMEM	*ctmem*
R01 = CARGOTREE	*fla*	R01 = CARGOTREE	*flaleft*
R02 = ARRAY	*flaarray*	R02 = ARRAY	*flaarray*
R03 = INTEGER	*trigstrt*	R03 = INTEGER	*trigstrt*
R04 = INTEGER	*varstrtnew*	R04 = INTEGER	*varstrt*
R05 = CARGOTREE	*flaright*	R05 = CARGOTREE	*flaright*);
R06 = CARGOTREE	*qbf*		
R07 = INTEGER	*varstrt*)		

Description

Creates an open QBF where the models correspond to selections of propositional formulas which together with the first input formula model the second input formula (in propositional logic).

The correspondence between models of the resulting QBF and selections from *flaarray* is as usual, cf. **ConsistentSelections**.

In other words: The models correspond to those selections k0,...,km where the propositional formula (*flaleft* & *flaarray*[k0] & ... & *flarray*[km]) > *flaright* is valid.

Parameters

ctmem	Memory used to create the resulting QBF within.
flaleft	QBF-Scheme. No quantifiers. Does not get utilised.
flaarray	Each entry in QBF-Scheme and without quantifiers. The formulas do not get utilised.
trigstrt	Start of the range of trigger-variables.
varstrt	Start of the range of new variables to use. Range-size via return-value.
flaright	QBF-Scheme. No quantifiers. Does not get utilised.

Return Values

ctmem	Passed through.
fla	Passed through.
flaarray	Passed through.
trigstrt	Passed through.
varstrtnew	Updated varstrt.
flaright	Passed through.
qbf	Resulting QBF.
varstrt	Passed through.

Chapter 9

Details on the Implementation of Reductions-to-QBFs

This chapter contains additional information on the Reduction-to-QBF Smute Package. This information is not required for using the Smute Functions of the Reduction-to-QBF Smute Package. Instead, it is intended to illustrate the implementation of functions working with recursively structured data via the Smute Language. It serves as showcase for the utilisation of various Smute- and Smute Language-components. Section 9.1 lists and documents the Smute source-code of a reduction-to-QBF. Technical remarks on the Reduction-to-QBF Smute Package are given in Section 9.2.

9.1 Documented Source Code of a Reduction-to-QBF

This section lists and explains the source-code of a Smute Function implementing a reduction-to-QBF for the consequence relation in the logic LP_m. This reduction has been introduced in Section 6.4 on pages 82ff. As the Smute Language is very generic, i.e., not designed with regard to a specific kind of functions, there are manifold variants for the implementation of functions working with recursively structured data. Thus it must be noted that for the implementation of new functions different approaches might be more suitable than to closely stick to the example-code presented in this section.

Smute Functions ThreeValT, ThreeValF, and ThreeValO, implementing $\tau(P, P', \phi, x)$ **(as defined on page 83)**

For the sake of simplicity and efficiency, $\tau(P, P', \phi, x)$ is specified via three different Smute Functions, named **ThreeValT**, **ThreeValF**, and **ThreeValO**, for $\tau(P, P', \phi, \mathrm{t})$, $\tau(P, P', \phi, \mathrm{f})$ and $\tau(P, P', \phi, \mathrm{o})$ respectively.

The recursively structured input, propositional formula ϕ, is expected in the form of a CARGO-TREE-instance in the so-called QBF-CARGOTREE-Scheme. The QBF-Scheme is defined by Smute Interpreter Logic Edition (cf. pages 87ff.). As the name suggests, the QBF-Scheme is a convention for the representation of Quantified Boolean Formulas. Propositional formulas are a special case of QBFs, namely QBFs without quantifiers. In order to avoid the necessity of conversion and distinction, there is thus no separate CARGOTREE-Scheme for propositional formulas. In the QBF-Scheme 32-bit integers serve as variable identifiers.

Instead of using two arrays P and P' of propositional variables a different approach is followed: INTEGER identifier ranges. In the resulting propositional formula the variable identifiers are integers of a certain range, determined by parameter *varstrt*. Propositional variable identifiers *varstrt*, *varstrt*+2, ... correspond to the input formula's variables (P), whereas *varstrt*+1, *varstrt*+3, ... correspond to the second array of distinct variables (P'). Note that it would

145

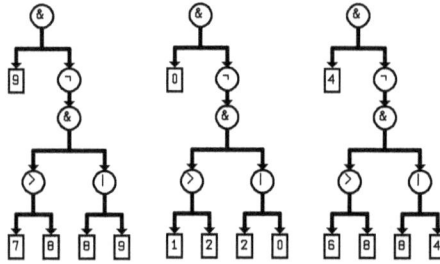

Figure 9.1: Occurrence-indices and Identifier Replacement

also have been possible to use a range *varstrta*, *varstrta*+1, ... for P and a range *varstrtb*, *varstrtb*+1, ... for P'. But then, in order to avoid overlapping ranges, the number of variables in P would have to be known, i.e., prior to calling the Smute Functions the number of variables occurring in ϕ would have to be counted. Thus, for the sake of efficiency the former "interwoven" variable identifier approach has been preferred.

The correspondence between variable identifiers *varstrt*,*varstrt*+2,... and the input formula's original variables is the so-called *correspondence-by-occurrence*. The principle is depicted in Figure 9.1. The leftmost visualisation is of an original input formula. The visualisation in the mid shows this formula with variable-integers replaced by the respective occurrence-indices. In the rightmost visualisation the variable identifier mapping is applied with a *varstrt*-value of 4.

Each of the three Smute Functions, **ThreeValT**, **ThreeValF**, and **ThreeValO** has the following interface:

- Parameters:

    - R00 CARGOTREEMEM *ctmem*: memory used to create the resulting formula within;
    - R01 CARGOTREE *fla*: formula in QBF-Scheme, without quantifiers, does not get utilised;
    - R02 HASHINT *hash*: hash with occurrence-indices, may be empty on calling;
    - R03 INTEGER *numhash*: number of entries in the occurrence-index hash;
    - R04 INTEGER *varstrt*: lowest INTEGER of the range variable identifiers are mapped to.

- Return-values:

    - R00 CARGOTREEMEM *ctmem*: passed through;
    - R01 CARGOTREE *flar*: resulting formula in QBF-Scheme;
    - R02 HASHINT *hash*: passed through and possibly altered (new variable-occurrences added);
    - R03 INTEGER *numhash*: updated;
    - R04 INTEGER *varstrt*: passed through.

The resulting formula is allocated from *ctmem*. Nodes from the input-formula are not used as part of the resulting formula, as indicated by the "does not get utilised"-description of the *fla* parameter. For variable correspondence-by-occurrence a HASHINT-resource gets used. For each hash-entry one additional data-field is expected, containing the occurrence-index of the according variable. The *numhash*-parameter specifies the initial number of hash-entries and may be zero.

The following listing shows the Smute Language code of **ThreeValT**. A description is given thereafter. The code of **ThreeValF** and **ThreeValO** is very similar to the one of **ThreeValT** and not printed here.

```
000   Label(ThreeValT);
001   GetNodeId(R01,R07);
002   JumpTab(R07,
003          QBF_NOT,100_qbfnot,
004          QBF_OR,100_qbfor,
005          QBF_AND,100_qbfand,
006          QBF_IMPL,100_qbfimpl,
007          QBF_PROPVAR,100_qbfvar,
008          QBF_CONST,100_qbfconst);
009
010   //100_qbfconst
011   Label(100_qbfconst);
012   GetVal(R01,R07);
013   NewIntImmSetVal(R00,R01,QBF_CONST,R07);
014   Return;
015   //100_qbfvar
016   Label(100_qbfvar);
017   GetVal(R01,R07);
018   HashIntAddImm(R02,R07,1,R08);
019   BEQ(100_gotit);
020   MoveToHashIntEntry(R08,R03,0);
021   Move(R03,R08);          //occurrence-index
022   Add1(R03);
023   BRA(100_occidx);
024   Label(100_gotit);
025   MoveFromHashIntEntry(R08,0,R08); //occurrence-index
026   Label(100_occidx);
027   LSL1(R08);
028   Add(R04,R08);          //add varstrt
029   NewIntImmSetVal(R00,R01,QBF_PROPVAR,R08);
030   Return;
031   //100_qbfnot
032   Label(100_qbfnot);
033   GetChildImm(R01,0,R01);
034   BRA(ThreeValF);
035   //100_qbfor
036   Label(100_qbfor);
037   Push(1);
038   MoveToStack(R01,0);
039   GetChildImm(R01,0,R01);
040   BSR(ThreeValT);
041   MoveFromStack(0,R05);
042   MoveToStack(R01,0);
043   GetChildImm(R05,1,R01);
044   BSR(ThreeValT);
045   Move(R01,R05);
046   NewConClsImm(2,R00,R01,QBF_OR);
047   PlugImm(R01,R05,1);
```

```
048   MoveFromStack(0,R05);
049   Pop(1);
050   PlugImm(R01,R05,0);
051   Return;
052   //100_qbfand
053   Label(100_qbfand);
054   Push(1);
055   MoveToStack(R01,0);
056   GetChildImm(R01,0,R01);
057   BSR(ThreeValT);
058   MoveFromStack(0,R05);
059   MoveToStack(R01,0);
060   GetChildImm(R05,1,R01);
061   BSR(ThreeValT);
062   Move(R01,R05);
063   NewConClsImm(2,R00,R01,QBF_AND);
064   PlugImm(R01,R05,1);
065   MoveFromStack(0,R05);
066   Pop(1);
067   PlugImm(R01,R05,0);
068   Return;
069   //100_qbfimpl
070   Label(100_qbfimpl);
071   Push(1);
072   MoveToStack(R01,0);
073   GetChildImm(R01,0,R01);
074   BSR(ThreeValF);
075   MoveFromStack(0,R05);
076   MoveToStack(R01,0);
077   GetChildImm(R05,1,R01);
078   BSR(ThreeValT);
079   Move(R01,R05);
080   NewConClsImm(2,R00,R01,QBF_OR);
081   PlugImm(R01,R05,1);
082   MoveFromStack(0,R05);
083   Pop(1);
084   PlugImm(R01,R05,0);
085   Return;
```

A note about the labels: They are prefixed (in this case with "100_") because labels are visible Smute Module-wide. In order to avoid label-collisions (a label like "qbfnot" is likely to be used in multiple Smute Functions of a Smute Module), it is recommended to use function-dependent label-prefixes.

In line 002 the different input formula cases get distinguished (is the formula a logical constant, a propositional variable, a formula $\neg\phi_1$, etc.). The JumpTable-instruction branches to the respective label. Node-ids QBF_EXISTS and QBF_FORALL are ignored, because the input-CARGOTREE must represent a propositional formula, i.e., a QBF without quantifiers.

For each of the different cases the treatment is very simple. For example, if a logical constant is encountered, then the resulting formula is just a copy of that constant. The code for this operation is printed in lines 011++. The value of the Int-node is read in line 012 (recall that logical constants are represented with Int-nodes in the QBF-Scheme, a value of 0 represents $\bot$, a value of 1 represents $\top$). A new Int-node is created, its value is set to the previously read value.

In the case of a propositional variable the occurrence-index of that variable is required. It is retrieved by trying to add a new hash-entry with the variable-identifier used as key. If a hash-entry with that key already exists, the occurrence-index can be read from the entry's data-field 0. Otherwise the occurrence-index is the current value of *numhash* and stored as data-field 0 of the new hash-entry. Then *numhash* must be updated, i.e., incremented by 1. Once the occurrence-index is available—here it is stored in register R08—the replacement value can be calculated. It depends on whether p_i or p_i' is required. As outlined above, in the first case the appropriate value is *varstrt+(occidx*2)*, in the latter case it is *varstrt+1+(occidx*2)*. Within **ThreeValT** only the first case is required. The multiplication by 2 is here performed via an LSL1-instruction in line 027.

Now to the more interesting cases of logical connectives. For connective ¬ recall the following definition:

$$\tau(P, P', \neg\phi_1, \mathrm{t}) := \tau(P, P', \phi_1, \mathrm{f}).$$

The appropriate specification is the code in lines 0032, 0033, and 0034. In line 0033 the child-node is retrieved—it is the root-node of the CARGOTREE representing ϕ_1. It is used as input to **ThreeValF**. This is a case of (distributed) recursive function-calls, because function **ThreeValF** could call **ThreeValT** again. If this actually happens depends of course on the input to **ThreeValF**.

Observe that the following two code-fragments have exactly the same effect, though the left one is shorter and executed faster (and thus used in line 034):

```
(1)  BRA(ThreeValF);        (2)  BSR(ThreeValF);
                                 Return;
```

For logical connective ∧ the following function must be implemented:

$$\tau(P, P', \phi_1 \wedge \phi_2, \mathrm{t}) := \tau(P, P', \phi_1, \mathrm{t}) \wedge \tau(P, P', \phi_2, \mathrm{t})$$

Basically this works the same as with connective ¬. Though here two subformulas must be translated (instead of one), and then be connected with ∧. Of course each of the two subformula translations is performed with the appropriate Smute Function call, i.e., a recursive call to **Three-ValT**. Here data preservation is required: After the first subformula has been translated, it must be possible to access the second subformula, in order to translate it as well. After the second subformula has been translated, it must be possible to access the translation of the first subformula, in order to connect it with the translation of the second subformula. The appropriate answer to data preservation during function-calls is of course a stack architecture. **ThreeValT** uses the Smute Data Stack resource for this purpose: In line 054 a block holding one register is pushed onto the stack. In line 055 the root-node-identifier of the CARGOTREE representing $\phi_1 \wedge \phi_2$ is stored to the stack. In line 056 the root-node of the left subformula is retrieved. With this node as parameter **ThreeValT** recursively calls itself in line 057. Then the root-node of $\phi_1 \wedge \phi_2$ is retrieved from the stack in line 058. The stack-place gets used for storing the translated left subformula in line 059. The root-node of the right subformula is retrieved in line 060. This formula again needs to be translated via **ThreeValT**, which happens via line 061. In line 065 the translated left subformula is retrieved from the stack in order to be used within the resulting formula. Then the stack-space is not needed anymore and popped in line 066.

The treatment of the other binary logical connectives follows the same pattern.

Smute Function Model3 implementing $m3(P, P', \phi)$ **(as defined on page 83)**

The Smute Function **Model3** expects a single propositional formula, whereas in the definition of *m3* an array W of propositional formulas has been used. There are two options for applying the translation to an array of propositional formulas:

- For array $W = [\phi_0, \phi_1, \ldots, \phi_n]$, pass $\bigwedge_{i=0}^{n} \phi_i$ to **Model3**.

- Write another Smute Function which accepts an array of propositional formulas.

149

When applied to a single propositional formula function *m3* takes the following form:

$$m3(P, P', \phi) := \neg\tau(P, P', \phi, \mathrm{f}).$$

This can be implemented rather simple: Function **ThreeValF** is called, and the resulting CARGO-TREE is then plugged into a ConCls-node representing a negation. For the ease of implementation, the interface of function **Model3** is almost identical to the interface of function **ThreeValF**:

- Parameters:

  - R00 CARGOTREEMEM *ctmem*: memory used to create the resulting formula within;
  - R01 CARGOTREE *fla*: formula in QBF-Scheme, without quantifiers, does not get utilised;
  - R02 HASHINT *hash*: hash with occurrence-indices, may be empty on calling;
  - R03 INTEGER *numhash*: number of entries in the occurrence-index hash;
  - R04 INTEGER *varstrt*: lowest INTEGER of the range variable identifiers are mapped to.

- Return-values:

  - R00 CARGOTREEMEM *ctmem*: passed through;
  - R01 CARGOTREE *flar*: resulting formula in QBF-Scheme;
  - R02 HASHINT *hash*: passed through and possibly altered;
  - R03 INTEGER *numhash*: updated;
  - R04 INTEGER *varstrt*: passed through.

The following is the code:

```
000    Label(Model3);
001    BSR(ThreeValF);
002    Move(R01,R05);
003    NewConClsImm(1,R00,R01,QBF_NOT);
004    PlugImm(R01,R05,0);
005    Return;
```

Smute Function ConsLP implementing reduction-to-QBF *ConsLP* (as defined on page 84)

Like *m3*, function *ConsLP* is implemented for a single premise formula only, not for an array of propositional formulas as in the definition on page 84. *ConsLP* is comprised of the previously implemented functions, plus two additional operations: universal quantification and the creation of formula $P \leq P'$. In the Reduction-to-QBF Smute Package general-purpose QBF-functions like these have been collected in a separate Smute Module called "qbf". The universal quantification occurring in function *ConsLP* can be performed with Smute Function **BigForAllB**, the formula $P \leq P'$ can be created with Smute Function **SubSelectionVarB**. Both Smute Functions are exported from Smute Module qbf. Refer to the Smute Module documentation (pages 126ff.) for the documentation of these functions, and for an overview of the available qbf Smute Functions. Obviously, Smute Function **ConsLP** just needs to call Smute Functions **Model3**, **SubSelectionVarB** and **BigForAllB** with the appropriate parameters and plug the results together according to the definition of *ConsLP*. The interface of **ConsLP** is laid out as follows:

- Parameters:

  - R00 CARGOTREEMEM *ctmem*: memory used to create the resulting QBF within;

- R01 CARGOTREE *flal*: formula in QBF-Scheme, without quantifiers, does not get utilised;
- R02 CARGOTREE *flar*: formula in QBF-Scheme, without quantifiers, does not get utilised;
- R03 INTEGER *varstrt*: lowest INTEGER of the range variable identifiers are mapped to.

- Return-values:

  - R00 CARGOTREEMEM *ctmem*: passed through;
  - R01 CARGOTREE *qbfr*: resulting QBF in QBF-Scheme;
  - R02 INTEGER *varstrtnew*: updated *varstrt* (determines the range-size of the resulting QBF's INTEGER identifiers).

Following next is the code:

```
000   Label(ConsLP);
001
002   // stack:
003   // 0 = CARGOTREE       qbfmod3r
004   // 1 = CARGOTREE       qbfr
005   // 2 = CARGOTREE       qbfmod3l
006
007   Push(3);
008   MoveToStack(R02,1);
009
010   Move(R03,R04);
011   NewHashInt(R02);
012   Clear(R03);
013   BSR(Model3);
014
015   // R00 = CARGOTREEMEM   ctmem
016   // R01 = CARGOTREE      flar    (resulting formula)
017   // R02 = HASHINT        hash    (passed through and altered)
018   // R03 = INTEGER        numhash (updated)
019   // R04 = INTEGER        varstrt (passed through)
020
021   MoveToStack(R01,2);
022   MoveFromStack(1,R01);
023
024   BSR(Model3);
025
026   // R00 = CARGOTREEMEM   ctmem
027   // R01 = CARGOTREE      qbfr    (resulting formula)
028   // R02 = HASHINT        hash    (passed through and altered)
029   // R03 = INTEGER        numhash (updated)
030   // R04 = INTEGER        varstrt (passed through)
031
032   DiscardHashInt(R02);
033   MoveToStack(R01,0);
034
035   Move(R04,R01);
```

```
036   Move(R03,R02);
037
038   FarBSR(qbf,SubSelectionVarB);
039
040   // R00 = CARGOTREEMEM    ctmem      (passed through)
041   // R01 = INTEGER         varstrt    (passed through)
042   // R02 = INTEGER         numtuples  (passed through)
043   // R03 = CARGOTREE       qbfr       (resulting QBF)
044
045   NewConClsImm(2,R00,R04,QBF_AND);
046   PlugImm(R04,R03,0);
047   MoveFromStack(2,R03);
048   PlugImm(R04,R03,1);
049   Move(R02,R03);
050   Move(R01,R02);
051   NewConClsImm(2,R00,R01,QBF_IMPL);
052   PlugImm(R01,R04,0);
053   MoveFromStack(0,R04);
054   PlugImm(R01,R04,1);
055   LSL1(R03);
056
057   FarBSR(qbf,BigForAllB);
058
059   // R00=CARGOTREEMEM   ctmem   (passed through)
060   // R01=CARGOTREE      qbfout  (universal-quantified QBF)
061   // R02=INTEGER        strt    (passed through)
062   // R03=INTEGER        num     (passed through)
063
064   Add(R03,R02);
065   Pop(3);
066   Return;
```

For better readability a Smute Function's return-values are inserted as comment after function-calls. As the function **ConsLP** is not called recursively, a lax stack usage is applied, reserving space for each of the values that needs to be preserved throughout the function, even if they do not need to be preserved at the same time. The three values preserved throughout **ConsLP** are:

- qbfr, an identifier of the second input formula CARGOTREE.

- qbfmod3l, an identifier of the CARGOTREE representing the formula where models correspond to three-valued models of the first input formula.

- qbfmod3r, an identifier of the CARGOTREE representing the formula where models correspond to three-valued models of the second input formula (for the type of correspondence see **Model3**).

It is important to note how the HASHINT-resource created in line 011 gets used as parameter to function **Model3** in line 013, and then reused as **Model3**-parameter in line 024. Only by reusing the hash are identical variables of the first and second input formula correctly re-identified in the resulting formulas. After the call to function **Model3** in line 024 the return-value *numhash*, i.e., register R03, contains the number of variables occurring in both the input formulas. This at the same is the number of tuples (p_i, p'_i) used in formula $P \leq P'$, and is hence passed as parameter to **SubSelectionVarB**. For the universal quantification all the variables from P and P' are used. If n

is used to denote the aforementioned number of tuples, then the number of variables in both P and P' is $2n$, which explains the multiplication by 2 in line 055. $2n$ is also the number of different variables occurring in the resulting closed QBF. The identifiers are taken from the INTEGER-range starting at *varstrt* (*varstrt*,*varstrt*+1,*varstrt*+2,...). Thus return-value *varstrtnew* is set to *varstrt* + $2n$.

Lines 035 and 036 show a typical phenomenon of Smute Function calls: Data needs to be moved to the appropriate registers before the function can be called. Although the effort for moving data to the appropriate registers can be reduced by designing "compatible" Smute Function interfaces (expecting parameters in the same registers), it is of course not possible to fully avoid such parameter preparation.

This concludes the reduction-to-QBF example specifications. The other Smute Functions of the Reduction-to-QBF Smute Package apply exactly the same principles as **ThreeValT**, **Model3** and **ConsLP**.

9.2 Technical Notes

Except where otherwise noted, all Smute Functions of the Reduction-to-QBF Smute Package can freely use all of the registers. Consequently, any data to be preserved during function-calls needs to be stored elsewhere (the typical solution is stack-storage). Parameters are usually passed in registers R00, R01, etc. The task of finding new, unused variable identifiers is supported by using integer identifier ranges. Many Smute Functions create formulas where variables are identified via integers of a specified range, i.e., from within a certain interval. If necessary, original variable identifiers are "mapped" into the range. This mapping is usually done by correspondence-by-occurrence, as depicted in Figure 9.1. Most Wrapper Functions create QBFs with an integer identifier range starting at 0. This is true for all translations creating closed QBFs.

The Smute Functions of the Reduction-to-QBF Smute Package utilise CARGOTREE parameters only where explicitly stated, by default there is no utilisation.

Chapter 10

Conclusion and Discussion

The *Smute Language* is a programming language for writing functions processing recursively structured data. *Smute* is the generic term for the Smute Language and related applications and conceptions. The functions implemented via Smute Language code, so-called *Smute Functions*, are directly exposed to users, so-called *Smute Function Users*, with the user-interface provided by Smute. Thus terms like "program" or "application", which are used with many other programming languages, are not used with Smute.

Currently there is one interpreter for Smute Language code, the *Smute Interpreter*. There is no compiler to date.

For authors of Smute Language code, so-called *Smute Function Developers*, there are many advantages over using alternative solutions. The following is a summary of important Smute features:

- Predefined functionality: For many of the operations typically occurring in functions processing recursively structured data there are predefined instructions and datatypes in the Smute Language. Examples are data instance manipulations and identifier-related operations.

- Abstraction from the implementation: Many specification-irrelevant implementation details, like the layout of data structures and the handling of error conditions, are hidden from the Smute Language layer.

- Efficiency: Smute Language code can be efficiently executed, with respect to runtime and memory-requirements. The Smute Interpreter establishes this efficiency.

- Non-restrictiveness: The Smute Language has a powerful repertoire of instructions. The Smute Interpreter implements the functionality in a non-restrictive way. For example, the size and recursive depth of recursively structured data instances is only limited by the computer's available memory and 32-bit integers/32-bit addressing.

- Function user interfaces: Reading and analysis of parameters is covered by Smute. On the one hand this guarantees uniform usage of Smute Functions, on the other hand it saves work for Smute Function Developers.

- Data I/O Support: Data I/O is covered by Smute where possible. For example, in order for a Smute Function to support textual input in arbitrary LALR-languages no parser needs to be written—the parsing is automatically performed by Smute.

- Recursive function-calls: Unlike most other programming-languages there are no restrictions, problems, or disadvantages for recursive function-calls. This is important insofar, as recursive function-calls are "natural" in the processing of recursively structured data.

154

- Modularity: Smute Language-code can be used in a modular, non-redundant way, based on (dynamic) linking.

- Auxiliary features for function development: There are several instructions in the Smute Language helping to debug or test functions. The most remarkable feature is a built-in tree-visualisation for arbitrary recursively structured data.

- Platform independence of Smute Language code: The Smute Interpreter is written in C, using only the ANSI Standard C library. It can thus be made available for most computer platforms. Smute Language code can be executed on any of these platforms, without any adaptations.

The *Reduction-to-QBF Smute Package* is a collection of Smute Functions implementing reductions for reasoning tasks from Classic Abduction, Equilibrium Logic, Paraconsistent Reasoning via Signed Systems, and Paraconsistent Reasoning via Three-Valued Logic. It includes Smute Functions for generic QBF-operations, which can be reused for the implementation of new reductions-to-QBFs. The Reduction-to-QBF Smute Package proves that the Smute Language allows for a concise and straightforward implementation of reductions-to-QBFs.

Although Smute is fully usable, some of the solutions are of a tentative nature. For all these solutions either the fully developed solution is of little significance or its realisation would have been too laborious (or a combination of these two factors applies):

- A Smute Assembler does not yet exist. A slightly less convenient solution is provided with the Smute Assembler Library.

- Currently there is no support for reading arbitrary binary input formats and to generate arbitrary output formats with Smute Functions. Though by using the CARGOTREE Exchange Format this can already be circumvented.

- Block comments are not supported by the Smute parser, due to the treatment of block comments in GOLD Parser Builder.

Furthermore there are features which can be regarded as "natural extensions" of Smute and should be considered for implementation:

- HASHSTR resource in the Smute Language (the equivalent of the HASHINT resource, with string-keys instead of integer keys).

- HASHSTRSTACK resource in the Smute Language (the equivalent of the HASHINTSTACK resource).

- Resources STRING and STRINGMEM, plus a set of Smute Language instructions for string-operations.

- Support for floating-point data-types and their according operations in the Smute Language, including new CARGOTREE-nodes for these data-types.

- Formal CARGOTREE-Scheme related specifications, including string-aliases for integer identifiers to be used in Smute Language code (most notably node-ids). This feature should be considered only after the Smute Assembler is realised. Within the same specification could there be visualisation-related information in order to support CARGOTREE-Scheme-dependent visualisations.

Another set of obvious extensions, with less relevance than the above mentioned ones:

- Type-checking for Smute Function parameters specified in the Smute Launch File.

- Support of passing Smute Function results as input to other Smute Functions "directly", according to appropriate specifications made in the Smute Launch File.

- Preprocessing Function and data-storage specifications in the Smute Launch File (could supersede the Wrapper Functions, which currently perform these tasks).

- Currently the parser of the Smute Interpreter is not recovering from parsing-errors, i.e., it cannot continue parsing after a parsing-error occurs (execution aborts). This means that multiple errors in the source can only be detected one after another, i.e., only after one such error gets corrected is the next one reported. Parsers with error-recovery are more user-friendly, as they can report multiple parsing-errors simultaneously. Thus the implementation of error-recovery is an option for ongoing development. It is however the author of languages and Backus-Naur forms who needs to specify the parsing-error-recovery behaviour. As a result, GOLD Parser could not be used any longer, as it does not provide such features. A completely new parsing-table generation system would have to be developed. For the small benefit of parsing-error-recovery this seems hardly worthwhile.

- The functions implemented by Smute Function Developers are directly used by Smute Function Users. There is a related task, where functions processing recursively structured data are used within an application, such as formula manipulations in mathematics software. Smute is not designed for writing application-functions. Though it can be abused for this task: Currently an application would have to externally execute the Smute Interpreter. This is of course a rather dilettantish solution. Thus the support of application-internal usage of Smute Functions is another potential extension of Smute. The minimal effort solution is to provide a library and interfaces for Smute Function interpretation. Though an application internally interpreting functions can be rightly regarded as peculiar. The best solution is a compiler for the Smute Language.

Due to its optimised direct interpretability the Smute Language must be regarded as lower-level language. Though a higher-level language is of course not ruled out by the Smute conception. In fact, the Smute Language could serve as base for a higher-level language, such that specifications in the higher-level language are compiled to the Smute Language. The following is a summary of important considerations for assessing the value and necessity of a higher-level language:

- Ease of function specification: Comparable to C, the usage of variables instead of registers, and the support of compound statements would definitely simplify function-specification.

- Readability/suitability for the publishing of specifications: For reductions-to-QBFs the situation is as follows: There is a specification with optimised readability which gets published. The implementation is based on this specification. Due to the abstraction provided by the Smute Language, the implementation-specification is already very closely related to the published specifications. Though it might be desirable to melt these two specifications into one: That is, specifications in the implementation language would have to be sufficiently readable for publishing. The Smute Language clearly does not meet this criterion. But even for a higher-level language this is almost impossible to achieve: A shift towards readability can usually only be made at the expense of expressiveness. In many computer-science books algorithms are listed in *pseudo-code* not only to be programming-language independent, but also because the comprehensibility of pseudo-code cannot be achieved with specifications in a powerful programming language. It is thus more reasonable to not demand the suitability for the publishing of specifications from a higher-level language, but to carry on with distinct specifications for publishing and for the implementation respectively.

- Efficiency: The convenience provided by a higher-level language is achieved at the expense of efficiency. Unnecessary loss of efficiency can only be avoided by sophisticated optimisation in the compilation. The realisation of such optimisations is however laborious.

- Compiler implementation: Some common compiler-principles cannot be used with Smute. Most notably, compilers usually reserve stack-space for local variables. As discussed on page 10, this is inappropriate for functions which get recursively called.

Readers interested in obtaining the Smute software should get in contact with the author, preferably via the e-mail address `norbert.pfaffinger@gmail.com`.

References

[1] aiSee. http://www.aisee.com.

[2] bdd (binary decision diagrams) library/boole. http://www.cs.cmu.edu/~modelcheck/bdd.html. Model Checking Group at The School Of Computer Science, Carnegie Mellon, Pittsburgh.

[3] GOLD Parser. http://www.devincook.com.

[4] Alfred V. Aho, Ravi Sethi, and Jeffrey D. Ullman. *Compilers, Principles, Techniques And Tools*. Addison-Wesley, 1986.

[5] Philippe Besnard and Torsten Schaub. Signed Systems for Paraconsistent Reasoning. *Journal of Automated Reasoning*, 20:191–213, 1998.

[6] Philippe Besnard, Torsten Schaub, Hans Tompits, and Stefan Woltran. Paraconsistent Reasoning via Quantified Boolean Formulas, I: Axiomatising Signed Systems. In *Logic in Artificial Intelligence: European Conference, JELIA 2002, Cosenza, Italy, September, 23–26, 2002. Proceedings*, Lecture Notes in Artificial Intelligence, pages 320–331. Springer Verlag, 2002.

[7] Philippe Besnard, Torsten Schaub, Hans Tompits, and Stefan Woltran. Paraconsistent Reasoning via Quantified Boolean Formulas, II: Circumscribing Inconsistent Theories. In *Symbolic and Quantitative Approaches to Reasoning with Uncertainty, 7th European Conference, ECSQARU 2003, Aalborg, Denmark, July 2-5, 2003. Proceedings*, Lecture Notes on Artificial Intelligence, pages 528–539. Springer Verlag, 2003.

[8] James R. Cordy, Charles D. Halpern, and Eric Promislow. TXL: A Rapid Prototyping System for Programming Language Dialects. In *Proceedings of The International Conference of Computer Languages (IEEE 1988)*, pages 280–285, 1988.

[9] Uwe Egly, Thomas Eiter, Volker Klotz, Hans Tompits, and Stefan Woltran. Computing Stable Models with Quantified Boolean Formulas: Some Experimental Results. In *Proceedings of the AAAI 2001 Spring Symposium on Answer Set Programming*, pages 53–59. AAAI Press, 2001.

[10] Uwe Egly, Thomas Eiter, Hans Tompits, and Stefan Woltran. Solving Advanced Reasoning Tasks using Quantified Boolean Formulas. In *Proceedings of the 7th Conference on Artificial Intelligence (AAAI-00) and of the 12th Conference on Innovative Applications of Artificial Intelligence (IAAI-00)*, pages 417–422. AAAI Press, 2000.

[11] Thomas Eiter and Georg Gottlob. Propositional Circumscription and Extended Closed World Reasoning are Π_2^P-complete. *Journal Of Theoretical Computer Science*, 114(2):315, 1993.

[12] Thomas Eiter and Georg Gottlob. On The Computational Cost of Disjunctive Logic Programming: Propositional Case. *Annals of Mathematics and Artificial Intelligence*, 15(3/4):289–323, 1995.

[13] Thomas Eiter and Georg Gottlob. The Complexity of Logic-Based Abduction. *Journal of the Association of Computing Machinery*, 42(1):3–42, 1995.

[14] Rainer Feldmann, Burkhard Monier, and Stefan Schamberger. A Distributed Algorithm to Evaluate Quantified Boolean Formulas. In *Proceedings of the 7th Conference on Artificial Intelligence (AAAI-00) and of the 12th Conference on Innovative Applications of Artificial Intelligence (IAAI-00)*, pages 285–290. AAAI Press, 2000.

[15] Kurt Gödel. Zum intuitionistischen Aussagenkalkül. *Anzeiger der Akademie der Wissenschaften*, pages 65–66, 1932.

[16] Georg Gottlob. Complexity Results for Nonmonotonic Logics. *Journal Of Logic and Computation*, 2(3):397–425, 1992.

[17] Arend Heyting. Die formalen Regeln der intuitionistischen Logik. *Sitzungsberichte der Preussischen Akademie der Wissenschaften*, pages 42–56, 1930.

[18] Henry Kautz and Bart Selman. Pushing the Envelope: Planning, Propositional Logic and Stochastic Search. In *Proceedings of the Thirteenth National Conference on Artificial Intelligence and the Eighth Innovative Applications of Artificial Intelligence Conference*, pages 1194–1201. AAAI Press, 1996.

[19] Jan Łukasiewicz. Die Logik und das Grundlagenproblem. *Les entretiens de Zurich sur les fondements et la méthode des sciences mathématiques 6-9*, 7 (1938):82–100, 1941.

[20] Terence J. Parr and Russell W. Quong. ANTLR: A predicated-LL(k) parser generator. *Journal Of Software Practice and Experience*, 25(7):789–810, 1995.

[21] David Pearce. A New Logical Characterisation of Stable Models and Answer Sets. In *Non-Monotonic Extensions of Logic Programming*, volume 1216 of *Lecture Notes on Artificial Intelligence*, pages 57–70. Springer Verlag, 1997.

[22] David Pearce, Hans Tompits, and Stefan Woltran. Encodings for Equilibrium Logic and Logic Programs with Nested Expressions. In *Proceedings of the 10th Portuguese Conference on Artificial Intelligence (EPIA '01)*, volume 2258 of *Lecture Notes in Computer Science*. Springer Verlag, 2001.

[23] Charles Sanders Peirce. Abduction and Induction. In Justus Buchler, editor, *Philosophical Writings of Peirce*, pages 150–156. Dover Books, New York, 1955.

[24] David Poole. Explanation and prediction: An architecture for default and abductive reasoning. *Computational Intelligence*, 5(2):97–110, 1989.

[25] Graham Priest. Logic of Paradox. *Journal of Philosophical Logic*, 8:219–241, 1979.

[26] Graham Priest. Reasoning About Truth. *Artificial Intelligence*, 39:231–244, 1989.

[27] Raymond Reiter. A logic for default reasoning. *Artificial Intelligence*, 13(1-2):81–132, 1980.

[28] Jussi Rintanen. Improvements to the Evaluation of Quantified Boolean Formulae. In Dean Thomas, editor, *Proceedings of the 16th International Joint Conference on Artificial Intelligence (IJCAI-99-Vol2)*, pages 1192–1197. Morgan Kaufmann Publishers, 1999.